OBJECT ◆ IMAGE ◆ INQUIRY

THE ART HISTORIAN AT WORK

We all are masters of wasting time. I often think of ants; if you watch an individual ant in the field, you will find it the most scatterbrained of creatures. It drags a dead fly with great effort for a few inches and lets it go; it crawls up a blade of grass and down again; it changes directions any moment. But with all this, ant heaps do grow and seem to be well organized. It seems to be similar with art history.

ERNST H. GOMBRICH

OBJECT • IMAGE • INQUIRY

THE ART HISTORIAN AT WORK

Report on a Collaborative Study by

The Getty Art History Information Program (AHIP)

and the

Institute for Research in Information and Scholarship (IRIS)

Brown University

Elizabeth Bakewell · William O. Beeman · Carol McMichael Reese

Marilyn Schmitt, *General Editor*

The Getty Art History Information Program

Santa Monica, California

Printed in the United States of America

To order this publication, please write:
The J. Paul Getty Book Distribution Center
P.O. Box 2112
Santa Monica, CA 90406
Telephone (213) 459-7611

Library of Congress Cataloging in Publication Data
Object, Image, Inquiry:
The Art Historian at Work
[Authors, Elizabeth Bakewell,
William O. Beeman,
Carol McMichael Reese:
General Editor, Marilyn Schmitt].

1. Art historians—Interviews.
2. Art—Historiography.
I. Bakewell, Elizabeth.
II. Beeman, William O.
III. Reese, Carol McMichael.
IV. Schmitt, Marilyn Low,
1939–
N380.025 1988 707′.2–dc19 88–1101
ISBN 0–89236–135–2

CONTENTS

Foreword vii

Introduction

DESCRIPTION OF THE AHIP-IRIS COLLABORATIVE STUDY xi

THE INTERVIEWS

Introduction 3

The Process of Art-historical Inquiry

ORIGINAL WORKS OF ART AND REPRODUCTIONS 7

PRIMARY DOCUMENTS AND ARCHIVES 22

SECONDARY SOURCES AND LIBRARIES 37

ORGANIZATION OF INFORMATION 44

WRITING AND PUBLISHING IN ART HISTORY 55

PRESENT USE OF COMPUTERS 68

PERSONAL FACTORS IN ART-HISTORICAL RESEARCH 72

FINANCES 81

TIME 95

WISH LIST 103

Art-historical Points of View

ANALYTICAL TECHNIQUES 111

CONNOISSEURSHIP 122

FORMAL AND STYLISTIC ANALYSIS 133

CRITICISM 139

STRUCTURALISM AND SEMIOTICS 140

ICONOGRAPHY 143

CULTURAL AND SOCIAL HISTORY 151

THE CASE STUDIES

Introduction 165

Roman Portraiture and Numismatics 169

THE SUBJECT OF INQUIRY PERSONNEL RESEARCH ACTIVITIES: THE ASSISTANTS RESEARCH ACTIVITIES: THE PRINCIPAL SCHOLAR ORIGINAL WORKS OF ART ORGANIZATION OF INFORMATION USE OF COMPUTER TECHNOLOGY SECONDARY SOURCES AND LIBRARIES POSTSCRIPT

The Palais du Tau 177

THE SUBJECT OF INQUIRY PERSONNEL RESEARCH ACTIVITIES: THE ASSISTANT RESEARCH ACTIVITIES: THE PRINCIPAL SCHOLAR PRIMARY AND SECONDARY SOURCES ORGANIZATION OF INFORMATION SECONDARY SOURCES AND LIBRARIES PRIMARY DOCUMENTS AND ARCHIVES TIME AND RESEARCH ACTIVITIES POSTSCRIPT

APPENDIXES

The Interviews

1. LIST OF SCHOLARS INTERVIEWED 185
2. SCHEDULE OF INTERVIEWS 187
3. CATEGORIES USED IN CODING INTERVIEW DATA 188
4. CATEGORIES STUDIED FOR THIS REPORT 190

The Case Studies

5. TASK SHEET 191
6. PARTICIPANTS' ACTIVITIES 192
7. PURPOSES OF ACTIVITIES 194
8. OTHERS INVOLVED IN ACTIVITIES 196
9. LOCATIONS OF ACTIVITIES 196
10. ANALYSIS OF HOURS BY MONTH 198

Foreword

In the spring of 1985 the Art History Information Program of the J. Paul Getty Trust and the Institute for Research in Information and Scholarship of Brown University began meeting to discuss areas of mutual interest. While the respective missions of the two organizations differ significantly, the common objective of applying computer technology to research in the humanities made for natural lines of cooperation. As we talked, a profound gap in our understanding became evident: if our aim is to foster procedures, systems, and user environments that will enhance the way scholars work in the future, should we not know a great deal about existing research practices? How can we aspire to satisfy the needs of scholarship and to marshal useful automated resources without better knowledge of what researchers do now? Both the development of specific projects and work with emerging technology presuppose a broad foundation of knowledge about the community of potential users.

In order to learn more about this community, we conceived a simply designed project that would examine the research process from two vantage points. First, we would ask scholars to *say* what they do when they engage in research. Second, we would follow their activities in practice and observe what they actually *do*. The study combined intensive interviews with nearly a score of art historians with examinations of two newly begun art-historical research projects. Drawing on expertise developed at IRIS, the orientation and method of investigation were derived from the social sciences, with particular emphasis on the interview techniques of anthropology. The selection of art history as the targeted discipline reflected AHIP's special commitment to research in the visual arts.

Lacking precedent for this kind of investigation, we were understandably concerned about the outcome of the project. Would the participants react badly to being the object of study? Would they take the inquiry seriously? Would they respond to the investigative techniques used by the staff? Two of the members of the interview team knew little about art history, while one had no training in the social sciences; could such a group work together successfully? Would the results give us a fresh perspective on research practices, or would we emerge with shallow descriptions of the obvious? These were just some of the risks that confronted the project.

Then too there were the inherent limitations of the study. In deciding to mine as deeply as possible the working methods of only two scholars, we consciously sacrificed generality. The eighteen subjects chosen for interviews were selected specifically for their diversity, rather than for the uniformity of their practices. Art history is only one discipline of the humanities; the participants in this study are but a small sampling of that field.

From our vantage point, and to our pleasure, the project accomplished what it set out to do. The reader will find many aspects of research practice explored in a way that is alive with detail and texture. In striking contrast to the widespread image of scholarly isolation, this study finds the participants immersed in a rich matrix of interactions—with objects of study, with colleagues, with institutions, with resources, and with a demanding professional tradition. Some of the interview passages and the events in the case studies could not be more personal or more specialized in subject matter. Yet in the obstacles and contradictions, the attitudes, intellectual strategies, and emotions described in these pages, anyone who has engaged in research will find strong reverberations of personal experience.

The strengths of this report are owed to the remarkable dedication of the project staff and the high level of cooperation offered by the participating art historians. For the better part of a year the staff spent much of its time living out of suitcases; both institutions—one in California and the other in Rhode Island—engaged in an active collaboration. Interviews were conducted both in the United States and in Europe. To be conversant with the specialized interests of the participants required extensive preparation. The six- and seven-hour interviews, usually conducted over two days, posed their own stringent demands. Consistent concentration, sensitivity, and teamwork were required to strike the difficult balance between eliciting detailed information about particular topics and promoting free-flowing discussion. The team's awareness of each interview as a onetime opportunity added to the pressure. The transcripts of the interviews and the data collected from the case studies resulted in a massive influx of information. Giving this information structure and shape while retaining the voice of the art historian was the most time-consuming phase of the study; it is surely one of the authors' major accomplishments.

It is also obvious from reading these pages that the art historians connected with the project did more than simply give generously of their time. For many of those interviewed, the project meant retraveling the uneven path of a lifetime spent in academic study. In covering this landscape, they proved open and thoughtful guides; the full interview transcripts (which extend far beyond the scope of this report) amount to the ontogeny of a scholar's career. For the art historians engaged in the case studies, the burden was more complex, requiring that they simultaneously carry out research and observe and comment upon the process in which they were involved.

This report raises several important challenges. For those charged with technical development and the creation of automated environments, the challenge rests in using this document effectively. The temptation will be to focus upon discrete applications that conform to today's computer tools or that affirm developers' existing directions. A more careful reading of the report, however, will suggest a different approach to this prospective user community. A grasp of the overarching objectives and thinking that condition research practices will be essential. The context of subject matter, attitudes, and politics that govern the art historian's experience must be understood and accepted.

Moreover the information needs of scholars are strikingly dynamic: what is suitable in breadth, amount, and quality of information at one stage of research may be inadequate or unnecessary at another. The manner in which literature and objects are browsed in the early formation of ideas, for instance, is very different from the use of these materials in formal arguments meant for publication. Existing computer applications typically begin and end at boundaries that show little regard for the stream of scholarly activities; those called for here would promote the transfer of knowledge through various stages of research. The section discussing the researcher's direct confrontation of art objects illustrates another sobering theme: if many aspects of the research process may lend themselves to automation, others are better left alone.

Equivalent challenges face authors, organizations, and professions charged with understanding and enhancing the research environment. This report is an initial exploration of the ways knowledge can be acquired and communicated. It raises issues of how that process can be facilitated and improved, of how the scope of individual effort can be enlarged, of how obstacles to access and barriers between realms of knowledge can be removed, and of how research practices can be made more efficient. What seems beyond question is that more studies like this one are needed to inform and guide us in applying new technology to the work of scholars. Considering the magnitude of the commitments that institutions are making to automation, we would be well advised to improve our comprehension of the constituency we intend to serve.

Michael Ester, Director,
The Getty Art History Information Program

William Shipp, Director,
Institute for Research in Information
and Scholarship

Introduction

DESCRIPTION OF THE AHIP-IRIS COLLABORATIVE STUDY

In January 1986 the J. Paul Getty Trust's Art History Information Program (AHIP) in Santa Monica, California, and the Institute for Research in Information and Scholarship (IRIS) at Brown University in Providence, Rhode Island, embarked on a nine-month collaborative study of the processes that art historians follow in the conduct of research. We sought to learn what kinds of information art historians need, where and how they search for it, how they collect and organize it, and what use they make of it. The study was intended to serve as a basis for discovering what kinds of automated tools would be of use to art historians.

We developed the study as two distinct projects that sought to describe art-historical research as it is currently practiced: an interview project and a case-study project. The former consisted of eighteen full-day interviews; the latter, of two five-month case studies. We devised the projects to give us what we hoped would be complementary information. The interviews provided insights into patterns of work that scholars had developed over lifetimes. The case studies, in contrast, provided an opportunity to observe art historians and their assistants in day-to-day work. Both the interviews and the case studies were exploratory in nature, and the scholars participated in an admirable spirit of self-inquiry.

The collaboration between AHIP and IRIS has been a fruitful one, for the two organizations share similar goals and offer complementary experience and expertise. Both are exploring new ways in which automation technology and information systems can enhance scholarly work. On the one hand, the university environment provides IRIS with a ready test bed for the analysis of the research process and the impact of computing technology. IRIS's Office of Program Analysis (OPA) applies the techniques of the social sciences to the analysis of the scholarly community's activities. On the other hand, AHIP has focused on a single discipline that poses complex technological demands. The quantity and variety of art-historical information—object information, images, archival documents as well as bibliographical data and text—especially beg for electronic aids to research. Both AHIP and IRIS are committed to enhancing not only the technology but also the understanding of the research endeavor in the humanities.

A collaborative team of three directed the study: Dr. William O. Beeman, director of the Office of Program Analysis at IRIS; Dr. Marilyn Schmitt, program manager in charge of scholarly coordination of art-historical projects at AHIP; and Elizabeth Bakewell, social science research analyst in the OPA office. All three developed the structure for the study and participated fully in its execution. AHIP art historian Carol McMichael Reese is largely responsible for transforming the initial report into the present study.

Dr. Michael Ester, director of AHIP, oversaw the planning and reviewed all of its details. Dr. John Logan, AHIP's program manager in charge of scholarly information development, participated in exchange meetings with IRIS's technical staff, including Dr. Michael Pear, manager of the support group; Norman Meyrowitz, manager of the scholar's workstation group; Nicole Yankelovich, project coordinator; and Paul Kahn, applications specialist. Transcribers and administrative and clerical staff at IRIS contributed valuable time and energies, as did the technical staff at AHIP. Erin Mills's oversight of the many phases of the report's production at AHIP was essential to the successful completion of the project.

Karen Jacobson devoted her considerable talents to copyediting the report, while Leslie Thomas of the publications department of the J. Paul Getty Museum created a sensitive and handsome design for the publication. We are also indebted to others in that department who contributed to the publication of the report, notably Andrea Belloli, Elizabeth Burke, Patrick Dooley, and Karen Schmidt.

We are grateful to Dale Treleven, director of the Oral History Program at the University of California, Los Angeles, for his valuable advice on the practical matters of interview techniques, and to Dr. Nicholas Olsberg, head of the Getty Archives of the History of Art, for his interest in this project and in the future life of its materials.

In addition we greatly appreciate the contributions of the following people in meeting the many demands posed by the project.

From Brown University: Dr. William Shipp, director of IRIS; Andrés Saldaña; Shirin Moid; Martin Michael; Sue Hahn; James Larkin; and Tim Farley.

From the Getty Art History Information Program: Gwen Levine, Peter Forman, Greg Kann, Brian Conway, Patricia Pharis, Raul Guerrero, Cindy Kemper, Derrick Hutchinson, Stefanie Reaux, Aletta Schaap, Karen Davis, Jan Porter, Karen Craft, and Robert Mendoza.

Finally, AHIP and IRIS shouldered equally the burden of travel, which constituted a significant demand on the staffs and resources of both institutions.

THE INTERVIEWS

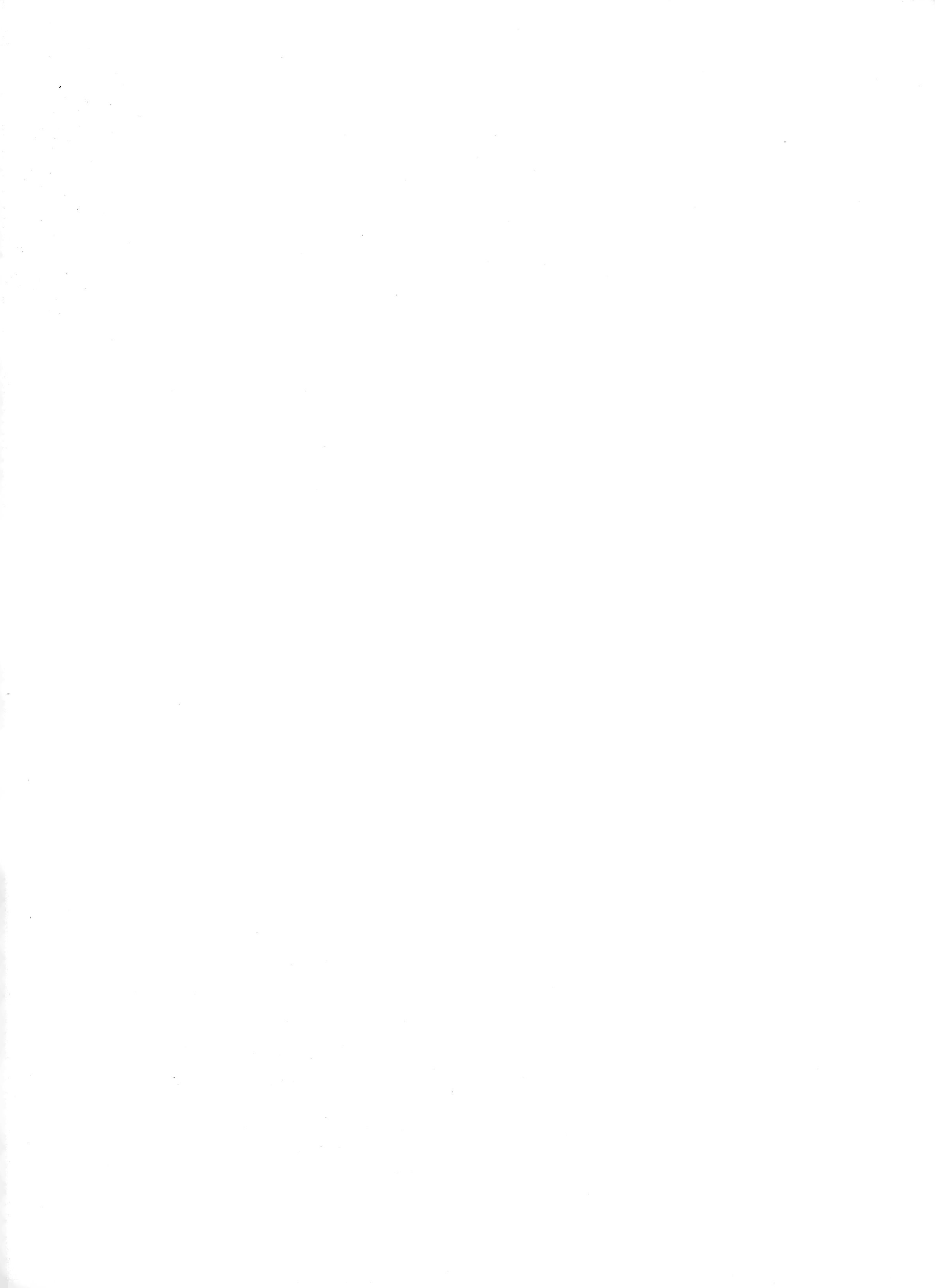

Introduction

The interview project entailed a broad investigation of the research concerns and practices of art historians. Intended to give texture and scope to the close, task-by-task observation of the case-study project, the interviews ranged widely, collecting interpretations as well as descriptions from the memories of the participants.

SELECTION OF PARTICIPANTS ▪ The eighteen scholars interviewed were chosen to represent a broad sampling of art historians active in research. Creating such a list was a formidable task. To assure variety in the selection, we established a set of criteria that guided our choices.

We interviewed both male and female scholars who lived and worked in a variety of locations in the United States and Europe. They included scholars from research centers, teaching institutions, and museums, whose areas of specialization ranged over historical period, geographical area, and medium. We interviewed specialists in such diverse fields as French Gothic architecture, Italian Renaissance sculpture, medieval Dutch manuscripts, contemporary American sculpture, and fifteenth-century German prints and drawings, to mention only a few. The range of scholars represented different conceptual approaches (formal, iconographic, psychological, and semiotic, among others) and a number of current art-historical concerns, such as patronage, the sociopolitical milieu, and the response of critics to art.

Preference was given to scholars who were heavy users of research materials, whether archival, bibliographic, or the works of art themselves; who were actively publishing their work; and who had in some way influenced their field. If the final list of candidates (see appendix 1) did not achieve a perfect mechanical distribution across these categories, we believe that it nevertheless yielded a rich diversity of points of view, interests, research methods, and requirements.

For all that diversity, it must be said that this study represents merely a slice of a much larger whole. Although the original plan for twelve interviews was expanded to eighteen (the maximum that staff and schedule could accommodate), to fill the gaps in our coverage would have required more than another eighteen. Even that expansion would not have assured a comprehensive view of art-historical research.

The predominance of American- and English-born and trained scholars reflects the fact that the selection was made by Americans representing sponsoring institutions in the United States. The choice of Europeans, moreover, was not intended to offer the most representative example from each country or to yield a comprehensive survey of every country where art-historical research is conducted. Instead the candidates' research interests often influenced the selection, since we believed that an insight into the scholar's situation in a particular country would emerge as a by-product of the individual's general concerns.

Thus we present this study as a portrait of a group of individuals, done at a certain time and from a certain vantage point, and with the selectivity and subjectivity that marks any interpretive endeavor. Nevertheless it is intended to be a mimetic likeness that depicts accurately a particular group of people in their work. We hope that it will offer insights into the process of scholarly research in the humanities, suggestions as to how such research might be aided, and a basis for further investigation. It is a first effort, not a final statement.

THE INTERVIEW PROCESS ▪ The interviews were conducted in several locations in the United States and Europe (see appendix 2). At times we met in the participant's office or home, but more often practicality dictated that we bring the individual to a central location. The length of the interviews ranged from three hours to eight; the average was six hours, extended over a two-day period to allow time for reflection and new recollections.

The interviews were intended to have no apparent direction, though the interviewers (Bakewell, Beeman, and Schmitt) had a "silent agenda" to be covered in the course of the discussion. We asked scholars to discuss their views of the research process in detail, for example, their methods of research on location, in archives, in libraries, in photo archives, in their own offices; their use and handling of field notes and photocopies, of notes from bibliographical searches, archives, and photographic sources; their writing process from first draft to publication, via the editing process, including interaction with publishers, choice of illustrations, and reception of the published work.

If the interview *agenda* grew out of the goals of the project, the interview *method* was modeled on the ethnographic interview, long employed by anthropologists as a tool for understanding diverse patterns of thought. The interview method stresses autobiographical content and indirect questions, followed by more precise questioning in areas opened by the free flow of conversation. This approach offers a study such as this a strategy for encouraging people to talk freely about what they know, do, and think about their own work and their profession.

The common thread that ran through the interviews was autobiographical. Even the most prosaic questions were designed to elicit personal recollections. Rather than asking, "How do you use an archive?" the interviewer might ask: "Can you 'walk us through' your first experience in the archives of Mantua? What was the first thing you did? What was your first impression of the place?" or "Pretend I am a student going to the Archives Nationales for the first time; how would you prepare me to find what I am looking for?"

This method yielded far more material than the project has been able to use. The autobiographical approach took us into many areas of inquiry that were beyond the scope of this study, yielding a panorama of the participants' professional histories. The interview records will be preserved for future study (see below).

TREATMENT OF THE MATERIAL • The interviews were tape-recorded, using standard portable equipment and tape cassettes. The tapes were then transcribed to a word-processing program by personnel at IRIS. The sixty-seven ninety-minute tapes produced about fifteen hundred pages, single-spaced, of transcripts.

The electronic texts were then reformatted and given line numbers by a software program called The Ethnograph (Littleton, Colo.: Qualis Research Associates, 1985). Developed for the purpose of reorganizing verbal files, the program allows text to be divided freely according to subject categories. After establishing a list of subject categories that included virtually all subjects discussed (see appendix 3), the three interviewers coded the processed transcripts, matching subjects to line numbers. Once the codings were entered, the program separated all the texts into component parts by subject. Because of the quantity of material and the limited scope of the project, however, only a selected portion of the complete subject categories was surveyed in this report (see appendix 4).

The tapes and transcripts are to be donated to two archives, where they will be available for further study: the Getty Archives of the History of Art (part of the Getty Center for the History of Art and the Humanities) in Santa Monica, California; and the Brown University Archives at the John Hay Library in Providence, Rhode Island.

The open spirit of inquiry that all the participating scholars brought to this project was truly remarkable. Their willingness to speak freely, indeed to allow the interviewers to invade their thoughts, provided the foundation on which the project could be built.

The Process of Art-historical Inquiry

ORIGINAL WORKS OF ART AND REPRODUCTIONS

For most of the scholars interviewed, original works of art are the starting point of art-historical research. Because art historians conduct much of their work at a distance from the artifacts that they are considering, they often use reproductions as substitutes for works of art. These substitutes are usually photographic reproductions, such as photographic prints, thirty-five millimeter slides, larger color transparencies, published illustrations, or microfilm and microfiche images. Reproductive images in other media, such as drawings, engravings, or lithographs, can also serve as substitutes. While reproductions can play a significant and even indispensable role in art-historical inquiry, firsthand experiences with the objects themselves are valued and usually essential aspects of the research process.

> You can look at pictures and slides of a cathedral, [but] that's not the experience of the building and how it works, . . . that's not the effect of the spaces and the shape and decoration. It's the same with a manuscript; a manuscript has a real character and quality and feel, which relate to its size and scale. . . . You don't get any of that from microfilm.

> The work of art has a kind of object-hood and physical presence which is very different from any [reproductive] image; even if the slide or the transparency were perfect, it's third-best.

> [Dealers] send you a photograph and ask you your opinion. I refuse to answer questions without having seen the original. Things look so different in photographs.

> [The study of buildings] is indeed physical; it is enormously direct and tangible, and you get dirty. . . . Buildings are incredibly complex and very largely

> hidden physical beings. . . . I would never pretend to study a building and publish on the building without having [crawled] into everything.

A reproduction may serve as an aide-mémoire and provide certain kinds of information, but one comes to understand the work of art in unique ways through immediate contact with it.

> In [a] collection [in Boston] is a picture, which—because it's great and important—always . . . interested me. There are some things about that picture which you . . . wouldn't notice from photographs at all because it has been overpainted.

> You use reproductions as reminders, but it's one thing to look at a photograph when you have a fresh visual image in your mind. I've been to Leningrad three times, [and] we've had *Three Women* here for a fairly long time. . . . So looking at a good transparency of the picture means something different [to me than to] someone who has never [seen it] or has seen it [only] once. . . . Then you try, if the picture is not on the other end of the world when you're through writing, to . . . double-check . . . text against picture.

> I was flabbergasted when I . . . discovered that there is an entire Roman city with enclosed palisades and garrisons under a coat of darkened varnish and dirt that is still lending its lugubrious brown, shadowy emotional quality to modern reproductions of this altarpiece wherever you find it reproduced.

A scholar may gain information directly from a work of art through a spectrum of analytic strategies that range from "subjective" to "objective" description. One scholar, for example, proposed a new historical reading of a medieval building based on sensory observation,

> I [sat] in [Beauvais Cathedral] and describe[d] it. I would move my chair around from one spot to another. I have pages and pages and pages of description. In that way you become very aware of what is where in the building: where certain pier types change and all the spatial aspects, . . . of the building changing gears. . . . On a Sunday morning [during] mass, . . . I was . . . forced

> just to sit there and not move, comparing with high-powered binoculars capital after capital. It became so very obvious that it was a sequence of change . . . from . . . west to east. . . . The more I thought about it, and the more I looked at the building, everything fell into place.

and he then supported his thesis with painstaking, measured architectural drawings.

> I am a great believer in the physical business of making a measured plan for the building and making measured sections of pier types. . . . For the dating of Beauvais [Cathedral] one of the best things I have is . . . the pier section . . . and the molding profile in the transept. . . . You don't get firm dating without careful physical analysis. . . . The main revelations I got out of Beauvais were as a result of this . . . and the plan, [which] took me four months of work—every day in the building—going back and back and back.

At times only repeated contact with the object under consideration will verify art-historical conclusions.

> You always face the problem [of making an incorrect attribution on] first impression. I force myself to be careful . . . to compare, to take my [magnifying] glass to look again and again. . . . I've seen that others reach very dubious attributions by being quick. And I fear to do the same.

One scholar trained his students to develop and sharpen their intuitions in the presence of the works themselves (see also "Connoisseurship") in the belief that sensitivity to originals was essential to the conduct of art-historical inquiry.

> To make wise and sensitive judgments about the value of things—I am not talking about dollars—involves a lot of different lines of inquiry. But at the very beginning it involves a direct response on [your] part. . . . One of the standard exercises I have had with students is . . . that they . . . make note of how they felt about something, whether they thought it was wonderful, ugly, confusing, clear, and so forth.

As central as works of art are to the work of art historians, access to originals is often difficult to gain. One may be at a costly distance from the objects of study (see "Finances"), or one may be restricted by their owners' limitations. To make the most efficient use of time and the most prudent use of financial resources, an art historian often collects and studies reproductions as well as primary and secondary documentation (see "Primary Documents and Archives" and "Secondary Sources and Libraries") before traveling to inspect originals. The discouragement that the author of a catalogue raisonné experienced when he was unable to see as much as he wished is not uncommon.

> I wrote hundreds of letters to museums to get photographs. I traveled then to see [the paintings], but I didn't see them all because sometimes they were in the basement, on the road, [or] under restoration.

If art historians encounter difficulties in gaining access to works of art housed in collections, they may meet even more formidable obstacles in studying objects outside collection walls. The experiences of a stained-glass specialist and an architectural historian illustrate the lengths to which scholars must sometimes go in order to confront originals face-to-face.

> You have to look at [the stained-glass panels] very closely with binoculars. In a way the method is very close to [that] one [uses] in a museum. . . . The idea is to get as close as possible to the panels themselves. Of course, when you can get scaffolding, this is the best. But it's not always possible. . . . It is awfully expensive. . . . You hire it and pay by the day.

> [To measure] the thicknesses of the walls [of a Gothic cathedral], . . . you climb up to the windows, and those are tall windows! You borrow an extending ladder. You put the bottom on the shiny floor, and you constantly have this image of the ladder skating away from under you.

Because of the difficulties, one may feel extremely fortunate to find the material one needs easily and to spend a good amount of time with it.

> I spent months . . . in residence in Bolton Landing [at David Smith's] farm called Terminal Iron Works. He lived and worked and had all of his amazing

> records [there], plus [many of] the sculptures. . . . It was very lucky that most of the work at the time of his death was unsold. . . . So . . . it came . . . falling like manna. Most of the [rest of the] work was on the East Coast, somewhere between Boston and Washington. . . . I did not have to go to . . . different countries. It wasn't [widely] dispersed yet. . . . Smith obviously wanted to keep [the larger] work[s] around him in the fields. . . . The smaller works were all in the basement, . . . so I could get them out.

ORIGINALS VERSUS REPRODUCTIONS ▪ Despite the primacy given to direct experience with original works of art, the scholars stressed that reproductions are essential to the conduct of art-historical inquiry. They were mindful both of the historic trust placed in the reproduction and of the constant danger inherent in assuming its veracity.

> Photography was a very crucial thing in the development of the discipline. . . . The Fogg Museum [of Harvard University] was originally intended to be a museum for an archive of photographs and occasional busts and reproductions, but not original works of art. It was felt that the only way to scientifically study art was to use scientific instruments.

> A photograph is anything but a neutral documentation. It entails, after all, a complicated chemical and optical process which is subject to severe manipulation at any stage along the way, including printing.

> Part of what is wrong with traditional art history is that . . . historians work from photographs rather than from actual objects of art. . . . [They] lose touch with what's wrong with . . . the slide itself.

The tension between the original and its reproduction requires the constant evaluation of appropriate use.

> There are certain things you can do with a bad photograph [of a work of art], certain things that you can only do with a good photograph, and certain things that you shouldn't do without the original.

> Ideally I don't believe one should make discoveries from photographs.

> I'd prefer to see the original, but I do a lot of things from slides or Ektachromes . . . or color Xeroxes. . . . One of the problems about people who are in systems is that they get hung up on the issue of faithfulness. In essence that's a kind of purist abstraction. . . . The issue is, you do the best you can because that's what we do in real life.

Reproductions raise special problems for the archaeologist, the architectural historian, the stained-glass specialist, the scholar of frescoes, and even the modernist, especially when they study the ensemble to which the work of art belongs.

> In the work that Leroi-Gourhan has done on Paleolithic painting, which is all about the analysis of the placement of the various animals in relationship to the various parts of the cave, . . . photography doesn't have any meaning.

> My first . . . professor of the history of art said, "Never look a long time at a [particular] photograph. Look at a lot of photographs and go back often [to the building]." And I think it quite true. . . . I go and take a short note, and I remember the atmosphere of the building, how it's lit, how it's displayed, the impression I have. And when I have to study the [stained] glass, I know the building itself.

> It is absolutely necessary to see the pictures [at the original site]. . . . For a cycle of frescoes it is possible [using reproductions] to have some ideas about the year, the culture of the painter, and so on. But the connection between the space and the picture is impossible if you are not in the place.

> Obviously photography becomes a very limited tool [in the case of] earthworks. . . . That had this very strange consequence, which was to pulverize the work, to fragment it, to disperse it into its documents. . . . The question of sculpture dissolving into nothing but its document became a problem.

ADVANTAGES AND LIMITATIONS OF REPRODUCTIONS ▪ Reproductions allow scholars to manipulate images of objects, but even as the scholars praised various types of reproductions, they acknowledged those substitutes' limitations. Diverse opinions about the efficacy of certain reproductive processes emerged in the interviews.

> [Microfilm] is a high-contrast, black-and-white object. [The quality] is so poor that I don't want to have microfilms of manuscripts except as a record of their contents and the relationship of images to the whole. . . . [Nevertheless] I microfilmed a great many Passion tracts [and] had a lot of them printed on copyflow paper. . . . I would then read through them and annotate them in the margins, right on the thing.

> I use slides because with slides [as opposed to printed photos] you have the options of printing them, blowing them up, using them with a magnifying glass. . . . I do all of that. . . . I have slides, prints made from them, sometimes even color Xeroxes made from them.

> A thirty-five-millimeter slide is simply too troublesome for research. You have to project it, and with a big transparency you don't. [The slide] creates a kind of artificial luminosity, which the pictures don't have . . . as a result of the darkness of the room and the light bouncing off the white wall. . . . Slide projection is a necessary evil.

> I have . . . a colleague [who] frequently sends me Xeroxes of manuscripts. And these Xeroxes tell me what I have to know. . . . I send Xeroxes . . . to colleagues all the time. It really tells me whether something is germane to what I'm doing, and that tells me if and when I will need a photograph or a slide.

Especially troublesome for many scholars was the importance of color and the frequent inadequacy of its reproduction.

> I'm going to have to postpone until I see the actual manuscript [rather than the black-and-white photocopy] to say more about what I think of it. . . . Burgundian manuscripts in the area of Beaune have a particular kind of palette and muddy color. The Ghent manuscripts have pastel blue colors as opposed to hotter, more vivid colors in Bruges. . . . Color is sometimes the definitive [characteristic].

> I had occasion to point out that certain colors essential to [a Jungian critic's] alchemical argument [about Jackson Pollock's work] . . . are in fact not in the picture at all and that she'd obviously seen a bad color reproduction and out of that she'd woven this thing. . . . Art history has become too much of a library science. . . . The young scholars dream up ideas and work in libraries.

> The whole history of art is being distorted by the selection made in the *opera completa* volumes, and you can predict what a student is going to do in a seminar because they . . . are lazy about seeking out photographs. . . . [These cheap serials] are marvelous books, but it is this selection of color and color detail that determines what a lot of students will actually focus on.

The art historians interviewed valued reproductions of works of art not only for their documentary, objective content but also for their artistic, subjective content. Historic photographs may be useful in revealing previous states, while contemporary photographs that are made with an express intention may enrich critical analysis of the object.

> You are always looking for the oldest photographs you can find of a given work of art . . . because pictures undergo amazing transformations over generations and centuries. We have photographs of works of art dating from the 1850s and photographs taken during the bad old days of wanton alteration—restoration of works of art—[which] are the most revealing thing we have got.

> [David Smith] performed an act of criticism with his own photographs. . . . The elegant [Ugo] Mulas views [were more dramatically] lit than Smith's work. . . . They were less informative, [more] percussive. . . . Mulas was probably also very aware of the way Smith photographed his own work [see figs. 1 and 2].

Indeed the study of reproductions, replicas, and copies as interesting objects in their own right and the examination of their relationships to original, sometimes lost works of art are fields of inquiry that have drawn the attention of scholars who work in other than modern fields.

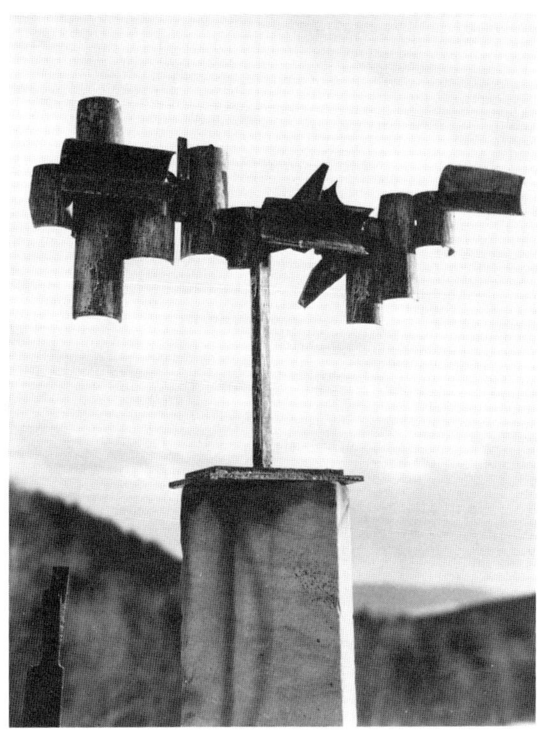

1. DAVID SMITH, *Bouquet of Concaves*, 1959, private collection, photo by the artist, courtesy Rosalind Krauss

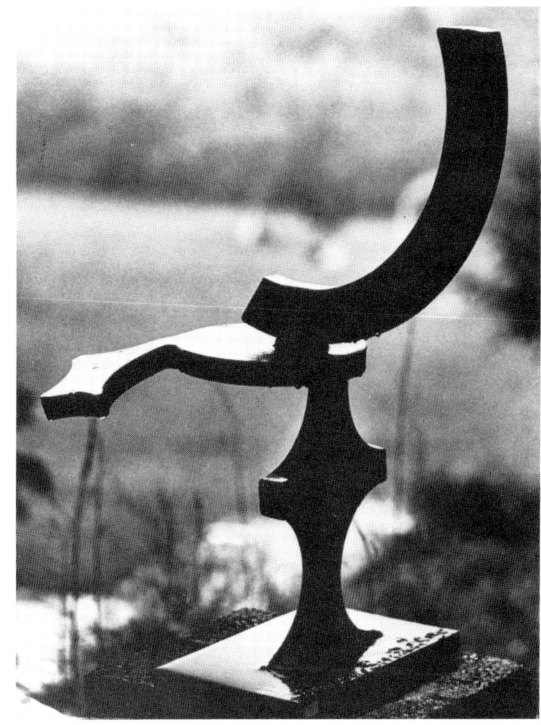

2. DAVID SMITH, *Albany III*, 1959, estate of the artist, photo by Ugo Mulas, courtesy Archives of American Art

> One of the things I described in my dissertation was the *Madonna with a Flower*, a very famous painting by Rogier van der Weyden, which didn't survive in the original but in a very fine copy in . . . Ghent and one very crude copy of a slightly altered version in Spain. What I tried to show was that reproduction—in the more or less modern sense—appeared in fifteenth-century art [when copies were made] after very famous paintings, which people obviously knew [through] engravings. I was able to show that this began not in German art, as was believed, but in Netherlandish art [see figs. 3 and 4].

Vintage and contemporary photographic prints made from the same negative present a modern-day dilemma with aesthetic, economic, and legal repercussions for both scholars and those involved in the art market. One scholar's determination to find photographs for an exhibition led her into such a problematic situation. When she was unable to locate vintage prints, she tried to locate negatives and obtain permission to have new prints made (see also "Connoisseurship").

> [I tried] to find the original photographs [that had been reproduced] in the magazines. Having decided that these [images] were very important, I couldn't put the magazines in the exhibition. There's this museological requirement that you have to find the original. . . . In the case of *Minotaure*, which was published by Skira, I called Madame Skira. . . . Indeed she did find about seven, . . . but that was all she could find. . . . In certain cases I found the negatives and had them printed. I had endless cups of tea . . . with Juliet Man Ray, for example, and finally got her to agree to let me go through the negatives in Man Ray's studio [where] I found . . . twelve images, [among them] the image of *Explosante-fixe*. I knew that there was no vintage print of that, and so I asked her if I could have it printed.

INSTITUTIONAL COLLECTIONS OF REPRODUCTIONS ▪ Archives of photographs in museums and research centers are an important source of reproductions for art historians. The best photographic archives were described as indispensable resources that had been carefully designed for scholarly use,

> The photo archive . . . at the Warburg [Institute in London] was always headed, and is headed to this day, by excellent scholars. . . . One of the great weaknesses in the Anglo-Saxon world . . . is that one always thinks of instruments of scholarship [as having been] created by some sort of glorified service staff, as opposed to knowing that the surgical instruments are built by people who know every motion that the surgeons are going to make with them.

or provided a panorama of information in conjunction with reproductions.

> The Documentation au Département Peinture [in the Louvre] . . . is a very important place if you work on paintings. In a certain way [it] is what a photo archive should be, . . . a collection of everything on an artist. They have boxes . . . with clippings out of newspapers, sales catalogues, and journals, photos that they get from everywhere, letters. . . . So if you look into these boxes, . . . you will find . . . thousands and thousands of pieces of information.

The large photo archive can offer a view of art seldom afforded in any other setting. Access to such diverse exposure can alter one's art-historical perspective.

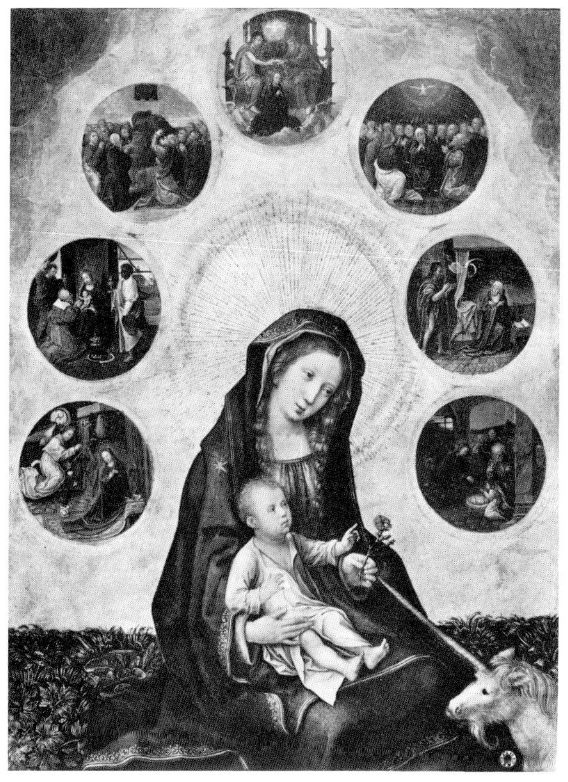

3. BERNAERT VAN ORLEY, *The Seven Joys of Mary*, sixteenth century, Galleria Colonna, Rome, photo courtesy Alinari/Art Resource, New York

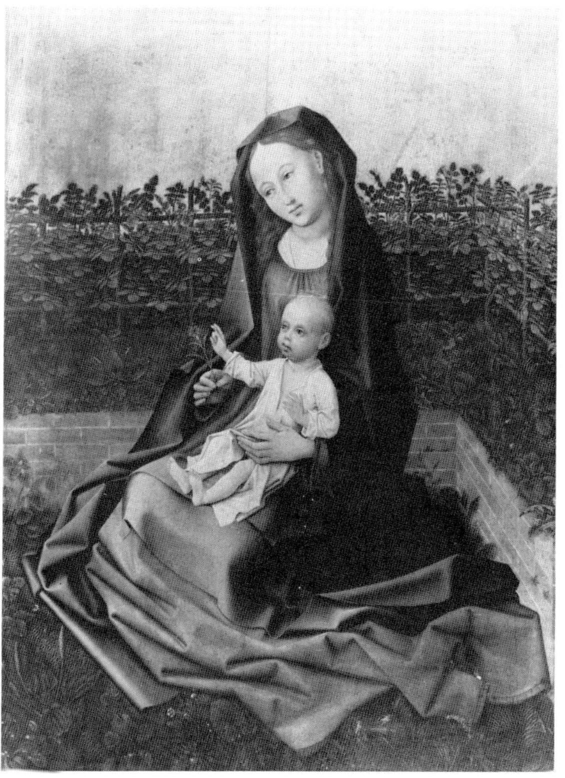

4. ALSATIAN MASTER, *Virgin and Child*, fifteenth century, Musées de la Ville de Strasbourg, photo courtesy Giraudon/Art Resource, New York

> In art history in the university you see the top, . . . probably less than 1 percent, of the total number of artworks floating around by the artists that are considered . . . important. . . . Your whole idea of the body of work is formed by the top. . . . When you work at the RKD [Rijksbureau voor Kunsthistorische Documentatie, The Hague, and] see this vast number of copies and replicas and questionable works and unassignable works, damaged things, fragments, you really come face-to-face with another kind of reality in the realm of art.

The art market also contributes to the fund of available reproductions by photographing works of art for sale and by publishing illustrated auction catalogues; these are invaluable resources for scholars.

> [When art] passes through the art trade, there are incentives for photographs to be made, typically. That is when the expertise is written. . . . And when the

> thing comes to light, it is published often in an auction [catalogue]. . . . When it goes back into private hands, things are usually quiescent. So that is where most photographs [that I need] come from. Now when [a work of art] is bought and goes into a public collection, you might not know about it unless it is published by the public collection.

PERSONAL COLLECTIONS OF REPRODUCTIONS ▪ Some art-historical periods are well illustrated by series of published volumes that furnish scholars with nearly encyclopedic collections of images, but these are the exception rather than the rule.

> There are two corpuses of paintings in Northern Renaissance art that one uses constantly. One covers everything from around 1250 to 1500. It doesn't reproduce every painting, [but] it's a selection that reproduces thousands, so it's representative. And [the second provides] the same kind of selection. Every year I must, in the course of my research, go through the eleven volumes of [the one] and the fourteen volumes of [the other] . . . in the sense that . . . I want to see the tradition. . . . I end up turning those pages again and again and again. . . . The reason I value [these corpuses] is because the material they've reproduced is the bulk of the tradition of German and Netherlandish art.

Most scholars must build personal collections of reproductions through their own efforts and acquisitions. One scholar's first attempt to form a photographic archive contributed profoundly to his growing knowledge and understanding of works of art,

> After the semester [that] I started art history, . . . I went to Italy . . . with another student. I photographed . . . architecture from the front, the back, and made thousand[s of] slides. . . . I was in a certain way prepared and organized. . . . We were looking at exactly the period we had [covered] in our seminars. . . . Just writing down what [the slides were], arranging them, classifying them . . . was very important . . . in my student education.

even though he later found the collection irrelevant to his work.

> I never used them [so I said] to my slide department, "You can use whatever you want." So they took [some], and the rest they threw away.

Art historians' collections compensate for inaccessible or deficient institutional collections and have the advantage of being personally selected and indexed. In addition they often contain hard-won images of objects that may not have been reproduced before.

> For each of those buildings I have thousands of photographs. I have my own darkroom, so I tend to be rather lavish with what I do, and I print it all up, generally small. . . . Then what I am interested in I print up large.

> The older I get, the more [slides I take]. . . . Sometimes what you didn't think was important turns out to be. Increasingly . . . I try and do as much as I can.

> It has been something like a policy: if you are there and you see it and you think it is going to be useful, and if it is not outrageously expensive, [get the photograph] now because you won't be able to find it again, you won't be there again.

> Modern art history is basically unmanageable without photographs because it's completely comparative by method. . . . [But] it's very hard to get the photographs; this is one of the great headaches of the field. . . . Every person runs into this whether you're working on ancient vessels or medieval architecture. . . . [Some] museums . . . will send you a photograph. They may charge you the world, but the money is the least thing in all of this. [If] you want something from [certain countries], . . . these things become agonies. . . . Part of the problem is they are understaffed, underfunded, and they have very cumbersome regulations which make it very hard to really accommodate people.

REPRODUCTIONS AND TEACHING ▪ Discussions of reproductions inevitably merged with conversations about teaching. Art historians who teach felt a responsibility to encourage their students to work with originals as well as with reproductions.

> Students are so needy; I mean students are dealing with substitutes all the time anyway, and what they need are unmediated confrontations with the real thing as much as possible and to have a mentor nearby to help.

> We rather discourage [students] from sitting around our libraries all the day. It is a bad sign if you see one of them there every day. It means they are looking at works of art [reproduced in books]; they are not out [looking at originals].

> [You can] perhaps study text on microfilm, but you can't study the book or the history of the book or the history of art. [Furthermore microfilms] are unwieldy in the sense that I find them tedious. And I don't want to have students [work] with microfilms and not . . . [with] art and manuscripts. So one uses them at times, but only as an aid.

The special role and requirements of reproductions for teaching emerged through both reminiscence and statements of current need.

> I took another type of photograph. . . . It's not to be published. It's more the atmosphere, general photographs of the [stained-glass] windows for my students.

> Most slides, for financial reasons, are duplicates; they're not original Kodachromes made in front of the picture. . . . [But even though I had access to original slides] I went around Europe myself when I began teaching in order to make slides, largely because [the available slides] had no details . . . [or not] the details you'd want to talk about.

WORKS OF ART IN THEIR CULTURAL CONTEXT ▪ The fallibility of reproductions and the fragmentary information that they provide led to discussions of the necessity of studying works of art in the full context of their cultures. For many the relationship between a work of art and its original context is integral to its elucidation. They wanted to reconstruct, if only verbally, the complex cultural matrix in which objects were produced (see "Cultural and Social History").

> I tried to establish where the *Isenheim Altarpiece* [fig. 12, p. 114] actually did stand and what use was made of it in this hospital for the terminally ill.

> The reason I got into manuscripts is . . . that I was very concerned with the context of works of art. In manuscripts you have the partial context of the work of art . . . the painting and the book for which it was made. You don't have the full context because the manuscript would have been used in a church [or] in a home for specific purposes, but you have enough to do things that you couldn't do otherwise. . . . One can argue historically for much more [contextual] evidence than [one can for] paintings that happen to be hanging on a wall in a museum.

Other scholars, however, seized upon the ability to place works of art in new contexts, such as museum exhibitions, in order to achieve new insights into meaning.

> Every time you readjust the relationship of pictures physically in space, they tend to speak differently in terms of one another. . . . There are parts of this collection that are extremely intricately installed from an art-historical point of view. . . . For example, there is a place where there is a Lipchitz sculpture next to a Picasso painting. I can't prove it, but I'm absolutely convinced that that sculpture was made in direct response to that painting. Lipchitz visited the studio while it was being made. His art before that was very different; suddenly it changed. I put the sculpture near the painting, and I think that people who are really visually oriented might see a connection between the two. . . . Because we had the works . . . I could make a series of direct and indirect relationships between works of art that is a kind of cat's cradle of intricacy.

REPRODUCTIONS AND INFORMATION TECHNOLOGY ▪ In the light of their considerable experience with public, private, and personal collections of reproductions, several of the scholars imagined automated image banks—some futuristic in conception—that might expand research possibilities (see also "Organization of Information," especially "Information Technology and the Future," and "Wish List").

> We fantasized a machine [in which] this entire slide archive was kept [and with which we could] get all the [architectural units with] a certain height, width, and length ratio. . . . And it would project these on a screen.

> The issue is that when you're studying Rembrandt and van Eyck, you have to have access to the traditions from which [they emerged]. You don't know the anonymous works and the minor works for centuries leading up to Rembrandt. . . . [Someday] we're going to have it on computer and video access.

SUMMARY ▪ Physical involvement with the original monument or work of art is seen as indispensable to the study of art history, especially in the areas of connoisseurship and the architectural environment. The manipulative nature of reproductions and the relative merits and deficiencies of various media demand wariness. Nevertheless the practical difficulties of traveling to and comparing original works have produced ingenious methods of using reproductions of all kinds. As works of art and as records of conservation history, older photographs have special value. Collections of reproductions, whether institutional or personal, constitute vital resources for the art historian. The comprehensiveness of the collection, the inclusion of less well-known works, the scholarly acumen used in cataloguing, and the difficulty of obtaining photographs were common preoccupations. Another was the absence of context that the photographic reproduction imposes on the work of art.

PRIMARY DOCUMENTS AND ARCHIVES

If works of art are windows on the past, documents can be keys that unlock the door of historical background. When one immerses oneself in archival materials such as correspondence, legal instruments, inventories, minutes and reports of proceedings, personal and household accounts, ecclesiastical and governmental records, and other types of written documents contemporary with the object of study, one enters a world apart.

> I never got over the kind of excitement that one gets in working with texts, and in a sense it is what I love to do best—simply to have a month in the archive and go through it bit by bit.

> I made myself into a sort of archival historian. . . . It's so enormously absorbing and really such fun. . . . You find that you are in very close touch with people of a thousand years ago who are dust now. You trace them through their particular dilemmas, problems, and happinesses that make them very contemporary, bring them right back to life.

> I always did and still feel very "grown up" when I visit an archive. It seems to me the only serious occupation of an art historian. . . . There one is in touch with the past.

The richness of archival material can be seductive, resulting in what some art historians consider to be unfortunate consequences: the texts themselves may displace the work of art as the focus of inquiry or may provide a daunting and distracting amount of information. One art historian who works frequently in archives expressed these reservations:

> It is bad on the eyes and it is bad for the mind . . . for the art historian to be in an archive most of the time. . . . You don't have to think, just collect, collect, collect. You are terribly happy when you are doing it, . . . and then when you actually look . . . at what you got, the euphoria can wear off. It is not quite so marvelous as you thought it was when you were reading it.

Some art historians are more heavily involved in the use of archives than others. The role that archival documents play in art-historical research depends on the questions being asked about the work of art, and certain periods and places are better represented by written records than others.

> [Early medieval] records are not precise [about glaziers' names]. . . . They are precise about money to justify [what was] spent. But quite exceptional are the contracts that tie the man asking to the man working.

> It is spectacular to be able to go to a pier [at Troyes Cathedral] and say Anthoine Colas cut that in 1462. . . . Having discovered [him in the written records, I went] to the building to establish firmly what it was that he had done [see figs. 5 and 6].

ACCESS TO ARCHIVAL DOCUMENTS ▪ In addition to making general comments about the conduct of archival research, many scholars stressed the differences between collections. These may arise from institutional policies, indexing practices, staffing, or conservation requirements. Gaining familiarity with an archive and feeling successful there are often uphill battles.

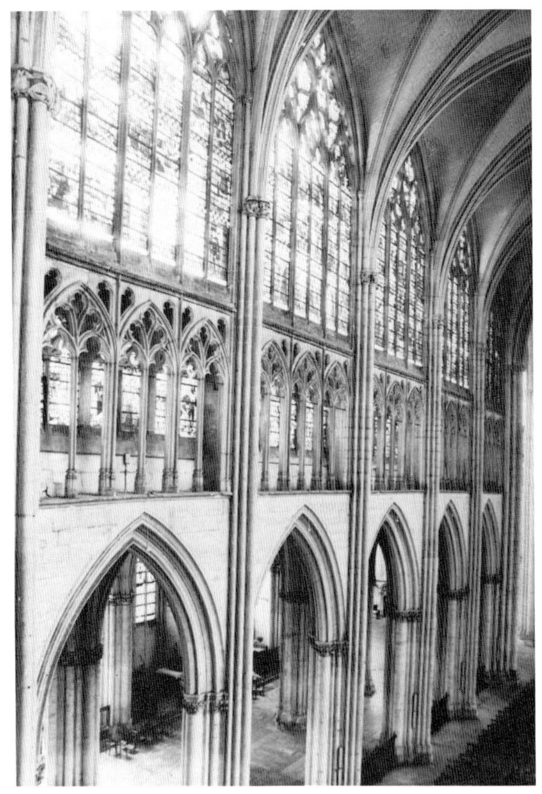

5. TROYES CATHEDRAL, interior of nave, north side, looking east, photo by Stephen Murray

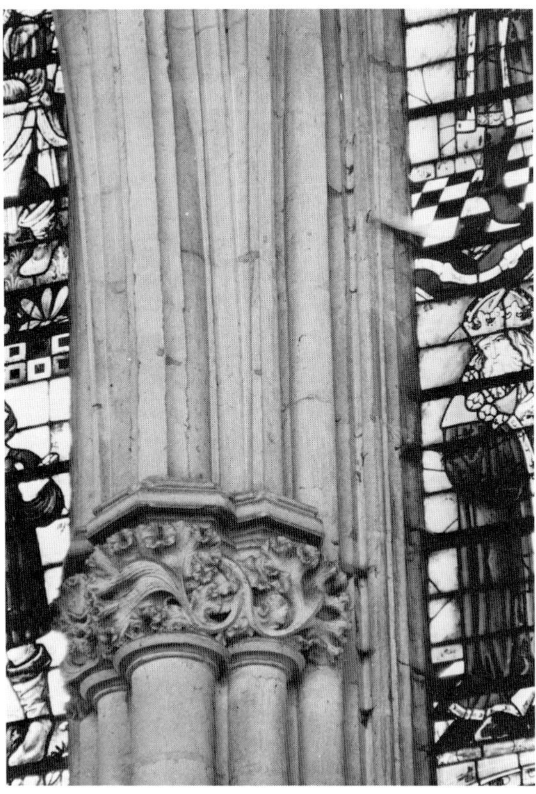

6. MASTER ANTHOINE COLAS, Troyes Cathedral, nave clerestory capital, circa 1470, detail of fig. 5 (second capital from left), photo by Stephen Murray

> This [archive] was a place terrifying to the foreigner. They were totally understaffed. . . . It was a place with . . . an enormous amount [of material], . . . and they have no people.

At the same time certain archives were seen as models.

> The Mantua archive . . . is a good archive to begin in because it is small and well organized and friendly, and you can get quite a lot done in a short space of time. . . . There are big [handwritten indexes] . . . and a typed, kind of rough guide. . . . It is all very homey. . . . So I was lucky that my first experience was a very pleasant, easy one.

> Holland was an incredible place to do research because . . . everything is accessible. It is public; they want to make it public. So I used archives for the

> city of The Hague [as well as for] smaller towns. Every municipality has archives which are well run. . . . It was just so easy.

Collection catalogues are the standard source that scholars consult to determine whether the information that they are seeking is in archival repositories. Indexes to some collections have been reproduced and are available in major research libraries. Yet scholars often found that these catalogues—whether published or on-site—did not portray a collection's holdings accurately.

> Access is through these indexes, which are *comme ci, comme ça*. Some were made by people who read every single act and summarized all names mentioned, all dates, and so forth. Others were indexed [less thoroughly].

> Once you start working in one of these archives, you realize what else they have got. You often can only know if you are there, because [they] are not turning out very complete or professional catalogues in the small towns.

> You still use the nineteenth-century indexes, which are tattered beyond belief. . . . And if somebody made a mistake then, that mistake is still there today.

One scholar discovered how useful a subject index could be, to the extent even of playing a creative role in his work.

> In the Bibliothèque Nationale [in Paris is a collection] called the Collection le Senne, which is card-indexed according to subject. . . . It's very extraordinary. . . . Once you begin, you then start to leapfrog from reference to reference. That, I find, is often the most fertile.

As the scholars stressed the importance of an archival catalogue, so too they emphasized the contribution to their efforts that those familiar with a collection could make. Curators, archivists, and fellow reseachers all aided in the research process. The time spent explaining one's work and cultivating scholarly exchange usually brought productive results. Researchers expressed deep appreciation for those who smoothed their way.

> I consider it terribly important to be right there on the spot, and by doing that, you learn all kinds of things you wouldn't know otherwise. I got to know the archivist rather well, and [he] helped . . . me revise and correct [my transcriptions].

> You walk into a [collection] and either just sit down and start ordering manuscripts, photographs, catalogues, and lists . . . or meet a curator and tell him what you're doing. . . . Sometimes I'll order manuscripts for two whole days, and the percentage of what's important . . . turns out to be one-hundredth. Then the third day the curator, [who] has been away, comes back and says, "Oh, . . . don't bother with the catalogue; I have my own list."

> In Mantua I used for years to talk with a retired supervisor of the study room. . . . You even invite [another researcher] for dinner and tell him the problem, . . . because there is a kind of knowledge of the stables which only the mice have.

Nevertheless archival research seems to require a high degree of self-sufficiency.

> [One] is always self-taught. There are a few people in the archive itself who are assistants, . . . who have a certain amount of training, and [with experience they become] walking encyclopedias of what may be found where. You rely a good deal on these people as you get started . . . , but mainly you do it on your own. You determine where the most promising fields are, and you begin to read between the lines.

DISPERSED DOCUMENTS ▪ The researcher's efforts are sometimes hindered by the fact that the locations of documents change over time and are difficult to follow. Knowledge of political history helps in understanding the present location of documents.

> [The chapter documents] are the main thing in terms of the medieval fabric because the chapter was mainly involved . . . in the construction of the cathedral. . . . During the French Revolution, with the dispossession of the church, these [chapter records] were removed [from the ecclesiastical archives] . . . , became state property, and are now kept in departmental

> archives. . . . It is just lucky that Troyes is the capital of Aube; it is nice [to study the documents] in the same city where the cathedral is.

> The archives of the Republic of Venice are more or less [similar to] all the archives in Italy, which is to say that what papers survived at the time that the Italian states collapsed (from the end of the eighteenth to the early nineteenth century) became the property of the successor state . . . [which] organized them into state archives, centralized always in the head town of each province. . . . And what you have today is essentially the archive as it was organized . . . in the nineteenth century.

A discouraging but familiar experience for the scholars interviewed was finding that portions of the records that they were studying were no longer in the archive. In cases where documents are sold as commodities, auction catalogues may lead to the discovery of their location. Personal contacts, dogged hunting, and serendipity are other important aspects of what one scholar called "the paper chase."

> Some [of the building accounts] were sold off in the 1830s. . . . Some are completely lost, [but I found some] through connections. . . . A lot of them were in the Phillipps collection . . . which had been in Cheltenham. . . . I got in touch with [a scholar who had traced the Phillipps collection], and he gave me references.

> Archives have a way of overflowing, so anybody who knows them has some sympathy for the desire to occasionally prune the trees. . . . When I worked on a small sixteenth-century town . . . , there was one very disconcerting statement in the introduction to the holdings of the archives which said that material which had no bearing on the history of the locality . . . had been weeded out . . . in the late nineteenth century. . . . Among the things that were missing were any payment records, any records of the actual day-to-day conduct of the building campaign. . . . [Through a tip from a friend,] I found them at the University of Kansas in Lawrence; . . . they were bought years ago as calligraphic samples of sixteenth-century Italian origin. . . . [This] is a good illustration that if you weed out, you may weed out some of the most valuable information for somebody else who comes along.

> I thought that everything I needed [would be] in the Civic Museum of Venice, . . . and I did find most of what exists there. . . . [But then I discovered that] . . . the department of maps [in the British Museum] had a lot. . . . I realized that I was in trouble, that the Venetian collection was not complete. . . . So I began systematically going to other places or writing to them.

USE OF ARCHIVAL DOCUMENTS ▪ Deciphering, translating, and transcribing records often require special skills beyond knowledge of languages. Fluency in the native language is usually requisite for productive work in a foreign archive.

> You must know French in a native way to work in the French archives; . . . you have to speak with a lot of people—archivists, neighbors working with you. . . . It's very important to get into this . . . special kind of community [of people] who are passionate about finding things.

One historian felt a spontaneous sympathy for the appearance of handwritten documents, which seemed to facilitate her work in the archives.

> I have a very strange hand[writing], . . . and I found that I could read other people's hands in archives quite well. . . . I made these sorts of marks myself.

Her experience, however, was uncharacteristic of the group. Indeed most of the art historians who undertake extensive archival research reported that they mastered documents only through trial and error; the process could be painstaking and frustrating, if ultimately rewarding.

> Your first document arrives, and you can't make heads nor tails of it because it is written in old writing; it's full of abbreviations. . . . You can sit there all day and really understand only three words. You think, "How do these people do it? What's the matter with me?"

> I took courses in paleography in London, but it doesn't really equip you. . . . There is nothing you can do other than just get the manuscript, start to transcribe it, and leave gaps. I started out sometimes having more gaps than

> words. . . . It is especially helpful if you can find things that have been transcribed, and then you can compare the transcription with the original.

> You make your own manual [of abbreviations peculiar to the period]. And that you get a handle on pretty quickly. More difficult are the formulae . . . [or legalisms that] exist in medieval and Renaissance acts, . . . and it takes a while to learn them. You must learn them because those are the things that get to be most abbreviated because they are always repeated.

> [In transcribing manuscripts, I use Adriano] Cappelli's small-format volume that summarizes the contractions in Latin words. Even when the scribes reverted from Latin into French, they went on using the contractions that had been used in Latin. . . . [The medieval fabric account was written in] a kind of shorthand designed to save space. Parchment and paper were expensive items, and one didn't want to [use] long words.

> [I had no training in paleography], which is really the old-fashioned pattern. Nowadays . . . we try to help students into a rudimentary grasp of paleography and codicology.

> Gradually you learn how to find [the archival documents], read them, rate their value, and estimate whether [you have] an original or a copy, a good or bad copy; all these things you learn by doing. In the end you can get to be quite good.

Even as he gained confidence, one scholar had persistent doubts that he had used certain documents to the fullest extent possible.

> I have gone back over and over that stuff now for the last ten years, and over and over I have said to myself, "There is a problem in that stage. Go back and reread it."

Preparing a transcription for publication may raise the issue of how a scholar can best represent the text.

> Basically there are two different positions. . . . I am an art historian, and I want to take the material out of these texts which is relevant for cathedral construction. And on the other hand, an archivist or paleographer is going to want a different kind of transcript which will not omit anything. . . . [They] are just going to have to accept the fact that the form of the texts that I am presenting does not conform to a critical edition. But what I am trying to do . . . is to bring these two sources together, the building and the texts.

As problematic as the tasks of deciphering, translation, and transcription of archival documents can be, most of the scholars felt that these undertakings lie within the purview of the art historian. Indeed one questioned the scholarly integrity of history written without intimate contact with the documents.

> The economics of the situation, the pressure of time, and the particular focus and relatively poor preparation of people who undertake [archival work] . . . has led to the most insidious . . . solutions where scholars . . . farm [out transcription] as a tedious and complicated sideline, which is best done by the locals. . . . It reproduces an old division which only amateur historians engaged in, and that is that the archiv[ist] does the dirty work . . . , and then the great historical consequences are the privileged insight of those people who don't dirty their hands with this sort of stuff.

Many of the art historians who spend a great deal of time in archives were keenly aware of the physical vulnerability of the documents that they use. Ideally these fragile records should be properly conserved and handled with extreme care, the kind of care accorded works of art. Because of lack of funds, however, archives are often unable to provide optimal protection for their records. Some of the scholars spoke of the contradiction they faced in wanting access to original documents and wishing to see them preserved.

> When you page them, you get a big box [with] fifteen parchments, and you have to unroll them, and everybody next to you growls at you because you are taking up their space and because the thing gets larger and larger. And then you are trying to find the top. And you get filthy, immensely dirty; everything is dust.

> The original handwritten parchment index that was used by the court continues to be in daily use in the modern archive and as a result is in an unbelievable state of disrepair. The index tabs [on which key words were written] have been torn off by people turning pages so often; the ink is worn away . . . from the upper right-hand corners so that you can't quite read the first line. It's ridiculous that you should be using such a thing.

REPRODUCTIONS OF ARCHIVAL DOCUMENTS ▪ Photographic copies on microfilm provide an alternative to using original records, but the scholars roundly criticized this reproductive method.

> I worked from microfilm, which was a truly sickening experience. . . . [After] flipping through microfilm, I would leave [the library] every night with this terrible sensation in my stomach. . . . It had been much easier just to deal with the papers. It's nauseating to have that [rolling image] disappear into your body, a text swimming past you.

> Alas, [newspapers] are now on microfilm. It was so wonderful to work with the huge, grand folio volumes. You stood at this great desk and turned the pages of the newspaper; it was magic. For me it was one of the simple ways back into the past. You got the whole picture; you saw the whole page; your attention was constantly straying from the Salon criticism to other things, in a way which was good. . . . Newspapers were wonderful, [but] microfilm tends to kill [them], unless it really does get to a level of technical reproduction and ease of use. . . . [Now] it's such agony sitting there in the booth, looking at these miserable images, that you treat it as an instrumental business. You're just going to look at what you're looking for, you're going to spare your eyes as much as you possibly can, and you're going to get out of the booth as quickly as you can.

ON TIME AND THE USE OF ARCHIVES ▪ Again and again we heard how time-intensive archival research can be.

> It is enormously time-consuming.

> I have worked [in the Italian archives] for fifteen years.

> I worked in the Medici archive later in my life, but never enough to be really satisfied that I had mastered it.

> It took a good six or eight years to be absolutely an expert.

In tackling archival work, scholars establish strategies for making the most efficient use of their time.

> You work out a complicated schedule to try to read [different] kinds of things; [for example, given a three-box daily limit, you call for] one box with the register of ten years' actions in a given court (that would take you days and days to read) and two boxes that contain separate little pieces in which you are fishing for the one piece you want. So if those two don't have what you want, you always have your register to fall back on.

Yet the vagaries of the archival situation make it difficult for the scholar to follow a research plan rigidly. When a search proves unproductive, one does not know whether one has spent too much time or too little. It seems that serendipity and luck influence success.

> Those [notarial] archives in Paris were . . . special. . . . [I worked with] the archives of lawyers of the sixteenth century. You have certain names [but no catalogues or indexes], and . . . if you go through all the papers [of several lawyers], you might [still miss] a document with your artist's name. You can work for fifteen years and find nothing, or you can work for three months and find everything.

> It is like being in a fog, where what is very close at hand is almost magically real, but everything else immediately melts away into an indistinct whiteness, and you have to grope around in it. Very often you make strategic decisions. You give up; you have spent one week there, and you have come up with absolutely nothing. Maybe you have stopped just the five minutes short that it would have taken, and there would have been the eighteenth box. By mis-

> placement it might have contained material that really belonged in the seventeenth box. It is, in that sense, like chance meetings.

In contrast there are sometimes tantalizing archival finds that one must either pass up or pass on to another researcher because one hasn't enough time to follow them through.

> I made a rather thrilling discovery after the [Second World War] in the Biblioteca Nazionale in Florence: the life of a Vallombrosan abbot who was in conflict for most of his life with Lorenzo de' Medici. . . . When one at last could get back to Italy again, in '48 and '49, I did then spend three months or so abroad and did go to the archives. [But] I found [that] to edit it or publish it, . . . [one must] go to Rome and find out the other half of the correspondence, . . . which I could never do. . . . It is hard work and long work.

ON USING ARCHIVAL DOCUMENTS AND WRITING HISTORY ▪ When faced with an overwhelming amount of archival data, the art historian must select and manipulate in order to control the material and mold it into substantive form.

> There is this sinking feeling that you get when you go into a well-documented situation. It is as if you had blown the dust of centuries into the air; it is total darkness, and it clearly dramatizes the fact that knowing everything about something is not what can lead to history. . . . History writing is the proposal of a construction which could make sense of these records because these records by themselves are so narrow. . . . They are literally like specks.

> If you are working on the artistic relationships between Venice and Mantua in a given period, all kinds of odd little peculiar things haven't been looked at, but you fit [them] together in a mosaic. I like the idea of working with fragments and fitting them together into something coherent.

The conceptual framework that one designs to control the plethora of material may range from statistical tabulations to sequential narrative. The choice and its intellectual consequences often leave the scholar feeling at risk.

> I did months and months and months of work in the Archives Nationales [in Paris] before I realized . . . what on earth I could do with this stuff. . . . I started out reading everything. . . . [I finally decided] that what I should do was some kind of statistical sampling, a very primitive kind, to try and work out whether there were any changes . . . between the nature of patronage before 1848 and afterwards. . . . But it took a long time for me to have the courage to decide that was the way this material deserved to be handled.
>
> When I started making transcripts, I followed two different kinds of patterns. One was to try and extract material that I knew would be helpful in a statistical sense. . . . So on the one hand, you've got the analytical approach, which demands you to use the same approach for each account. . . . I like to think of that as a kind of cross section. On the other hand, there is a kind of longitudinal approach, which has to do with simply following the sequence of work. . . . And that is where one's intuition comes in and one's common sense. And that is where the reader is just going to have to rely on my ability to go to where the key material is.
>
> I had a colleague and friend . . . , a very eminent archaeologist . . . , [who] lived on the same floor, and it was the case of old friends getting together all the time. He was working on August[an] Rome. . . . [We discussed] politics and architecture. That was very stimulating, . . . [and] I found some interesting parallels [in my] work. I had all the written material. I knew what Napoleon himself said about the Arc de Triomphe. . . . We often discussed whether to have documentation is really to have an advantage. . . . It's more complicated when you have so [much] information about the subject to pull together. You realize there is not [just] one answer.

The sheer quantity and inclusiveness of documents pose problems. One scholar described the difficulties that he faces with archival data that he has collected over many years.

> I have lots of projects which are elephant babies. . . . [I] build up a stock of notes, typically taken in archives. [Photographers are usually not available, and] I cannot Xerox the delicate materials, [so] I have to transcribe them.

> Xeroxing would be no good [anyway] because they are harder to read in the copy. Often the ink has bled through, and then you can hardly disentangle the writing on one side from the writing or the blotches on the other side. So you actually have to try and decipher this right then and there, and that yields folders of notes. . . . [After fifteen years] I have literally thousands of sheets of paper. . . . So one gets back to the disconcerting thing, which is not so much how one's interest naturally shifts, but also how hard it is to read one's own notes.

Despite the minutiae collected in the archives, these scholars' goals involved broad historical thinking.

> To find one particular desired piece of information, you may have to plow through heaps of stuff which presumably doesn't bear on this matter. But the reward is somewhere else in that you find out about a lot of other things that you would never know you should know about . . . from dietary habits to the social perception of food to the metaphorical valences of weather and what it brings about in human life.

> [In the archives] I have learned a lot about slaves, dwarfs, dogs, falcons, money, salt. But this all mattered. I mean, I am a better art historian; I can write things that [other] people can't write because I do know about these things.

> I am a worker who has some problems with separating collected material and working on it in an intellectual way. [Another] scholar would for a year collect everything about the architect, and then he would write two volumes about . . . the building. . . . I did that for [the painter Joseph-Marie] Vien, . . . [but] I won't do that anymore. My collecting of material [on the Arc de Triomphe] was guided by certain ideas. So there were many folders [of archival material] . . . which I just dropped, discussions of the scaffolding, for example.

> It is not so good, it is not so useful just to find out some [piece of information] about this picture or that picture. The problem is, why Cardinal Francesco Barberini was interested . . . not only in . . . the remains of classical antiquities

> but also in the remains of fourteenth-century art. . . . The problem is always how to use a source. It is possible always to look for only a piece of evidence, a quotation, a name, a date, a year. But it is more interesting to understand the global [significance].

Archival documents would seem to supply an endlessly renewable art-historical resource.

> What escapes one may not escape another and vice versa. . . . It is rather arbitrary who looks at what. . . . It is very hard to get to the point where the object would be much the same even if you work on the same project. . . . Every scholar has to study [these documents] again. . . . That is like we all have to live our lives. It is not [through] a compilation of all mistakes made by everybody [that] we can avoid them. Then what would we do? We would have canceled the effort of living.

SUMMARY ▪ As repositories of documents and even original works of art, archives yield information integral to some art-historical inquiry. Immersion in documents contemporaneous with a work of art often gives the scholar a heightened sense of the past. But some art historians worry that this immersion may displace the direct experience of the art object. Moreover the plethora of information contained in an archive can frustrate the researcher whose goal is selective discovery. Ease of access varies from institution to institution, depending on staffing, attitude toward the public, and adequate indexes. Because archives are often idiosyncratically organized and incompletely catalogued, curators and veteran researchers frequently provide crucial assistance. An understanding of the history of a collection and the political history of the region in which it resides may be necessary to trace documents whose locations have changed over time. Skills required for archival research include knowledge of paleography and codicology and fluency in ancient as well as modern languages. Success in an archive seems to depend as much on patience, intuition, and serendipity as it does on hard-won knowledge and experience. Despite the frailty of archival records and their need for conservation and restoration, most scholars prefer to work with original documents, since reproductions, such as microfilm and photocopies, can be undependable in quality and difficult to manipulate. Although it is time-consuming, archival work provides many scholars with an opportunity to engage the past and the challenge of imposing an intellectual structure on the fragments of history.

SECONDARY SOURCES AND LIBRARIES

We asked the scholars how and to what extent they kept in touch with the secondary literature of (1) their fields of specialization and (2) the history of art in general. We learned that they used secondary sources in different ways and to different degrees according to their subject matter and methodological interests (see "Art-historical Points of View," especially "Analytical Techniques"). The art historians read secondary literature, for example, to examine relevant theoretical issues, to gather biographical information, to study the cultural context, or to interpret the meaning of a work of art. Many felt it necessary to throw the research net wide.

> I find that information about works of relevance to art history, criticism, and theory is often found in journals in literary studies and anthropology as well as in archaeology.

> I just gathered all of the references that I could find. I'd just go through libraries; I'd gather words and themes which had some kind of connection with the subject, which would spring out of the page at a given moment. . . . I tried to work this up to a picture in my mind, some kind of whole.

LOCATIONS OF RESOURCES ▪ The specialized subject libraries on university campuses may limit an art historian's purview, as one scholar experienced during her undergraduate education,

> [The art library at my college was a] wonderful resource . . . but . . . cut you off, in a way, from other possible resources. . . . I was more and more encouraged to be involved in the art library. [As a result] it took me a long time to learn about Clement Greenberg, who had written quite important criticism but never published it in art magazines. . . . It wasn't until his book *Art and Culture* floated into the art library that I discovered [him].

or may fragment the research process, making it less efficient for a scholar.

> The library is very frustrating because information on Minoans was split . . . ; they could never decide whether this was archaeology or art history. So you'd get to a certain point, and then you'd have to go across the street.

When art historians are unable to get the materials they need in the libraries at their institutions, they often must depend on interlibrary loans (see also "Finances," especially "Costs of Travel"). The process of interlibrary borrowing, however, can be less than satisfactory for scholars. One European scholar expressed frustration with librarians who administer research collections.

> The administration of resource material overcomes the possibility of scholarly access. Research is more and more burdened by the requirements of librarians. I see that everywhere. . . . Sometimes it takes a long time to get [books on interlibrary loan], so I order several books. Yesterday I got ten books at the same time. I have to give back those ten books [in two weeks]. Because it took two days for them to arrive and will take two days for them to be brought back, I have in fact a week to get through all those books. . . . Why is this required? [There are] restrictions on photocopy[ing], on how many books you can have, on library hours—restrictions of all kinds.

Even as the same scholar criticized certain libraries, he praised others that facilitated his work.

> Working in European libraries is not that fun. They're always too full, and if you don't get a place, you don't get a book. . . . I could have written this book . . . only in the United States. . . . The libraries [at the research institute] were, first, excellent and, second, easily accessible.

It is often difficult for a scholar to have concurrent access to primary and secondary sources; yet such proximity may be helpful if not crucial (see also "Finances," especially "Costs of Travel").

> The whole framework of . . . reference sources is necessary. . . . [In the archives] there are unpublished volumes of medieval documents for Troyes, and if you have got a particular name out of the fabric account that you want to follow up in the other sources, you need the library right there.

> [In the archive] you are sitting on top of an ant heap of documentation, but you may need a particular [source that isn't there]. Or over here [in the

library] you have only what you gleaned from there, but you may have the world's literature at your fingertips. That is the kind of inevitable oscillation which only in the rarest of circumstances actually coincides.

Given the time lag in processing books in the libraries I use, I seldom have the feeling that I am operating at the cutting edge of new published scholarship. This is in fact one of the reasons why I feel more assured as a scholar dealing with primary rather than secondary material.

BUILDING A BIBLIOGRAPHY ▪ Strategies discussed for developing a bibliography ranged from the systematic to the informal. Union catalogues, catalogues of individual libraries, and indexes of periodical literature facilitated more methodical searches for secondary sources. The scholars were keenly aware, however, of the limitations of the bibliographic tools that appear in print.

On-line *RILA* [*International Repertory of the Literature of Art*] is going to be a very good thing for me. . . . The lag time with [published] *RILA* is frustrating [as is the] invariable attention to abstracting.

The Bibliothèque Nationale catalogue is so new they . . . are only as far as the letter *R*. *The British Union-Catalogue of Periodicals* came out in the 1960s, I think, and they are on the fifth or sixth supplements, so you have to take down volume after volume.

I never use bibliographies; that is, I use them only as a last check when finishing something or starting something new. They are too late and are not helpful.

I have always found the so-called comprehensive bibliographies tedious and cumbersome, so never use them. [But] I regularly consult [some] specialized bibliographies.

Yet there were benefits to be derived from using bibliographic indexes. One scholar recognized the contradiction implicit in wanting careful abstracting yet timely listings.

[Although] the abstracting is crucial, . . . what I want is the citations right up there as soon as they appear.

In response to the time-consuming nature of bibliographic research, scholars developed their own shortcuts and methods of locating items. In some cases these strategies can be precisely described and duplicated; in other cases they are more difficult to define, more idiosyncratic, and harder to replicate or delegate.

> What I do when I'm not writing is read journals in a very systematic way. I not only pick up articles that have newly appeared, but I read their reviews and get notices of books that have newly appeared. . . . I keep a typewritten list of the journals I want to keep track of. I have no idea how many titles there are, maybe two hundred. I annotate in this list what is the last issue I've seen, because otherwise I would never remember.

> What helps me a lot are [photocopied] table[s] of contents. The first time I ever came across th[ose] was [when] the Fogg Library [at Harvard] circulated [them]. We [went] through those as if they were the morning newspaper.

> Experience counts, obviously, [and] a sense of what you're looking for, which you probably could not spell out to another person . . . because . . . you only become aware of it in the process of doing it. . . . You could say . . . to a research assistant, . . . "By the way, if you see anything else that strikes you as interesting or important, copy it." But that's a daft instruction to an undergraduate.

One scholar worried that she was not methodical enough in her efforts to stay abreast of current research developments and adopted a tactic that took her outside the library.

> The procedure I follow in [keeping up with secondary literature] is rather haphazard, and I am indeed frequently rather worried that I will not be aware of important new material or developments. For this reason I have been rather willing to accept invitations to colloquia—mainly of an interdisciplinary nature—because the opportunity to meet colleagues in other fields always means a connection to areas of intellectual production of which one might otherwise have remained unaware.

Indeed the art historians interviewed described a wide variety of informally structured activities that may contribute to their awareness of secondary source material, especially current literature; of particular importance was maintaining contact with colleagues,

> In general I am not shy about going to the typewriter and writing either to my regular correspondents or, occasionally, people I don't know who have published something that interests me. I also get spontaneous letters from others, which I have trained myself in the course of time to answer promptly.

> I do some keeping up with the discipline as a whole just by . . . talking to students and colleagues worldwide; I travel a great deal.

> In the area of new problems, I ask colleagues in other disciplines for references to material which might otherwise escape attention. I profit greatly from consultation with colleagues.

as well as reading publications sent to them by colleagues and other authors not personally known to them.

> If you are known, you get offprints and review books from everyone in your field of specialization.

Other informal strategies included attending professional meetings; visiting publishers' booths at these meetings; subscribing to journals such as *The Times Literary Supplement*, *The New York Review of Books*, and *The New York Times Book Review*; perusing university and other scholarly press catalogues; serving as departmental liaisons to university libraries (in this connection some read the journal *Choice*, which recommends books for library purchase); and consulting *The Worldwide Art Catalogue Bulletin*, an international listing of selected Western and non-Western exhibitions and descriptions of exhibition catalogues.

During the most informal and least systematic of searches, some scholars experienced information gathering and bibliographic construction as rewarding, creative acts.

> I feel very strongly about the need for browsing—serendipity, if you will. I sometimes just turn pages of old periodicals. I did that much more when I

was a graduate student at the Warburg Institute and had the luxury of time to do it and learned more accidentally that way than I do now.

> It is very much a matter of detective work. I looked at my bibliographical file last night . . . but even my files didn't really tell me how I'd compiled the bibliography. And I think that it is because you do it in a very ad hoc, detective, intuitive way; you're absolutely in the middle of this material after a couple of days in the library. . . . You get on certain trails, on the scent. There is an openness to chance all the time.

If the thrill of discovery and the excitement of structuring a successful search were the pleasurable parts of bibliographical research, the frustration of tracking down citations sometimes overshadowed that enjoyment. Here experience is essential, and the ability to travel to research libraries can be critical (see also the case study "Roman Portraiture and Numismatics").

> The problems of finding things are created by other scholars who cite things in a way that isn't right. The worst offenders . . . receive an offprint from somebody and then in writing their own contribution, will write a footnote [that says]: "Rossi, The Communal Palace of Bologna, 1927." Rossi is like Smith in Italy. If you already know the basic literature on the subject, . . . you [go] through bibliographies on Bologna . . . and you find that there is no book by Rossi by that title. So obviously this is an article of some kind. And how do you find it? First, consult *RILA* [for more recent material] or *Répertoire d'art et d'archéologie* for that year and the year before and two or three years after. Second, consult published library catalogues of specialized fine arts libraries that in fact will catalogue, and put on their shelves, separately bound articles they received. . . . Once I get to Bologna [I will] look in the public library there; it's a marvelous bibliographic tool. . . . [You] go to the subject catalogue and pull out the drawer that is called "local history," . . . and there you will find things that no one has ever cited.

TAKING NOTES FROM SECONDARY SOURCES ▪ Once a book or article was found, the task of absorbing its information carried the scholar into another phase of activity, to be treated in the following chapter ("Organization of Information"). One remark, however, demonstrated that for some, making notes on secondary sources was not simply a process of data gathering but one that in retrospect constituted a history of their own intellectual interests.

> If you went home and took Hegel down from my shelf, you would find it very heavily annotated in the very wide margins, which invite such doodles. Whereas otherwise I don't mark things in books. I stick in papers. . . . I mark the pages where there is something interesting on the inside cover so that . . . I can go to the book, and in a sense I do a scan of the hot spots where the intellectual geysers came up twenty years ago. . . . [One is] able . . . to check what struck you or interested you . . . and then look at what they are in the context of today [when] altogether different aspects of these texts are interesting. And you [may] barely recognize or . . . remember . . . the one thing you reacted to.

In conclusion art historians use secondary source material to link works of art with their contexts and traditions.

> The making of connections is all there is to it. It's a puzzle. Yes, you try to piece things together.

While these connections may be facilitated through access to primary and secondary sources of information, intuition, erudition, and wisdom play the key role in identifying significant relationships.

> I have always thought that the Giorgione in Vienna, *Three Philosophers* [fig. 7] (it's a look at a cave), [is related] to [something] Aristotle said—that from the bottom of a well or from within a cave you can see the stars in daylight. . . . This is how an interpretation can . . . click, because one remembers something. But you couldn't search for it because you wouldn't know what to search for.

SUMMARY ▪ The desire to achieve the widest contact with bibliographical materials often conflicts with the wish to have those materials close at hand. The library and its services can be seen both as offering indispensable access to research materials and as obstructing that access through restrictive or inefficient practices. The gathering and organizing of bibliographic references may be done with systematic tools such as indexes and library catalogues, but timely information is often gleaned through informal contacts with colleagues. The search for bibliographic materials can be laborious and frustrating when citations are misleading, or creative and exhilarating when it is successful or results in unexpected finds. One's bibliographic memory sometimes serves as a map of one's intellectual development.

ORGANIZATION OF INFORMATION

For the art historians interviewed, the question of the systematic organization of information is a vital one. Some described a constant, often irrational struggle with fear and self-doubt about keeping track of information.

> My trend is to lose everything, every little sheet of paper. I have lost days and days, making the same thing three times.

> I have a problem with [my method of working] because you can have too many things in front of you. . . . I tend to work with piles of material around me, and at a certain point [when] I can't find anything, I have to put everything away—or not everything, because I am too scared to put things away. I think [that] if I put it away, it is going to vanish.

Controlling accumulated information can be a matter of professional survival and success. One scholar spoke with gratitude about the organizational skills that she learned in graduate school.

> [My mentor] had a very highly refined system [for his bibliography cards and other note cards]. . . . Many graduate students were working with him [on a certain project, and] he showed [us] how he kept his notes because he wanted . . . the material [left with him] to be in the same mode. . . . Very often I talk to graduate students early on about how they are keeping notes. . . . If you are ever going to be able to come back to material, you have to have stored it in some way that is meaningful after the fact.

DOCUMENTING AND CATALOGUING VERBAL INFORMATION ▪ For many scholars the act of structuring files represents a creative stage in the process of intellectual inquiry.

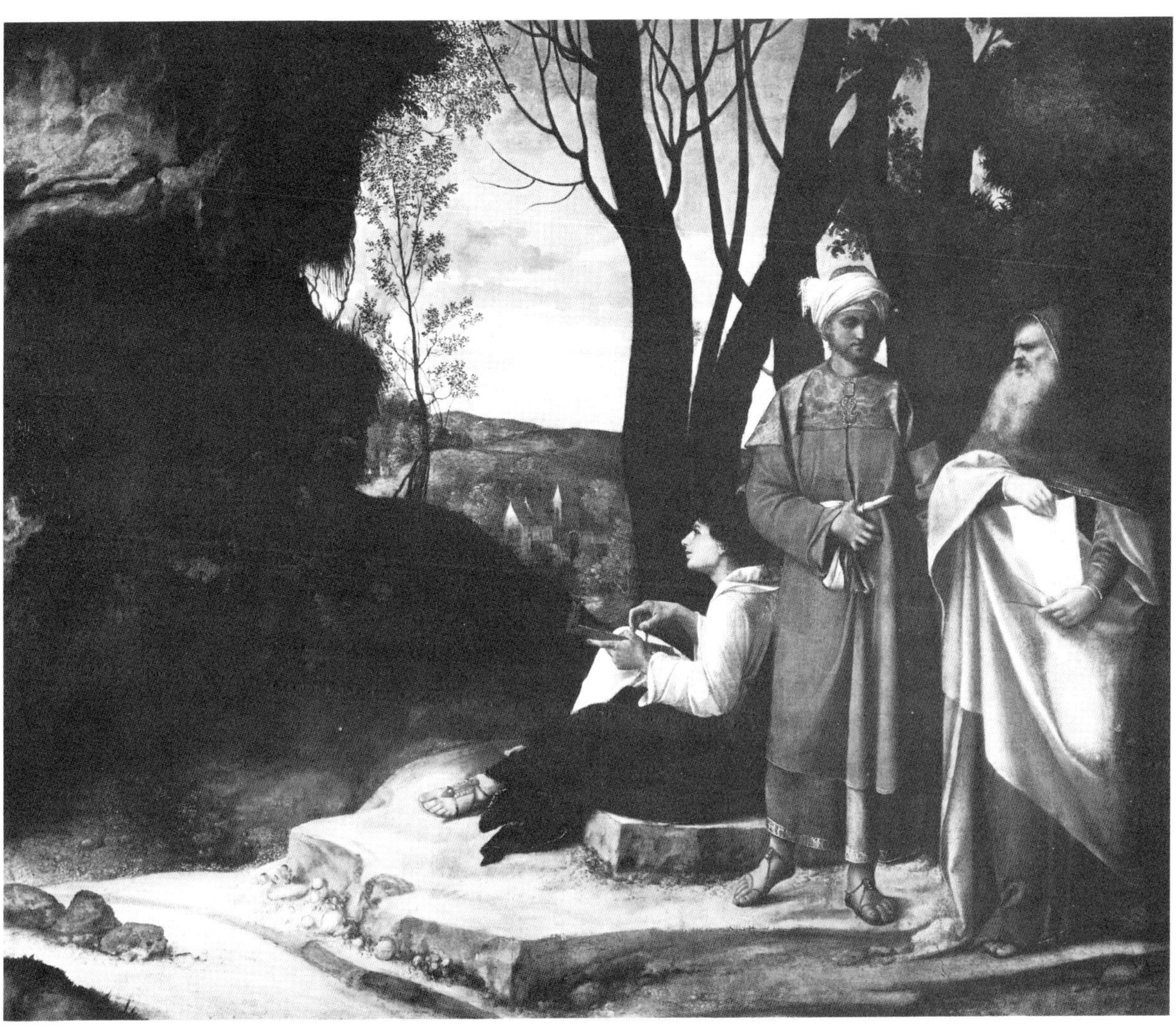

7. GIORGIONE, *Three Philosophers*, circa 1508, Kunsthistorisches Museum, Vienna

> The question is: "What are you looking for? What are you trying to get out of [the material]?" You have to come up with the organization and the contents that are going to give you [the answer].

> I've never been successful with keeping notes on [an entire art-historical] field or [on everything] that seems interesting to me. Unless I have a problem to attach [a note] to, it just gets lost.

Once the problem-solving process has begun, approaches to the collection and organization of material can range from the formal to the informal.

> I always keep . . . notebooks, which are numbered and [dated].

> I can design—have designed—and am forced to design for different projects a kind of work sheet, which is the list of information that I am concerned with recording in a systematic way. But it differs with different projects.

> I just bought regular spiral notebooks and—without concern for order, I didn't try to format them in advance—wrote down in the upper right-hand corner what the source was and took notes. . . . I wouldn't make an index, . . . but I'd copy out bibliographical references, and anything that struck me as relevant I'd summarize and comment on.

Many scholars separated bibliographic references from other information, often by making distinctions in the sizes of files used. Not all the scholars maintained a permanent general bibliography, but those who did found that it saved time when making scholarly citations and retrieving materials from libraries. Apart from general bibliography, information was organized largely on the basis of projects, with a strong emphasis on subject categories tailored to the research effort under way. Systems for filing information tended to be organic, growing and branching as the project developed.

> [I used] three-by-five[-inch] cards for bibliography only. . . . Then I had another series of cards which were five by eight for material. . . . I used a short-form bibliographical citation on the second line [of these] and [on] the thicker line at the top would be the subject. . . . I have boxes for all of these

> things. . . . Sometimes I have cross-referenced them, . . . but I can tend to lose things more easily than I would like because I have thousands of these cards . all divided by subject matter.

> I work onto file cards when I'm engaged in a big job. . . . And the principles of selection and arrangement . . . change and evolve as the project goes on. You start out with some obvious kinds of categories, but other categories appear, and then some categories get so elaborate that they have to be broken down into others.

The relationships between a scholar's various projects affected the evolution of filing systems. Some scholars treated each project as an isolated effort and closed the files when the project was finished. Other scholars were interested in the correspondences between or among projects and designed systems that facilitated the making of connections. For the scholars who emphasized the relationships between their projects, filing systems became highly organized. One such scheme is worth noting here:

> [Major] categories for the work I'm doing on Venetian urbanism are . . . ancient, Islamic, [and] medieval [history]. Medieval has a subcategory Venice, [with] subcategories: . . . documents, . . . chronicles, and other general Venetian history sources. There are other major categories: . . . economic history . . . and social history. . . . These are similarly subdivided. Then there is architecture, where the subdivisions are not only by period but also according to category: secular architecture, sacred architecture, ornament, Eastern-Western relations, and so forth. . . . There's a section called urbanism, and then there are period divisions. Under that section [is] . . . all the topographical material, area studies, as you say. . . . I also have bibliographic material on individual cities filed alphabetically, city by city, or under urbanism. Under building types are palaces, rural houses, urban houses, again subdivided by periods. And for medieval I subdivide by countries. . . . When they cross over, I tend to make two or three cards and put them in two or three places. . . . There are building types—palaces, castles, towers—and categories also for what are urban features—ports, markets, and so on. I annotate these cards to show where the thing is if I need it.

Often the collection, organization, and analysis of information proceeded simultaneously. Scholars described a need to open files concurrently so that they could synthesize their material.

> You've got to keep thinking about the material. You've got to keep . . . trying to elaborate and clarify your questions. So I'm constantly making notes to myself, not on note cards but on sheets of paper, which go fairly higgledy-piggledy into files, other kinds of files. In other words, I'm writing as I go, sometimes in a formal way.

> I had this basic structure that I made up at the beginning, . . . and that did not change. The intellectual content changed, but the actual structure is something I decided on in advance, just working with the paintings. I filled in these files with all of the information that I came upon, and I consulted them continuously. I was always thumbing through them and reading and rereading the material. Any time I came across a connection or name that looked interesting, I would run through the files and try to find out more about it.

The media for keeping files varied widely, as we have heard, from notebooks to file cards to data sheets structured in advance of collecting project-related information. Although some scholars have begun to use computers for both word and data processing, existing software applications do not always meet research needs.

> I keep [notes] . . . on my own PC [personal computer]. I don't have a data-processing [program], so it's not about data. It's more just reading a book and taking notes and starting to synthesize that way.

> What I want to [have is] a constantly accumulated index . . . interweaving alphabetically but also by subject matter. And that I haven't found a way of doing yet. One could design it, but I haven't found a commercially available data base that lets me do it automatically.

Other scholars, however, were reluctant to change from paper systems, with which they were comfortable and successful, to more technologically advanced systems.

> No one will take my [file boxes of cards] away from me. That will never be automated.

> It is very hard for me to work with a computer because it is not all there on the screen at that moment.

In handling their material directly, they felt a sense of security and control. The intellectual processes of ordering and reordering information seemed tied to its physical presence. Moreover the relationship of pieces of information plays a crucial role in conceptualization, even, at times, emulating spatial relationships.

> [Using note cards] enables me to switch everything around. All your information can be moved from place to place, so you can reorganize things very easily by taking something out of one category and putting it in another.

> My memory is very topographical, as long as I can put things in a spatial rapport to one another, even spatial by high degrees of abstraction. . . . The piece of information has a physicality about it. . . . This translates into assembling, let's say, an argument on the wall; I have the different pieces, and I am trying to build an argument out of it.

Indeed some antagonisms to new technologies may be related to unpleasant experiences with older technologies, namely microfilm. As one scholar complained,

> It's very hard in a microfilm situation to have a kind of spatial relationship to [the material. Working with paper one can ask] how far down in the pile of paper is the thing that you're trying to look back to find, or is it in this pile or that pile. [Microfilm creates an] abstract space. . . . [The material is] sequential, but not necessarily in any way that you [can make sense of].

CATALOGUING VISUAL INFORMATION ▪ Collections of slides, photographs, and other reproductions of works of art made different kinds of organizational demands on the scholars interviewed. They developed various systems for filing visual materials that responded to the needs of both teaching and research.

> I'm not a slave to system. If I'm working on a specific project, I'll have a notebook that has slides organized [topically]. . . . I [also] have boxes of slides . . . put in the sequence in which I discuss them in my lecture. . . . I do other things with photographs and . . . slides. For example, . . . I have notebooks . . . arranged chronologically and by style. . . . So I have [duplicated images arranged] in different systems. . . . I design the systems to the project.

The art historians' comments about their files of reproductions again illustrated a distinction between projects that are open-ended and those that are more finite in nature.

> I have a vast filing system on [each architectural feature], each capital, each base [that is] important to me.

> I was very interested in Vuillard and Bonnard and artists of that generation who made screens. "Art Nouveau screens" was a kind of category [of reproductions] I had for a while.

Often, however, the pressure of time prevented the scholars from cataloguing their personal collections of reproductions as fully as they might have liked.

> One of my major intentions was to document the site photographically. So I built up a slide [collection] of these things, some of which is now useless because I didn't always label them. [I learned by] trial and error.

> I had a research student remounting [my photographic archive] and found a lot of mistakes.

Because of the nature of art-historical research, teaching, and publication, an ideal organizational system would seem to be one that interfiled and coordinated a scholar's collections of verbal and visual materials.

> I go to The Hague a lot, like everybody in the field. I sit there, pull down the boxes, go through them, and make files and notes. The most valuable things in my working files [are] my notes [about individual photographs], taken over

> all my different trips to The Hague on sheets of paper, and files of copy photographs made there.

INFORMATION TECHNOLOGY AND THE FUTURE ▪ Although current technology has made it possible to record visual data electronically and to wed verbal and visual materials, such mixed-data banks are not yet widely available (see also "Wish List"). The art historians interviewed, however, imagined the leaps forward in scholarship that they could make with computer-aided indexing, cross-referencing, and analysis of reproductions.

> If one could theoretically push a button and get information about all the occurrences of blue cloaks in eighteenth-century German painting [for example] and then use that as a basis to work, that would be the general best thing—the ability to cross-index information.

> I would like access to visual traditions . . . and to me that means electronic and computerized, so that you can slice the pie there and get different permutations and combinations [making] images accessible according to iconography, time, region, artist, and owner. . . . The issue is not just indexing; it's accessibility. And that means articulating indices, giving you different ways of organizing material and slicing it, and also efficiency of access.

> [If we had computerized our data on architectural measurements,] we would have been able to put things into equations, so to speak, and then get immediate results. We could have had a real data base compiled with great accuracy and precision.

The scholars envisioned the increased utility of standard published references through the computerized sorting of visual materials.

> [I wish] these photographs [in two major corpuses of Northern Renaissance art] were . . . arranged . . . iconographically . . . or by a given artist . . . or within a given time frame. . . . We have such things, but not comprehensive. The Warburg Institute has [for example] an Annunciation file, and most of it is fifteenth-century.

They also hoped that data banks might one day make unpublished information generally available.

> One could imagine having a thing where [if, for example,] you want to see all the Rouaults in public collections in France, you just tap into it, and you get a sheet of color Xeroxes. . . . Then you'd be able to go a little further with those pictures that particularly interested you.

> Gathering of information is a long-winded business. . . . If we really did have . . . electronic availability, . . . wouldn't it be wonderful to have access to . . . some sort of network reaching to the major museums and to find out what the museums' holdings were. . . . It would save months and months of work. . . . The process of finding out where pictures by these [minor Cubist painters] are is incredibly ponderous . . . , and there's no guarantee of any success when you begin. It's very much a matter of word of mouth. . . . Even the crudest kind of black-and-white accompanying visual would be tremendously valuable.

And those who taught the history of art imagined the computer in the slide room as a tool that would allow them to introduce a broader range of images in the classroom.

> [It] would be so helpful if you could go into a slide room and use a computer to find your slides. . . . [For example, because architecture is filed geographically,] if you want to find a [certain] Frank Lloyd Wright house, and you don't know that it is not in Chicago—it is in Oak Park—you can't find it. You ought to be able to [have] a list with the dates so you could get one that is close to what you are looking for.

Nevertheless most acknowledged that even in a utopian world of research, where information was ideally organized, the process of inquiry depended in part on what the scholar brought to it.

> I think order and creativity are not completely linked. There's a gap in between. You also need inspiration to be really creative.

INFORMATION NEEDS OF THE PRESENT ▪ In general the most desirable research enhancement discussed was not the electronic processing of information but the creation of scholarly catalogues.

> It would be very important for us to have not only name catalogues but also subject catalogues . . . [and], for example, to ask for information on Gothic art in Pisa and to get not only information concerning publications but also concerning . . . drawings, correspondence, and so on.

> When you realize that most manuscripts . . . are not described, photographed, or indexed, you realize what lies ahead of us. [Do we] really have access to the tradition, and can we speak with authority? I've [studied] thousands of manuscripts, [but] that's very subjective still [because] I can't document them [properly]. The real task is to come out with a catalogue and make it accessible.

Those interviewed identified the absence of detailed cataloguing and cross-indexing of information as an impediment to research, whether in museums:

> The indexes [to the print collections] are only by artist. [When the artists are unknown, the prints are listed as] "Anonymous, sixteenth-century German" or "Anonymous, fifteenth-century Netherlandish," for example.

in archives:

> Just to have a good inventory of an archive could obviously help. . . . It would obviously capture only certain categories, because if it captured everything all the time, it would become again opaque.

in libraries:

> [I would ask for the catalogue] and literally call forth every manuscript that looked feasible. . . . [But] most cataloguing apparatus is very primitive, if not hopelessly inadequate. So you simply work as best you can with and around it.

or in slide libraries:

> In the slide library [some aspects of] twentieth-century art pose particular indexing problems: When did performance art start? Do you put performance art near happenings? And is that part of sculpture? Or is it part of theater?

Finally, one art historian aptly characterized the ambiguity that a scholar often feels about the information he collects during the process of research. The goal, after all, is to produce a publication or a lecture; neither the amount of material nor one's carefully worked out systems of organization must overtake that goal.

> Is there some way in which you can keep hold of the totality of your information without it all just stacking out in some mechanical, dead order, and having it be accessible to you so the writing can keep going, flowing? That is the problem which drives people to "Ah, to hell with the notes! I've got to write!"

SUMMARY ▪ As information is amassed, the fear of disorder increases. The scholar's organization of information may reflect idiosyncratic intellectual concerns, range in structure from formal to informal, and take many different physical forms. To be of long-term benefit, however, a system should be flexible enough to accommodate unexpected finds as well as shifts in the direction of research. The separation of full bibliographic citations from other materials does not obviate the need to maintain a relationship between sources and data. Indexing and cross-indexing of information not only offer access to materials for work in progress but also organize them for future retrieval once the project is completed. Simultaneous consultation of any number of files or categories of information is integral to the process of creative synthesis. Apprehensions about the computerized manipulation of data stem from the need—especially during the writing stage of a project—to work with more information than appears on a conventional screen. Furthermore the physical handling of information is perceived to enhance both the intellectual control of data and the construction of arguments. The organization of reproductions presents the need to link visual and verbal research materials. Filing systems for slides and photographs followed patterns similar to those used for written information, except that the separation between teaching and research materials was less clear. Dreams of computerized scholarly data bases of both verbal and visual resources in museums, archives, libraries, and slide libraries, indexed by all categories, including subject, were rife. The improvement of existing scholarly catalogues remained a preoccupation, yet most scholars recognized that organizational systems were no substitute for inspiration and creativity.

WRITING AND PUBLISHING IN ART HISTORY

The presentation of research is usually the goal of art-historical inquiry. The scholars talked about the processes of forging a text from notes and ideas and disseminating that text through publication. Conversations ranged widely over such topics as predoctoral research projects, doctoral dissertations, dissertations reworked for publication, current writing projects, manuscripts and the publishing business, and reviews of the scholars' manuscripts and publications. There was an emotional edge to many of the art historians' comments on writing and publishing as vital aspects of the scholarly endeavor.

> Writing for me is painful; it's excruciating. I am a very constipated writer, so I dread the thought of having to write anything. I approach it dutifully as a requirement, but I'd much rather talk about [my ideas]; talking is a much more natural mode of communicating . . . for me.

> I wrote it without really realizing that I had done it; it was painless.

Many of the scholars described special states of mind that seem to overcome them when they are fully involved in writing.

> I am . . . in the material; I have some things written so I know where I am going. . . . I think I have got to have it all in front of me, to keep it all in this buffer zone . . . [in] which I feel like my brain is shrinking and the material is growing.

> I'd written all the [early] chapters before I realized what was really going on. And I went back and rewrote the entire thing. It was really a period of six months of very intense work. When I finished I looked back, after delivering the final pages in June 1984, to where my thinking . . . was in April 1984; I almost got dizzy and fell. It's like a tightrope walker realizing that he's [traversed a wire] high up in the air.

Deep involvement in a writing project stimulated one author to envision future projects.

> The honest truth is that whenever I'm in the advanced stages of writing a book . . . I know that there's another book I'm going to want to write and have to write. I know the subject matter, [but] I don't really know the form it's going to take. And I may even know the subject of the third book ahead, but I don't know the form.

Some authors shun finished pieces, whether out of discomfort with the image of themselves reflected in the work or out of an urgency to move on with the work at hand.

> I never read anything I have written again. . . . I don't want to look at it. . . . I find it astonishing to see things there [in print] with my name on them. . . . Sometimes I wouldn't even tell a student to read something [by me]. . . . I am reserved that way.

> I barely read my texts again, the written or published texts, except to look up something or rather more often some [question] people have raised. I have things quoted at me, and I think, "Did I really say that?"

BUILDING AN ART-HISTORICAL ARGUMENT ▪ The process of structuring a written argument by no means spells the end of the research effort. Two scholars illustrated the close interaction between the formulation of an argument and ongoing research.

> I find that everything I've ever written, in a way, is like a novel. It writes itself. I start with a certain idea . . . of the kind of answer that the article is going to provide. And as I go along all kinds of ugly contradictions raise their heads. What I thought was the answer becomes less and less tenable. Finally I have to rethink it. I start on a new tack. Then some issue I hadn't even realized becomes crucial in the article, and I do research about that. [But then] the second answer won't work anymore, and I have to start a third way. I come out with a work that is 180 degrees from what I intended.

> I wrote it twelve or fourteen times. I was struggling. . . . The hardest part of the thing was getting the ideas on paper, because I had this big picture, a lot of facts, a lot of connections, things I was convinced of, things that were less important. How do I put this together? And I put it together in a lot of ways. I started out with all sorts of different points of entrée, and . . . mostly it came out muddy. I would read it through, and it wouldn't—as they say in the advertising business—track. . . . So I considered the literary part of this; just isolating that part of it [was] perhaps the most important of all. And it influenced the research also. Because once I started writing, I realized what kind of claims I wanted to make. I realized that I didn't know enough to back them up. So I would go back into research . . . and start all over again.

Not all the scholars whom we interviewed worked in such fluid ways. Some spoke about the establishment of a priori conceptual structures that governed the course of work, either as the scholars began research or as they committed themselves to writing.

> [My spouse] is one of these extraordinary people . . . [who's] organized: has an idea . . . , lays out an outline . . . , goes out and does research . . . , writes the book according to the outline, then publishes it. . . . It is really like a general's campaign: he takes out a map; he finds what are the strategic points; he masses his armies; he designs the [troop] movements. . . . The cities fall. I can't do this. I'm like a guerrilla; I go all over the place taking potshots at this and that.

> What I find I have to do when I write out of a mass of material [is] map it . . . with a list of references. . . . I put down enough of a notation [so] that I know in each case what the essential point is. I refer back and back to this list, trying to think of an order in which this material might [fit].

REVISION ▪ No matter how systematically the art historians approached their material, most revised their texts during the writing process. The procedures that they followed, however, did not seem to follow predictable or uniform patterns.

> I tend to avoid writing drafts; I want what I'm typing to be the final copy, which means that I go fairly slowly sometimes, develop a pattern [while] writing the first page [perhaps] ten times, and I finally get [my] voice.

> I don't type, . . . and so I write in longhand. I'm constantly changing it and making arrows. . . . I have a secretary here who is capable of deciphering the most complicated signs. Then I take [the transcription], and I usually rewrite something four or five times; I mean, I go through it four or five times making changes before I'm satisfied.

> If I showed you what my manuscripts looked like you would be horrified. It is just a battlefield of cut and paste renewed over and over.

Although the act of revision seemed to occasion some chagrin, it also brought deep satisfaction as the scholars improved their texts.Two art historians emphasized the creative aspect of making revisions; they drew compelling analogies between writing and painting.

> My method of writing an article is extraordinarily peculiar, to the point that my [spouse] sometimes thinks it's sick, which it is. But I write it, and I write it again, and I write it again, and I write it again. . . . I write the way Titian painted, . . . which is to say that often as not I will write something and then put it away because in some way I'm not satisfied with it. (With one article, I remember, two years passed before I went back to it again.) Then suddenly I understand how it really should be. I read it as if I were unfamiliar with it. I see it anew, and I can suddenly penetrate to the problem and do it right.

> I write longhand. . . . It's very important for me that the thing becomes a palimpsest, and you can see previous versions of it. . . . [T]he idea of this manual aspect [of writing is comparable to] certain [other] representational practices. It's like oil paint; I like the idea of it being manual yet rather clumsy and intractable. . . . You're aware of what you've altered, and you're overlaying something which is still obtrusive and still there and resisting the alteration.

But at least one author wondered whether too much revision might have a negative effect on the work.

> This was a tough book to write, and it was entirely rewritten afterwards. . . . It's always better if you're able to write more directly and with less second thoughts. But sometimes it's not possible.

TONE ▪ The scholars credited the revision process, in part, with making them more self-aware as writers. If they struggled with form and content in their writing, they also searched for an appropriately expressive tone. For some the challenge was to produce a manuscript that might engage an audience as the work or works of art about which they wrote had engaged them.

> The hardest thing going is to write vividly when you are writing thoroughly, and I don't know how to do that except not to be afraid of the affective power of works of art. I don't know how to do it except by running some risks.

> Looking back on the way things happened, I see a real contrast between the sheer pleasure, joy, the very rich quality of the material and the discoveries, and the first form of my manuscript, which was written in this dry archaeological tone, as dull as anything. What I gained . . . was being able to pull out that much more narrative approach and ultimately to incorporate it. . . . What I searched for with the Beauvais [Cathedral material] was some kind of way to let the reader know that in fact it isn't . . . antiseptic.

One scholar reflected on the different styles in which he had written his books, placing them in an autobiographical and historical perspective.

> Those previous books . . . were written at a certain historical moment and had a great deal of confidence, you know, devil-may-care kind of attitude. The moment provided a certain kind of style, tone, way of writing. The problems were vivid. The late seventies and early eighties weren't at all like that. I was very much more firmly within academe. . . . It would have been death to try for the same kind of tone that the previous books [had]. . . . So a lot of effort went into trying to find a way of writing . . . which was honest about the limitations of what one was doing. There was a sort of utopian flavor to the previous books, which just would've been absurd for me to reproduce. . . . I still wanted the book to be intransigent, . . . but I wanted a tone which would be intransigent without laying claim to the things that it would be preposterous to lay claim to.

FOOTNOTES ▪ The art historians occasionally complained about the constraints that the requirements of scholarly writing and publishing placed on them.

> The hell I have with writing is not with writing or having ideas or material; it is doing footnotes, which I dislike intensely. [They cause] me tremendous stress because I am absolutely chaotic, not mentally, but physically, and I have things on bits of paper and in little notebooks.

But some saw the scholarly format as a creative opportunity.

> The footnotes, for instance, provide a kind of narrow-gauge railroad parallel to the heavy-gauge tracks, which presumably represent the main argument. The little nervous choochoos move on the footnote level. That is why footnotes basically are intriguing . . . and contain arguments sometimes which are not part of the main body of the text. That is why I find footnotes which merely indicate more or less dutifully where some of the information is coming from profoundly disappointing . . . as opposed to footnotes which are like the ballast in a ship, that give it a certain firmness of keel, a certain weight, a certain speed.

ILLUSTRATIONS AND ART-HISTORICAL TEXTS ▪ Art historians generally illustrate published manuscripts and public lectures with reproductions of works of art. Often these illustrations play a fundamental role in the scholars' conceptualizations of a problem, a role that in part distinguishes the practice of art history from that of other humanistic disciplines. One art historian characterized what he believed should be the relationship between visual and textual material:

> Ideally, when you deal with the sort of evidence art historians are dealing with, you ought to be able to lay out your argument almost like assembling a skeleton of an animal with your illustrations. And then you flesh out the connection between these things, and you shape the nature of the argument with this material. . . . Our arguments have in a very essential way to spring from the [illustrations] and not the other way around, where the [visual] material becomes a kind of stamp which is glued in to add yet something else to an argument.

What might be described as a pictorial outline can form the intellectual framework for the writing of a manuscript,

> I always tack [the illustrations] up on boards and discover as I do that maybe there is a flaw in the argument because [for example, two illustrations may] work but the third somehow doesn't hang in there right. And I realize that in the very early stages of trying to shape the argument, rather than at a later stage, when it becomes a question of the layout of illustrations or something.

the transformation of a spoken lecture into a written piece,

> So many of my books or writings originated in lectures, and the lectures had slides. [The publication process] usually starts with slides.

the assembly of an exhibition,

> In any exhibit or installation, while you're jockeying things around, you discover some things that you didn't know . . . in a serendipitous way. Installation is for me as interesting as writing.

or the arrangement of an exhibition catalogue.

> I truly think of the layout of the catalogue, . . . for which I wrote no text, as art history without words. The particular juxtapositions of reproductions in there were meant to tell a story, and it wasn't just laying things out in some chronological order.

Securing permission to publish illustrations, however, can present a stumbling block to authors.

> The proprietary nature of ownership . . . just means that you put in a lot of labor every time you write, . . . [even for] an article with [as few as] twelve illustrations.

The cost of illustrations can also hinder publication since publishers frequently require that authors pay for them. The following anecdote shows that forbearance and ingenuity are sometimes necessary to secure essential illustrations.

> Because the [drawings] had been confiscated after the Second World War, [the curator of the collection] was afraid that if anybody knew where they were there would be a scandal [and] that the heirs of the family would try to get these things back. So he didn't want them to be published, and he told me, "I am working on them." That went on for about two years, and he finally agreed that I could buy [photographs] of them. I think he charged me something like fifty dollars a photograph. I decided, "I don't want to pay this much money. It is not worth it. This is ridiculous." [But I needed the photographs,] so I made an agreement with [a museum]. I bought the prints and sold them to the museum, and they have them now.

FINAL PRODUCTION ▪ The art historians described deep involvement with the production phase of their manuscripts, from footnotes to illustrations and diagrams to translations and transcriptions. The costs were great, however, in terms of both the time spent on proofreading and other editorial tasks and the frustration of being unable to wrest exactly what they wanted from their publishers.

> This [book] took a long time to come out because the manuscript was finished and all the proofing was done by . . . the summer of 1982. It came out a year later. That's not bad. But I'd been involved with proofing for at least a year before that because there were so many diagrams.

> Last summer I went through all my transcribed texts and marked them up with the intention of showing what syllables I had added. . . . I talked to my publisher about doing it, and [he] was so anguished at the thought of trying to set all that in type that in the end we agreed that we would just flesh it out, without any indication of the [added] syllables.

Many of the scholars expressed frustration about their lack of control over the quality of illustrations once a publisher accepted a manuscript.

> The variable quality [of illustrations] is everybody's bane.

> You can print photographs [in such a way as] to make them useless. [A certain university press] is capable of destroying any photograph in reproduction.

> This incredibly important stained-glass window was photographed when it was in this De Stijl exhibition . . . , and they couldn't filter all the light . . . so it came out yellow. It looks as if there is a fire at the back of it. . . . But I wasn't in [a] position [to object]. Maybe [other authors] can't either. . . . I was so grateful to have my book published that I [didn't make] many demands.

Not only the quality of illustrations but also their relative size and position within a manuscript can affect the power of an art-historical argument. The scholars wanted some control over the layouts of their manuscripts. One, for example, was determined that the proportions of the illustrations not dictate the form of the book.

> The reproductions [were] largely horizontal in format. . . . I was horrified at the idea that I was going to have a coffee-table book. I didn't want a horizontal book no matter what.

Indeed the scholars seemed to be particularly sensitive to the effects of various formats, an acuity that they perhaps gained through the visual analysis of works of art.

> When I first started publishing, it never occurred to me that I had to give some guidance to the editor on [layout and scale of illustrations]. To my astonishment some things would come out much too small and other things would come out unreasonably big, and an illustration that was supposed to be compared with another was on the wrong page. So I've come now, in my old age, to the habit of usually sending a layout with an article. That is to say, I make a dummy, like for a book. I put in lines where there's supposed to be text, and I draw an illustration. Generally they are grateful for it, but they don't always follow it.

WHERE TO PUBLISH? ▪ Many authors expressed dismay over the conventional review process that publishers who specialize in scholarly manuscripts prescribe.

I hate having to search for a place to publish something. . . . Society's erected these extraordinary structures that make it almost as difficult to . . . publish something as it is to write it in the first place. . . . If you want to publish in an American journal, . . . the editor sends it out to readers and . . . they, being other experts in that field, of course have a primary interest in showing you and the editor how much more they understand about the subject than the poor bloke who wrote the article. Therefore it comes back with . . . suggestions [for] revisions. . . . So you rewrite it, it goes back for further reading, there are still a few more suggestions, and finally it's accepted. Then you can wait [up to] two and a half or three years for the presses to grind it out. I have always thought that this was really for the birds. . . . So I'm really an awful opportunist and try as much as possible to circumvent this procedure.

Especially in the modern field, the more "popular" (or less "academic") journals and presses provide a welcome alternative.

Most of the articles that I've written, including some pretty scholarly kinds of things . . . have usually appeared in what we call the "art mags," because you don't need to present your text a year in advance and because they reproduce things in color. . . . A reasonable minority of Americans feel [they have] a legitimate place.

Choosing a country and a language in which to publish can also be strategic decisions for scholars, with implications that range from the audience one seeks to the monetary gain one anticipates.

If an art historian in Austria produces a book, a catalogue, for instance, it is produced for seven million people. If you write a book in England, then you write that book for fifty million people. If you do the same in the States or in Russia, then you do that for two hundred million people. And that makes a difference. It's the same work, but the chance of multiplication of your work is so different. . . . There's also a difference in whether you can do it originally in English or whether your editor does it. [Then] there's somebody in between who cuts you for more than 50 percent.

PUBLISHERS AND THE STATE OF THE DISCIPLINE ▪ If the authors described their symbiotic relationship with the world of publishing in somewhat negative terms, they also acknowledged what they construed as positive influences exerted by their publishers on the practice of art history at various times and in various places.

> In art history the kinds of things that have been rewarded in the past have been fairly traditional and remain largely so. But there are signs that that's changing too. The proliferation of new journals in art history over the last five or six years has been very good in the sense of opening the field up.

> The fifteen professors who did art history in the Italian universities at the time, perhaps, were not so interested in Hauser. But it was impossible for them to influence the publishing houses. I remember, there was not academic terrorism in Italy at this time. . . . Einaudi [the publisher], with the publication of Hauser and Antal, started a new interest in the methodology of art history in Italy. After, with the publication of Gombrich and so on, the methods of art history began to be discussed and known and important in intellectual life.

REVIEWS ▪ Many of the authors interviewed have both published criticism of the work of other scholars and seen their own work subjected to criticism. Aware of the double-edged sword that criticism represents, they have learned to benefit from the valid objections of their critics,

> [The reviewer] made some negative criticisms of the language which hurt me but which helped me a great deal. . . . It hurts to be caught out in a rhetorical . . . ploy, but I thought afterwards, "He's right." These things stick in your mind for years and years, twenty years now. But it helped me in my [subsequent] writing to keep my feet on the ground. . . . I got boosted up with the few very nice, positive remarks, but I did take negative criticism . . . to heart.

and to be prepared to rebut the criticisms that may come.

> One always has to have something in one's pocket, so if the first critic is against you, you have counterarguments. It isn't necessary to [write] everything.

MAKING CHOICES ▪ The scholars also responded to intra- and extradisciplinary judgments about the relative values and impacts that different kinds of art-historical studies may have. One scholar touched on the professional, economic, and even moral implications of writing about works of art that are on the art market. Because scholarly exposure can raise their prices, marketable works of art can be sensitive subjects for art historians.

> I have never heard of a museum scholar's reputation being hurt or [of] the future of a museum [being] endangered by having published honestly things that weren't right. The other side of it is that there have been museum types who have been overgenerous and whose reputations have suffered as a result. . . . Most museum people generally avoid publishing works of art that are for sale and avoid publishing adverse opinions of works of art in private hands, [but] not because they object in principle to doing so. The opportunities just don't arise that often.

We heard admonitions about publishing for publishing's sake.

> I do think you should reserve yourself for something fairly important. . . . The trouble is that once . . . rubbish . . . is published we all have to read it. . . . You can't ignore it because the poor old student is going to home in on this ghastly article . . . [and quote] something absolutely crazed, and you have got to have read it too.

They described a typological spectrum of subject matter, which ranged from descriptive catalogues to monographic studies of artists or works or themes to critical syntheses of a broader historical nature. One spoke of his choices as a dialectic.

> I tend to switch as a scholar almost in absolute alternation between what I call idea pieces—interpretive issues—and cataloguing projects. I get stale if I do just one all the time. . . . Cataloguing projects . . . in the thought of our discipline [are] less sexy. Everyone wants idea pieces. They have a lot of . . . intellectual justification. The reason I do cataloguing projects is simply because I work in areas in which a great deal of the primary material has never been analyzed or presented. . . . One of my teachers said years ago that most of

> what art historians do is reshuffle the same deck of cards. . . . It's much more exciting to me to add new cards to the deck.

As a group the scholars expressed overriding commitment and dedication to their writing; they hoped to make lasting contributions to art-historical inquiry.

> [Scholarship] is highly creative. . . . Ultimately the historian is a writer, an artist, as much as a novelist in the sense that what you're doing is what one calls an ordering of experience. A novelist, or any creative writer, is guided ultimately by standards . . . that are fixed within the literature. . . . These patterns are the controlling constraint. The historian, on the other hand, doesn't have so much patterns, poetic form, and the like. He has facts. They are the constraint. His creative idea has to be disciplined by the unbendable facts . . . and must survive the fire of those facts.

SUMMARY ▪ The topics of writing and publishing raise emotional issues; special states of mind often accompany the act of writing. Far from being discrete stages in a process, research and writing continually interact. Whether the approach is systematic or disorganized, revision is usually integral to writing and may even play a creative role, increasing the author's sensitivity to both form and content. The achievement of a tone appropriate to art-historical tradition, to the subject matter, and to the intended audience poses a particular challenge. Footnotes may be painful to produce from disorganized notes, but they can provide enriching subtexts. Illustrations often form the initial and fundamental framework upon which art-historical arguments are built, whether for lectures, exhibitions, or publications. Cost and difficulty in obtaining publication rights are barriers the art historian constantly faces in choosing illustrations. The quality of illustrations and their visual relationship to textual material—as expressed in the graphic design of the final publication—cause deep concern and involve many art historians in the production phase of publishing, as do preparations of transcriptions for publication. The choice of publisher and language may have considerable impact on a scholar's career. The prepublication review process of most academic presses, which often delays the appearance of scholarly manuscripts, can sometimes be circumvented through more popular presses. Both publishers and reviewers may influence the direction and quality of art-historical inquiry, but the scholars too ponder issues that affect the lasting value of their contributions to the discipline.

PRESENT USE OF COMPUTERS

When asked how and to what degree they were presently using computers, the art historians responded with a broad range of answers. At one end of the spectrum were those who hesitated to use computers at all, even for word processing.

> I will admit to being Luddite about [using a word processor]. I'm not entirely convinced that a computer operation would save me an enormous amount of time. I can see that it would enable certain kinds of flexibility. . . . I'm a terrible typist. And one gets stuck in one's ways. . . . I certainly don't think I could convert to writing onto a keyboard and a screen. . . . I've no doubt at all that people who start their writing career with an electronic machine will devise all kinds of personalizing operations, [but] I don't think it would work for me.

There were others who appreciated the changes that word-processing technology had made in their work, although they did not operate machines themselves.

> [My assistants] have put the checklist of the exhibition into the computer [including] credit lines, facts, and sizes; everything is constantly changing. It would have been just an incredible headache to have the secretary constantly make changes [on a typewriter].

> I am very lucky because I have help clerically, and I can dictate or write longhand, and it gets typed [on a word processor]. . . . I don't need to spend my time at a keyboard. Given my advanced age and my hardened habits of composing, I think I am not about to write better at the keyboard. I am still so in love with the idea of being a reviser. I am a terrible, compulsive reviser, and so the word processor has made life a perfect torment for everybody around me.

Still others used word-processing programs themselves, but their commitment to this technology varied.

> After I have handwritten [a piece], I use [the word processor] to edit. I can write a letter on it, but I can't write [manuscripts]. . . . I don't know, maybe it's possible; I can always hope.

> I started this long before any of us began to think about computerization, and I have a vast bulk of handwritten [research] material, which had to be carried back and forth [to Europe] with me. And then as book projects developed, I translated that . . . into typewritten material, which then I would also take back and correct and recorrect and check folio numbers and read again and wonder if I had the spelling right. . . . I wish that five years ago . . . I had put my typewritten version on a disk.

> I'm using [my computer now] for two or three things. The most important is descriptions of manuscripts [for] my corpus of Dutch manuscripts. . . . Since so much of this is technical—folio numbers, superscripts, and things like this—the number of mistakes that one makes is enormous. Having the luxury on the computer of just changing it like that, being redeemed, not having to retype or mess up a typed page, especially if you're fastidious like I am, is wonderful. . . . A project like mine takes years. And right now I can be describing my manuscripts in a given format. I may decide before I publish it that . . . I want to change the format. . . . The fear of investing a lot of time . . . is gone. So it gives you much more confidence and freedom to record things and [give] structure [to them], knowing you can change them.

A few of the art historians interviewed had begun to demand more of their computers than solely word processing. These scholars had tackled problems that required the sorting of information and thus needed software that incorporated both data- and word-processing capabilities. One scholar described the development that had occurred in his work as he mastered first one and then another such program. The second program was better suited to the increased complexity of the later, more ambitious project. He evaluated both programs in the light of his experience with them.

> I started with WordPerfect 4.1, which delighted me . . . , for word processing and sorting. I used it doing the catalogue of [an] . . . exhibition where I was dealing with a hundred paintings. It does sorting by alphabet, number, line, and character. . . . I was able to produce lists alphabetically, chronologically, [and] in size order, which for an exhibition is very handy. . . . But I did discover . . . that you have to revise these lists. . . . Maybe with a lot of experience you

> could construct your information as you put it in, so that you could get exactly what you want.
>
> And now I'm working with dBASE II, putting information in it about the image of the black in Western art. I had taken notes on about three thousand paintings. . . . [As I found it, the information] was just a jumble. . . . They did what scholars usually do. There were a few big chunks for the largest categories, then the rest got [put] into a mixture of thematic, chronological, and other categories—and size order: big and small things. So by the time they finished, one had no idea of what paintings there were on what subject or by what painters or [from] what countries. And with dBase, I got to [sort] this all fairly well. [But] dBASE II can only do two files at the same time, which is not enough [editor's note: the scholar did not yet have dBASE III]; you have to be able to search throughout all of them at the same time. . . . I do not think that many other art historians would be as thrilled as I am with these systems. I know that I have always wanted a computer. . . . But I also know that I'm working more or less at the limits of my ability to organize things in advance well enough [for it] to . . . be really useful to me.

Another has gone through elaborate preparation in anticipation of establishing an automated project that will be useful to colleagues.

> I have had to design my system . . . , ranging from the sequence, [to] the headings [that] I'm going to have, to how much information I'm going to give the headings . . . . I've been putting a lot of this stuff on the computer. I've experimented with different systems, and I've been mailing them around to colleagues all over the country saying, "What do you think? Tell me how you think I might change or improve this."

But another scholar's disappointment in being unable to structure a tailor-made program at a critical juncture in his research showed that the conceptual formulation of the problem can be more important than technical knowledge.

> It became obvious that we would actually have to do this survey, measure as many buildings as we could. At the same time I took a course in computer

> programming . . . so that I could tabulate all this mass of numerical data I was getting. . . . It didn't help because I couldn't really articulate what it was that I needed.

From those who made extensive use of computers in their work as well as those who did not, we heard cautionary remarks about the role that computers should play in art-historical research. All were adamant that mechanized access to information should not substitute for inspection of original works of art and documents and that quantitative analysis of information should not replace creative synthesis. They regarded the computer as a tool but not an actor in the research process.

> I am a skeptic about computers. I don't think that it's a creative act, no more than doing a plaster cast, . . . or a print of a drawing.

> A substantial part of the time that anybody would put into research would be mechanical, and that part would be cut down [using computers]. The cerebration—I don't see any shortcut to that.

> In the end I'm really deeply skeptical about a lot of the enthusiasm about the computer from my fellow academics. . . . So much of it is . . . thinking, discovering what your questions are, and pursuing them. . . . You can have all the data you like, beautifully arranged before you, but if it doesn't come together in some intuitive order, if you've asked dull questions, you will have a massively dull book as a result . . . , and there's no way of computerizing that dimension to inquiry.

SUMMARY ▪ While art historians who write longhand or have secretarial assistance seemed slower to embrace word-processing technology than those who type and compose at a typewriter, both groups appreciated the impact of computer technology on the work of preparing manuscripts for publication, notably the tasks of revising, editing, and meeting the requirements of a scholarly format. Data processing was still rarely used by the scholars interviewed. Experience with computer technology often led to the wish for more sophisticated programs, although some recognized that software was no substitute for a sound conceptual scheme for manipulating data. Most saw the computer as a tool that enhanced the research process mechanically but did not contribute to the creative dimension of inquiry.

PERSONAL FACTORS IN ART-HISTORICAL RESEARCH

Throughout this study one impression has come forward with great strength: that of the art-historical pursuit itself as an art, with a sizable component of craftsmanship. This impression is in part conveyed by the personal enthusiasm and conviction of the speakers; theirs is not a dry recitation of procedures but a search for new questions, better answers, and satisfying solutions. Many experiences, although they cannot be classified under "process" or "method," had crucial impact on the formation of the scholars' attitudes and practices.

MENTORS ▪ For most of the scholars graduate school and their early careers served as a kind of apprenticeship during which they learned the craft of the profession, sometimes under the tutelage of a "master" whom they deeply respected. Many remembered with gratitude the encouragement that their mentors gave them and the intellectual doors that they opened.

> I went to see [Ernst Gombrich] at the Warburg and said I was very interested in the way he did things. He was very nice to me. He took me round the library and showed me things, like documents. I was very interested in archival work, and he showed me facsimiles and said, "Why don't you come here [to study]?" . . . And so I developed a Warburg sort of slant before I was finished.

> We were not treated like amateurs; we were treated like budding scholars. Julius von Schlosser [my teacher] said, "Here's an ivory. I've often wondered what it is. You'll just have to work on it." So if you ask me what my first work was, it was in fact a Carolingian ivory pyxis, which had been considered to be fifth century. I gave a seminar report in which I said it was Carolingian, and [he] said, "Yes, you are probably right. Why don't you publish it in our [journal]?" I was in my second year, you know. It was how life was.

> [Meyer Schapiro and I] talked about . . . new and exciting things . . . like semiotics and how that related to the past of the discipline. He talked a lot

> about his experiences and the changes in his own theoretical and methodological orientation from the thirties to the present. But just sitting in his study, which was a great sea of books and papers, . . . or just listening to him talk was quite fun. The fact that he would do this for me—an anonymous beginning teacher who wasn't his own student—gave me a sense of the discipline and also at the same time a sense of its history.
>
> Jim Ackerman had an enormous impact on me throughout my life. The article he did on Milan was something I deliberately set out to try and emulate. . . . He influenced me also in terms of inviting me to Harvard when he was chairman. . . . That was a great transition for me in my life. . . . [I went] to Harvard for a semester. . . . That was really when I decided to not be a bureaucrat after all, but to get back to my scholarship.

One scholar was especially grateful for the demands that his mentor made on him, which he met with an increasing sense of self-reliance.

> He was the toughest guy I ever [studied with], the most difficult person to please I ever thought possible, the most impatient with students. And that in itself was an interesting challenge, and [he] loved the material.

Another shared a bittersweet memory of the paces that his mentor had put him through.

> I asked [my mentor], "What are your ideas on [my dissertation] subject?" And he said, "It's your thesis. You have to get at what it is. I can't tell you anything." So I worked for about a year, maybe a little more, and I found perhaps ten prints from which I could develop ideas about the beginnings of reproduction in the fifteenth century. . . . I went to [him] with all the photographs [of examples and comparative material] I'd collected. He opened [his own file, and in it] he had everything that I had found [except one]. Can you imagine? . . . [But] I think he was right . . . , [even though] he could have saved me a year or more. . . . [My time] wasn't wasted.

A few of the scholars had developed an interest in—if not a passion for—the history of art even before their university training began.

> I had been interested in . . . art as a schoolboy. . . . Vienna has marvelous museums. On rainy Sunday[s] we went to the Kunsthistorisches Museum in Vienna, and I "caught fire." We had also had a good library at home. . . . So it was natural to be interested in art.

> I, from the age of ten and a half, did art history as a part of my art training. I did homework in it, and I took a state scholarship in it. . . . I decided that I would like to be the world's greatest living expert on [something art-historical,] no matter how small an area!

Others were attracted to the history of art while undergraduates, inspired by the erudition and warmth of senior scholars.

> I was . . . indebted to Johannes Wilde. . . . [He] knew the great Venetian paintings intimately and had examined them technically. . . . He gave a very remarkable series of lectures on Titian, which had a great deal of feeling. . . . He identified always with old artists—late Michelangelo, late Titian—and that is probably one of the reasons why I turned to Venetian art.

> The second semester [of the survey course] was taught by [Horst W.] Janson. . . . Janson was really exciting, interesting, made things live, and he was always sharing fascinating secrets with kids. He didn't treat you as a kid at all. He treated you as an intellectual equal in discussion. It was overwhelming, but it was also flattering and fascinating. . . . That really gave me the idea that art history had everything in it to engage me and keep me fascinated.

In contrast the same scholar's reaction late in graduate school to what he perceived as the constraints of academic art history had important consequences for his career.

> The last year [of my graduate training] I taught a section of . . . a survey course. . . . You get up in front of these freshmen, and you have to parrot [the professor's] inanities about [works of art]. . . . This was the contrast between the application of high intelligence and tremendous resources to fascinating problems at the frontiers of knowledge, and . . . commonplaces in front of a

class of freshmen. So I tried to boost the level of these sections . . . , and [the professor] got furious with me. . . . I said, "Teaching is not for me!"

COLLEAGUES ▪ After graduate school, associates became increasingly important sources of inspiration and stimulation to the scholars, although some continued to maintain close contact with their mentors. For many, relationships with colleagues affected their professional development as well as their understanding of themselves and of their field.

> My first job was as [professorial] assistant at the institute. Those are positions that are related to professors but in which you also do administrative work. It was a very important moment in my career. . . . I was in a certain way the link between the professor and his students. I prepared the seminars in terms of organizing them, speaking with the students about their reports. . . . I was also his discussion partner. . . . I learned how he prepared his books, his lectures. He would give me his lectures to read. . . . At the same time I was the head of the library, deciding what should be bought. . . . I really came to know what was happening in the field.

> At crucial times [my mentor] has had a very important impact on me as a teacher, as somebody who opened up a lot of exciting things, but methodologically I am not all that close to him. . . . From the moment I left graduate school . . . , I worked with somebody else who was equally strong as he was. . . . Now [at my current university] there is [someone else] hovering. [They are] very different people.

> I had the great benefit of [a colleague]. . . . I learned that I had a better eye than he did, which was exciting, but he taught me a hell of a lot about how things work. He taught me to not be too tight and fearful about stuff I didn't know, that I should just enjoy it. . . . I went to dealers with him; I really had a kind of crash couple of years in the practical life of collecting. He was a private collector himself . . . and had a very unstilted and uninstitutional view of art and collecting art, which was helpful to me.

The art historians who teach were particularly concerned about the dynamics of collegial interaction within their universities.

> One of the things about being in a conservative department is that we lack a certain culture of open discussion. And I love that; it's part of one's everyday life as an academic. You should be arguing and discussing, having your ideas torn to shreds. . . . [At a former university] I had younger colleagues, essentially the people I'd hired, who were wonderfully cantankerous and demanding and stimulating. And we had a great measure of common ground.

> I've always been involved with forming art forums and discussion groups, just to get people talking. . . . [In] academia . . . , you really become a kind of business person, marketing something in your own shop. The reasons that I—very idealistically—thought academia was exciting are seldom there.

Institutional encouragement of narrow specialization and concomitant professional competition were seen as barriers not only to collegial relationships but also to personal intellectual growth.

> I never could take a job where the university said, "You have to teach [only] French nineteenth-century [art]." And where a colleague said, "Don't come into my field of [French] eighteenth-century." . . . It shouldn't be done this way.

Some scholars found less exchange of ideas than they would like in the larger national and international art-historical community and expressed dissatisfaction with the traditional forums of annual conventions and letters to the editor.

> An awful lot of our conferences are geared to the world of art and the world of the museum. I don't believe that that world is conducive to open, unsparing critical debate. . . . Ultimately art history is too affirmative, celebratory, genteel, well mannered. . . . [Other disciplines don't have objects] that the culture lays claim to, which are big business, big money, and which are symbols of extraordinary prestige, cultivation, culture. CAA [the College Art Association's annual conference] is not enough, even in its very laudable attempts to . . . become more of an intellectual forum. . . . We need more places in which people can publish.

> Controversy is not something that is welcome in art history. . . . There seems to be very little discussion of anything. . . . You write a paper, and who knows what the reaction is to it.

Research institutes sometimes served as catalysts for collegial interaction by bringing groups of scholars together for extended periods of time.

> I feel isolated at my [institution]. This is an exaggeration, but being at [a research center], being able to speak with people in completely different disciplines, is far more challenging. [At home] I have interesting colleagues, but we don't have an intellectual discourse because we are always speaking about business.

> The [research center] did foster things. Everyone was required to give a colloquium paper during their year there, to report on the work they were doing. . . . There were about eight or nine of us. We very quickly formed a very closely knit group, people with compatible interests. We spent a lot of time talking about the discipline, about current theoretical writing; that also was fortuitous. And we did a lot of things together socially. . . . In terms of my getting work done it was a very, very productive period.

Truly collaborative scholarly effort was uncommon among the art historians interviewed. Two scholars, however, described situations in which they authored pieces jointly.

> [A colleague and I] set out to write a history . . . and theory of caricature, a book which . . . has never been published. . . . We would get together every evening. . . . We started writing. Sometimes he held the pen, and sometimes I held the pen. We really worked together.

> When [my graduate student] worked with me on various articles on Giulio Romano, . . . we stayed in the same *pensione*; . . . we talked constantly about it; . . . we wrote it into the machine; we tried to formulate every sentence as we went along. . . . It was . . . genuinely and totally a collaborative work. It is very hard. Not many people can do that because you have to be willing to . . . suspend deeply ingrained mechanisms.

And another is currently involved in a satisfying cooperative project.

> I had a problem with the personal papers of [Joseph-Marie] Vien, which were still in the family. Vien wrote his autobiography, and this was published in the nineteenth century but only [in] part. I spent a lot of time trying to find out where it was. . . . Then [by chance] I met this person . . . who had access to the family and the memoirs and the autobiography. . . . [Our acquaintance] turned into a real friendship. We are working together. . . . He is writing the biography . . . , and I am writing about Vien's work. We are such good friends that there's no problem; we share. [The book] will come out [under] two names.

Finally, several scholars stressed the contributions that relationships with students made to their work.

> The questions, the observations, the suggestions made by people who haven't, in a sense, fully nested inside the discipline . . . can be enormously productive. . . . An advanced graduate student's participation . . . may be more than merely an echo, it may be an active participation. They should be given credit for that. And I think there should be much more of that.

CHOICES WITHIN THE DISCIPLINE ▪ The scholars described various intellectual and philosophical attractions that the field held for them as young historians. Some felt the magnetism of certain genres of art.

> I realized . . . that if I went to a museum, I always had to do the Dutch paintings last. If I started with the Dutch paintings, I wouldn't have the patience to look at other kinds of painting. It just seemed to me that the Dutch dealt with the visual world with a kind of thoroughness, honesty, and humor which engaged me so much that other kinds of painting looked a little pretentious to me after that. . . . It made me aware that I had a fascination with Dutch painting.

Antipathies to certain types of subject matter and aspects of artistic style as well as to various analytical approaches could also contribute to definitions of interest and approach.

> Central Italian art [was] ruined for me by [two of my teachers] who saw everything from the point of view of perspectival construction. . . . I thought [this was a] false sort of manipulation of pictures to fit theories.

> [In] these glamorous court portraits [of Louis XIV; see fig. 8] the values evoking material, office, [and] splendor [were] things which I was absolutely uninterested in and thought were kind of a negative part of art, which I really didn't want to know about, because my interest in art had to do with much more important cultural and aesthetic values. Modern art, which set the tone, was rebelling against society and setting society examples rather than glorifying the head of [some] ridiculous, pompous state.

Experience outside of graduate school—notably in first full-time jobs—often caused the scholars to rethink decisions they had made regarding the arena in which they practiced art history.

> I did realize . . . fairly quickly during the first year [of teaching] that I was really a lot itchier for the things that you do in musuems: . . . the worldly side of things, the choosing and hanging of pictures, . . . giving popular lectures. . . . You get, in a museum, . . . immediate, privileged access to works of art—new works of art, even things that nobody's ever seen before. . . . You can keep your hand in the game sitting in the university, but it's a bit of work, and you're conscious of being a bit out of it.

The questioning process was seen as essential to intellectual growth. Commitment to one area of the discipline did not necessarily preclude a shift in interest to others. One scholar described a dramatic engagement with a new field in midcareer that seemed to hold great excitement and challenge.

> I'm very interested in certain aspects of Mayan architecture and sculpture. That interest was triggered by going down there and seeing the stuff and reading and thinking about it since. . . . It's an extraordinary experience for somebody coming from nineteenth-century French art history. There's so little known; it's unknown territory, and the questions are wide open, waiting to be asked. . . . I'm casting around.

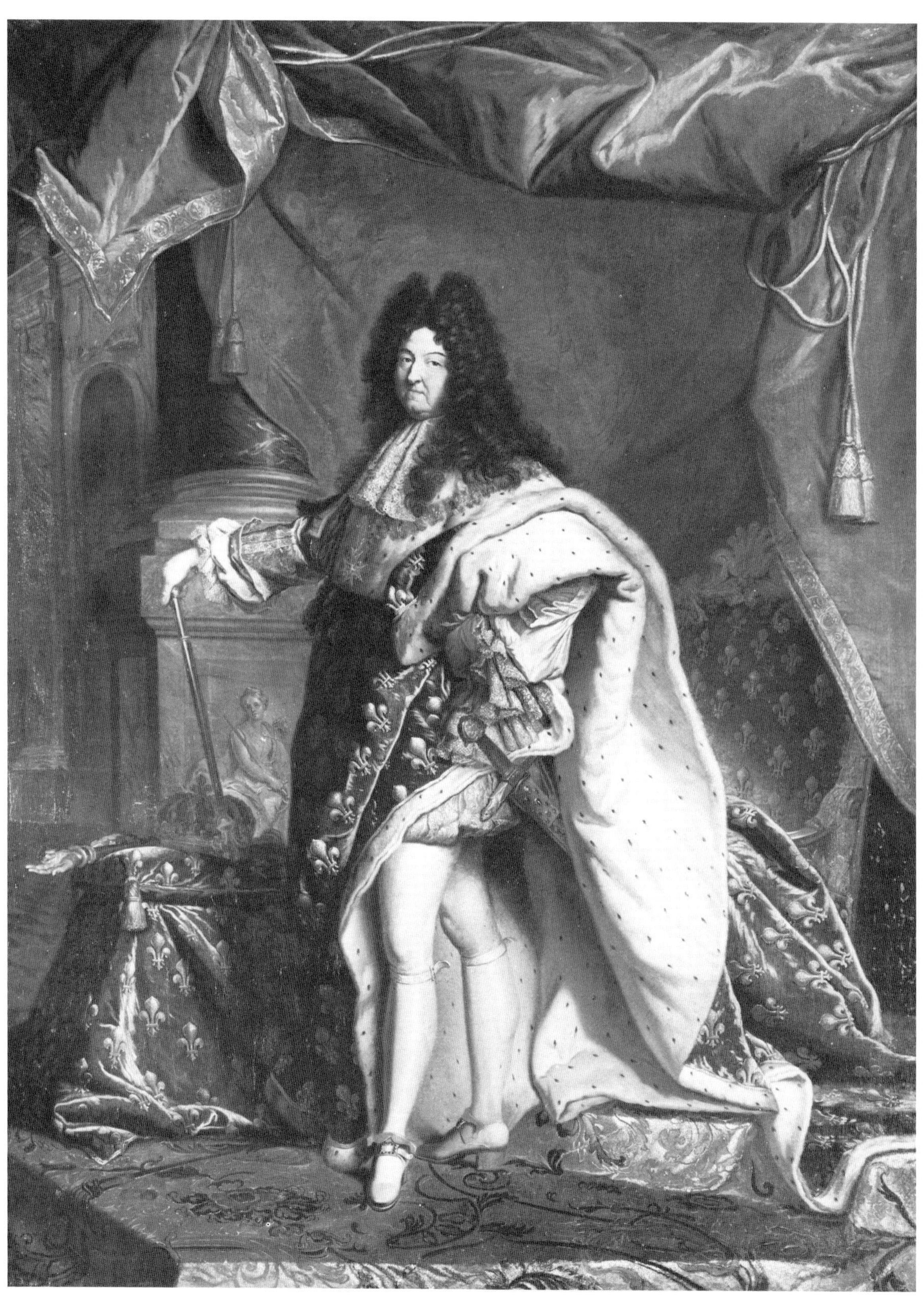

8. HYACINTHE RIGAUD, *Louis XIV*, 1701, Musée National du Château, Versailles

SUMMARY ▪ Personal associations with senior scholars affect the learning and practice of the discipline. Mentors were often credited with attracting their students to various fields of study, with influencing their choice of analytical approaches, with guiding the course of their careers, and with challenging them through demands or even neglect. Although an early appreciation of art was sometimes a factor, exposure to the history of art as a discipline usually occurred in university-level courses rather than in grammar- or high-school curricula. University professors served as role models for both professional and personal directions, but after the completion of formal studies, colleagues became increasingly important as sources of inspiration. Although a thirst for intellectual collegiality is seldom satisfied by the academic community or professional conferences, research institutes appear to offer the desired environment for open exchange. While art-historical research is characteristically a solitary pursuit, some scholars have been involved in collaborative projects. Emotional considerations can determine choices of fields of specialization and career paths. Midcareer changes to new areas of interest provide stimulation and intellectual growth.

FINANCES

The scholars interviewed reiterated what is perhaps common knowledge: American, British, and some European art historians are not, in general, well remunerated for the work they do, whether they are employed in universities, museums, libraries, archives, or research centers. Most art historians find it difficult to support themselves, let alone a family.

> English pay now for academics, [especially] for married [people] with kids, is not a very exciting prospect.

Even more troublesome, however, may be the impression that the low compensation reflects general societal attitudes about the value of the pursuit of art history.

> Being an art historian—this is the old part of the game—is not considered to be time-consuming. . . . It's not the general opinion that it is serious work. That concerns our research also; normally we don't get one cent for [most of] our publications.

> I don't understand why a lawyer makes a report for a company and gets a lot of money, when I give [art-historical] advice all the time for nothing.

SALARIES ▪ In many cases the successful academic finds little advantage in the marketplace. A German art historian described the process that governed incremental raises in salaries in his country's universities:

> You bargain, but this is not free bargaining. It is completely outlined by the state: for the first outside call [from another university] you get 200 marks more, for the second outside call you get 350 marks more, and for a call from another country, you get 500 more. It's not very much, I can assure you. I have had outside calls, and I can say it didn't change my life at all.

Indeed the successful senior academic may find that at the "top" of the profession, one may be priced out of the market and find the range of job possibilities limited.

> A very eminent [academic] . . . wanted to come here because his university system has got completely hellish with an open system, whereby students who have no preparation in anything can just sign on anywhere they like. And there is a lot of politics involved in his job. He is constantly in committees. . . . He could only assign his students so many books a week to read. . . . He said he would like to come to a system where he would be free to impose whatever kind of style. . . . In the end . . . he couldn't afford it, so we lost him.

One scholar had done more than grumble; he had dedicated himself to raising the consciousness of fellow academics.

> I have been an active member of the American Association of University Professors. . . . [How many of us] have ever considered what the implication is of paying a full professor twenty-eight thousand dollars a year after that professor has taught for fifteen years and is at the height of [the] profession? What we are seeing is a profession that has been going down. . . . The buying power of professors . . . has . . . bottomed out.

SOCIAL AND ECONOMIC CLASS AND THE ART HISTORIAN ▪ Several of the scholars discussed what they interpreted as a social mystique surrounding the art-historical profession. Works of art, the discipline's traditional focus, have gained extraordinary monetary as well as cultural value. Therefore a privileged social status may accrue to those who care for and study these objects. Two scholars reminisced about how uncomfortable they felt as initiates to the haut monde.

> I found it very alien. I had no money and no clothes, and people were very well dressed and beautiful. . . . It still is so. Art history tends to attract narcissists and the vain.

> The Institute [of Fine Arts] had a very overwhelming reputation. . . . I followed a few lectures [there] when I was at NYU [New York University]. . . . The atmosphere of the place intimidated me: this tobacco mansion on Seventy-eighth Street, marble sculptures and secretaries from high society, and the idea that it's a precinct built by the very rich in which you're supposed to behave yourself and behave as if you belong there.

One memory illuminated what the scholar saw as an insidious relationship of economic class to the discipline.

> The secretary of the department . . . arranged for me to live with a distant relative of hers, . . . a rich old lady living in this big house. . . . But she kicked me out one fine day . . . [because] I bought a [used] sports car. . . . She said, "Poor boys don't drive cars like that." . . . I've never really thought much about it . . . , but it certainly has deeper significance with certain relationships—art historians coming from down below, being trained, and serving the interests of very rich people, [and] very rich institutions. Now these days they let the poor boys drive cars like that, I suppose, but there are other thresholds.

ADDITIONAL INCOME ▪ Most of the art historians interviewed felt that their salaries were not sufficient to meet their needs and wants. Some took on additional work. But moonlighting presented them with dilemmas, notably those concerning the popularization of intellectual discourse.

> One of the things that's the advantage, and possibly the disadvantage, of working in twentieth-century art is that there's the endless seduction applied

> by dealers. . . . [A dealer] asked me to write about grids [for an exhibition he was doing]. . . . So I had this problem: how could I write about grids such that it would be for me an interesting issue?

> If I was a civil servant, I would be earning a lot more. If I was a state museum person, I would earn a lot more, so we are on quite low pay, but we all moonlight, . . . take on an exhibition . . . , [go] on radio or television . . . , do journalism. . . . I can earn a lot by lecturing, but I don't wish to do that too much—to do what I call hack lecturing, . . . drawing the crowds and putting on a big show.

Outside work brings other rewards, of course, than financial gain. One profits from both increased recognition and personal contacts as one's circle widens.

> There is pressure [to join the lecture circuit from] professional duty, curiosity, and money. The pressures are very clear. A lot of invitations are very well paid and attractive. . . . This place seems very interesting or this conference has some interesting people.

GRANTS ▪ The pressure to win grants and fellowships begins in graduate school and continues throughout one's career; scholars expend a great deal of time and effort seeking support for their research. Although many scholars have periodic access to research funds through their institutions, these monies are usually not substantial enough to allow one to take time away from routine duties for a significant period.

> The British Academy funds are for scholars who are in full-time employment in universities. . . . I don't think anybody applying here would be turned down. There is no great glamour in getting it because you would be very surprised if you didn't; . . . you would be really worried. But they are not big sums of money.

The harder-won awards may require scholars to make difficult personal as well as professional choices. One person's recitation of her past year's activity highlighted both the frenetic effort she had made and the somber realizations the process had unveiled.

> This year . . . I applied for a Guggenheim. . . . I had had an NEH [National Endowment for the Humanities] . . . so I didn't apply for [that]. I applied for an ACLS [American Council of Learned Societies]. . . . I also applied for a Fulbright. I don't think I bothered with the AAUW [American Association of University Women]; that was such a long shot. I applied to CASVA [Center for Advanced Study in the Visual Arts at the National Gallery in Washington, D.C.] and to the [Institute for Advanced Study in Princeton]. I did not apply to the Research Triangle [in Raleigh, North Carolina]. . . . I applied to the Howard Foundation, which was this one-year possibility for art historians. . . . I didn't get the Guggenheim, . . . ACLS . . . , [or] Howard grant[s]. So that was it for the possibility of staying home where my work actually [was]. . . . I gave up the Fulbright. . . . I also gave up the grant to CASVA, thinking that the institute would probably be better for the little bit of time my husband could be with me. He would be near New York. . . . My institution . . . doesn't have a sabbatical policy. . . . I really am stymied by what is going to happen to me in the future. . . . I think that is the most significant problem [for] women as [they] come into the profession, because you will have gotten all those things [like] ACLS and Getty grants for young Ph.D.s. And then there you are in midcareer, when you probably will have a young family and when you aren't flexible. . . . I think what people will have to do in my position is take time unpaid.

Indeed scholars sometimes underwrite their own research, either without assurance that reimbursement for expenses will be forthcoming,

> A friend of mine who was the assistant director of [a museum] got very excited about the material and said, "Oh, it would be a wonderful exhibition. Why don't we do it?" So I [agreed] because I had done exhibitions before, and I knew from past experience that this was a wonderful way of traveling on somebody else's "nickel." . . . I didn't know that [the museum] didn't have a "nickel." [I decided to conduct my research for the exhibition anyway] on a sabbatical . . . hoping that [the museum] would get the grant that they had applied for.

or with the knowledge that supporting funds will not cover the expenses.

> I have had various grants . . . , but a huge amount of that weight you simply carry out of your salary. A grant very rarely pays for your stay in France.

COSTS OF TRAVEL ▪ Many of the art historians saw the costs of travel to consult source materials as a constant problem.

> Maybe 60 percent [of the research materials I needed] Berkeley had, and maybe another 12 percent you could get on interlibrary loan, and the rest was simply unavailable. You had to go to the Library of Congress or the New York Public Library. You had to save up your needs and do this on one or two trips a year. That was at least doable for faculty members, but of course it is not doable for a student.

The need to see special exhibitions posed a particularly compelling financial challenge.

> [I had a Kress grant] to go to see an exhibition in Texas, which was about abstract art in Hannover in the 1920s, where they reconstructed for the first time Lissitzky's Proun room [see fig. 9].

> All exhibitions are [finite], and I think a certain percentage of them are undoable again, so that you would want to bring scholars to exhibitions. . . . I can't tell you how many [people] from Europe . . . regretted that they couldn't come [to the Picasso retrospective exhibition] because they couldn't afford it.

Although the scholars may continually face the question of how they will finance travel, they do not doubt its necessity.

> I see art history and art as being absolutely inseparable. . . . I have traveled all over to see one [Bellini]. I have even spent hundreds of pounds on a flight to go and see one.

> I'll go into debt to go to Europe and look at stuff . . . but it's not an extravagance. To me it's an investment in [my]self.

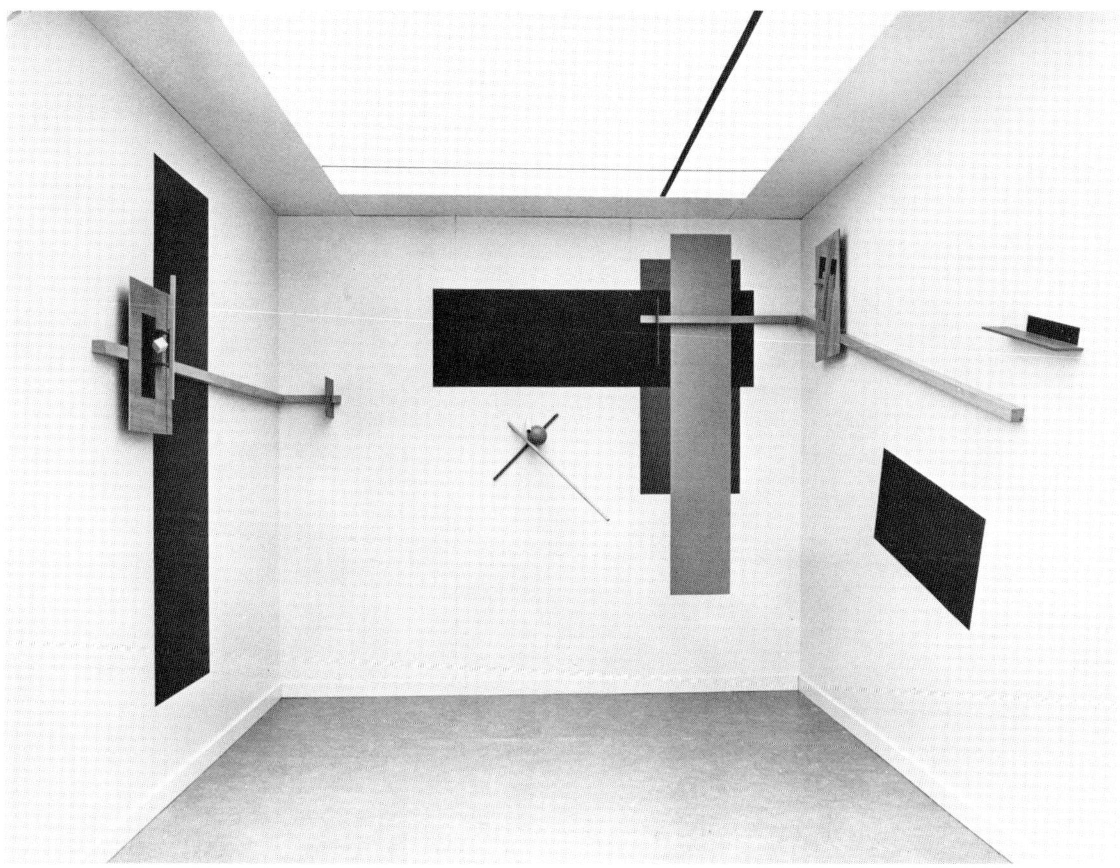

9. EL LISSITZKY, *Proun Space*, 1923 (reconstruction, 1965), Van Abbemuseum, Eindhoven, photo by Martien Coppens

> Doing research abroad in other countries is necessary for an art historian. If he is working in the Italian field, he has to go to Italy. [The way I did it was to] stay most of the time in a German university and travel for a week or two or three [to Italy and Paris] every once in a while. It's evident that for me it was more complicated, [because I had a job and was not on a fellowship] than for those people who had the chance to live for several years in Italy.

Many saw the extended traveling they had done during their student years as the most important of their careers. Those scholars who had done graduate work in England spoke of the advantage of being able to travel cheaply to the Continent to study.

> The fortunate thing was that I was a graduate student in London then, and I used to simply put my motorcycle on the boat and cross over to France. I

used to stay in the youth hostel in Troyes. I could afford that at very low cost—to go and spend entire summers there. So I wasted an enormous amount of time and stumbled around, and it took me a long time to feel confident about reading and transcribing.

> I was too poor to fly, but within twelve hours [from London, I could be] in Italy at a ridiculously low cost, except the wear and tear of traveling all night in a third-class coach. This meant that I could teach myself a broad knowledge of Venetian sixteenth-century painting, the major works of the artists, their styles, the qualities of an autographic work and those of the school work, and so forth.

Graduate students in America were not at a total disadvantage. One scholar remembered the years that he was in graduate school as a time when American students encountered few difficulties in funding travel. The students of which he was thinking, however, were privileged in that they attended institutions where the history of art was favored and financially supported, and at a time when adequate funding was offered to students.

> [A travel fellowship] was the birthright of every art history student in America in the sixties. There weren't too many students; there was money from the Kress, this, and that. Everyone agreed that art history students had to go abroad; it was one of the secondary advantages.

If one was lucky enough to find such a project, a well-funded exhibition might provide travel benefits.

> I had a lot of opportunities because of the De Stijl exhibition. I had access to . . . photographs but also was sent to Holland a couple of times and to Paris. So I had an opportunity to do on the spot what otherwise would have been much more difficult. . . . That was a fortuitous thing.

While many American graduate students depended on grants to spend extended time abroad, a few were able to parlay the skills that they had developed in research and language facility into job opportunities in foreign countries.

> The summer of 1964 I spent in Rome with the *Encyclopedia of World Art*, doing editorial work. . . . [A friend] had been doing copyediting for them in New York. . . . He introduced me there, and I got this job.

> I started doing free-lance translating. . . . In the beginning I didn't know what to charge. At first they [paid] me one cent a word, which was really horrible—one Dutch cent a word. The going rate was four cents a word. But it went up very quickly.

The passion for travel might lead to odd jobs.

> I had been working in a factory spraying beds to get some money to go back to Italy.

In one case displacement to a foreign country led to a career in art history.

> I started studying the history of art [accidentally]. I was a newspaper reporter. I started in San Francisco after graduating from college, and I worked in the city room. I did suicides and fires and things. I was so successful they promoted me and made me editor of the religious page. . . . Having saved a thousand dollars, . . . I decided to go to Europe. I ate up my thousand dollars, and I needed a job, so I got a job with United Press in London. . . . I started taking an evening course [at the Courtauld Institute]. That got so interesting that I thought, "You don't want to be a journalist; you want to be . . . another Jacob Burckhardt."

A determination to master foreign languages and a belief that they were essential to the study of art history characterized most of the art historians whom we interviewed.

> During the second [year at the Courtauld Institute in London], I made more effort to learn Italian, and then I developed friends . . . , a family of art historians from Bologna. I lived with them, and I became an Italianate from then on.

> I started English at school. . . . Now I am very interested in reading . . . not only art history books [in English but also] novels, nineteenth-century espe-

> cially. . . . When I started [to study German as a university student, I read] only art history publications. . . . German was more difficult, but . . . it is impossible to write or to study art history without a basic knowledge of German. . . . Spanish is not a problem for Italians. Dutch is more difficult, [but] with English and German and a dictionary it is possible.

Language fluency could be an important factor in appraising scholarly ambitions,

> For my thesis on Andrea Pisano it was not possible not to read [or] to understand the German publications.

> I was going to do a study of [Dutch] humorous subjects . . . to show how the attitude toward humor underwent evolution from a kind of . . . bitterness in the middle of the sixteenth century to a kind of mirth, through changes that reflected religious and spiritual changes. . . . It gives me a little shudder to say it, because it . . . [was] certainly undoable by any twenty-two-year-old American with one year of Dutch behind him.

and in the guidance of students.

> We have language specifications as well; we don't encourage anybody to do this [special course] if they can't read Spanish or French. [But] we can't say, "You must have Flemish; you must have Dutch." That would be too unrealistic.

COSTS OF EDUCATION ▪ Financial circumstances did act as a constraint on some of the scholars' choices of undergraduate and graduate schools. None of the scholars, however, expressed regret about an alma mater.

> You had to walk a tightrope between what your parents could afford, what the circumstances would permit, [and] what you wanted to do. . . . It was rather more economical to study in Berlin in the cold winter of 1956–57 [than] in Zurich. In 1958 in Florence or in 1959 in London, you could do very well as a student, . . . come home with lots of books.

> [I went to Berkeley because] it was the local college. . . . One just went to Berkeley because [it was the] good old college that was free . . . for the top 10 percent of the high-school graduates.

> I didn't know whether I wanted to go to graduate school in art history. If I did, the logical place to go would be the Institute [of Fine Arts], which after all is attached to New York University, [where] I was doing my undergraduate work. . . . [My mentor] said, "Do you want to go [to graduate school at Johns] Hopkins? . . . He didn't think I could get a scholarship for the Institute. He said I could get admitted, but I'd have to pay my own way. . . . In American graduate education in those days, when someone wasn't rich, you needed a scholarship. Getting admitted wasn't the big thing; it was the scholarship that was the big thing.

At particularly well-endowed universities with strong art history programs, students could look forward to a variety of financial aid programs that enabled them to get the most out of their graduate training.

> At Yale a lot of people got supported. . . . It was a fellowship, and then if you were a teaching assistant, you got paid.

Some of the scholars were fortunate enough to receive substantial aid from their parents so that they could afford not to work or to take unsalaried or low-paying internships.

> I was an intern in the museum-training program at the Guggenheim Museum. The first time I was an [unpaid] intern, and then I went back and had a small salary. That was wonderful. That was probably the best thing I ever did.

> I stayed in Florence for five years. . . . I had no post, [but] my father gave me money just to live in Florence . . . as a [postgraduate] student.

For most, however, financial need meant completing student work while commencing a teaching career.

> I started to teach long before I finished the dissertation. There was no question of finishing a whole dissertation fully supported.

COSTS OF PUBLISHING ▪ Art historians must often sacrifice financially to publish their work, especially as younger scholars without established reputations. Publishers may expect an author to assume all the costs of securing illustrations, for example (see also "Writing and Publishing").

> I paid for all of the things in this book in terms of photographs: . . . for the rights [to publish], . . . for the color plates, . . . for the black-and-white ones.

One way of cutting costs is to build one's own collection of reproductions, but this assumes a substantial investment in photographic and even darkroom equipment, as well as travel.

> I do have a pretty good photographic archive of my own. . . . When I am printing in my own darkroom, I tend to print everything on a postcard size of four by six [inches], so I can get four of those on a page. Then when I come to publish, I have a negative number transcribed beside the print, and I simply print up a full plate or a half plate or whatever I want.

Authors may bear additional costs; hiring a research assistant to help with the preparation of an index, for example, can be a significant expense.

> There are always students wanting to do work. So if you're able to pay for it entirely out of your own pocket, then I'm sure you could get somebody. But, you know, it's a considerable amount of money.

The prepublication review process too can prove to be expensive when reviewers ask to be sent reproductions to illustrate articles.

> I learned never to send original photographs no matter what journal is reviewing your book, because I have lost things that way. . . . You could spend your life getting these things reproduced at twenty dollars a shot.

Most of the scholars described a trial-and-error process by which they learned how to protect their rights as authors and find financial assistance for their publications. A sense of hesitancy seemed ever present, however, and those who received even moderate support regarded themselves as lucky.

> I wasn't in trouble myself. I had a good salary, and I had some money, so I did not need to ask for an advance. . . . I didn't negotiate for that. I probably should have. . . . Very often universities can help. . . . At [Johns] Hopkins I was able to get money to have the manuscript retyped. I had money for a graduate student to proofread it. . . . Perhaps they could have helped me, if I really needed it, with photographs. . . . I think we are very dependent on our institutions.

> There came a fairly arbitrary moment in which I decided it was time to write. . . . [My mentor] made me the first recipient of [a] research fellowship . . . [and got me] a literary agent . . . and an advance.

Especially in Italy one finds commercial subventions for academic publications, but these are rare in the overall picture.

> The Bank of Trento is paying for the book . . . because the banks in Italy are very interested. It is a form of advertising. They publish wonderful books of art in Turin, in Milan, in Rome.

In general one is very much on one's own. There is a constant struggle to advance one's reputation so that financial aid will be forthcoming.

> These first books were a success. . . . They were widely reviewed, and the publishers said, "This is a good property we've got here, and we'll give him an advance on another book." An advance was just about enough to live frugally for a year.

ECONOMIC STRAITS OF UNIVERSITIES ▪ A scholar's sense of well-being can depend not only on his ability to find sources of funding for research and publications but also on the larger financial fortunes of his institution.

> They brought in a new dean [of fine arts] about five years ago, . . . and he was a very aggressive person, really interested in making the art history program . . . the best in the country. . . . It's a very, very positive feeling.

> Suddenly there were these drastic budget cutbacks. . . . Our means to support [graduate students] were so limited that we ended up with, number one, not very good graduate students and, number two, the standards that were enforced . . . were below what I thought acceptable.

Ironically the offer of a better-paid position at a more heavily endowed university may not solve a scholar's financial worries if costs of living in the new community are significantly higher.

> Frankly I don't know how we are going to [make this move]. I have been looking at property and considering the balance-of-payments crisis at the end of the month. There is no way that the increase in salary would cover [the new mortgage]. . . . Certainly financially it will be a very difficult thing to live with.

Finally, the interviews seemed to suggest that many art historians felt that they were doing two jobs, one of which supported the other. Any effort to vary this model proved difficult, as we heard from one independent scholar.

> I began inventing this structure in my mind based on American academic life. You do teaching and you do research. And the teaching pays for the research, as it were. You have to devote 60 or 70 percent of your time to teaching in order to spend 30 percent of your time on research, and if you throw sabbaticals in, it works out to about fifty-fifty. [I thought,] "I'll do the same thing except not using teaching [but] work in publishing, translating, and so forth to pay for this half-time that I was going to do." . . . I called it a publishing company, but I told myself that [it] was not my first priority to set up a company, or to establish continuity, but just to make good books and to make enough money out of it to pay for this dream of mine of being able to do research, writing, which I loved. And it didn't work out that way, because publishing is at least as demanding as working for [someone else].

SUMMARY ▪ Low pay is a persistent problem for art historians in America, Britain, and some European countries, especially in the face of the expenses that they incur for research and publication. Because the discipline is expensive to pursue and is concerned with objects of high monetary value, an air of elite social status conflicts with the usually modest remuneration. Outside work (exhibitions, lectures, journalism) may tempt one to lower standards or may stimulate broader interests. While grants are relatively numerous, the application process is burdensome, and they seldom cover expenses fully. The costs of travel, so necessary for the study of original works of art and for work in archives and libraries, can be alleviated only slightly by interlibrary loans. The temporary exhibition that represents a onetime gathering of dispersed works of art poses an acute need for special travel. In most cases the art historians absorbed these expenses, while looking back nostalgically to the cheap travel, abundant grants, and odd jobs that characterized their student days. Fluency in foreign languages, a requisite for art-historical study, sometimes affected the choice of what to study. The cost of education—defrayed by family, grants, the state, and jobs—could influence the choice of university. Publishing one's research represents a significant expense because of the standard expectation that the art historian will assume the costs of secretarial assistance as well as those of securing publication-quality illustrations and the rights to publish them. The economic straits of institutions affect the individual scholar. Moving to a better job is a mixed blessing if the change involves a higher cost of living. Most scholars regarded their jobs as means to subsidize research.

TIME

Most of the art historians interviewed need large blocks of time to conduct the research and produce the publications that contribute to their scholarly achievements. Those who teach often use the summer holidays and extended periods between terms to do the work that they are unable to accomplish when classes are in session.

> The English vacation system . . . has quite a lot going for it, because you do have those two real chunks of time at Christmas and Easter . . . , which really can be used . . . [as] working vacation[s].

TIME AND RESEARCH ▪ Original art-historical research can rarely be achieved without travel away from one's home base to study works of art or to work in libraries, archives, and museums for lengthy periods of time. To use their time at home and abroad efficiently, most scholars construct a careful balance between library work best done at home, which serves as preparation, and work done in the field, which in turn sends one back to the library.

> Time in Europe is required for the gathering of material. . . . It's not required for the thinking and writing, although the thinking and writing go along with it, alerting you to the fact that you need more information and have to go back. . . . At the beginning there was a period of three or three and a half weeks of working in the archives in Parma, working in the libraries of Parma, . . . going to Milan to see the collection of topographical materials, and so forth. . . . Then came a period of many months when, working part-time, I was reading books I could get hold of in this country. A year passed, and I had an opportunity to go back to Italy again, and I carried a checklist of specific things I needed, books I had not been able to get in America. Now I realized I needed dimensions of individual buildings. . . . I must have spent a month or so on these aspects.

The scholars described the strategies that they develop to work in the "field," far away from the offices, studies, and libraries that they routinely use. Photocopying allows them to transport essential materials to the sites of their work abroad.

> You don't need a whole library if you have the right Xeroxes. You can leave certain details and footnoting to be filled in later when you get back, rough it out. I don't have the library [abroad]. Mostly what I do is read and write there.

Modern techniques of reproduction also make it possible to take home copies of documents or portions of documents that seem crucial. Yet the technology is not without its drawbacks, for the scholars may feel overwhelmed by the amount of information that they have gathered and have not found time to analyze (see also "Primary Sources and Archives" and "Organization of Information").

> Duplication . . . is actually a strategy of deferring. . . . I have at home cardboard boxes full of Xeroxes made over the past twenty years, and I have never read [them] yet. The fact that you can copy . . . allows you to defer dealing with it now.

> When you have such a massive overkill of copied documentation, how much time are you actually saving?

FELLOWSHIPS AND SABBATICALS ▪ Fellowships at research institutes may enable scholars to pursue their work under optimal conditions, freed from the distractions of their usual jobs and in proximity to library, archive, and museum collections that support their work.

> In terms of location [the Center for Advanced Study in the Visual Arts] was ideal, because of the Library of Congress and because of the National Gallery Library itself, which was very good. Because my apartment was literally across the street from the Library of Congress, I was there all hours of the day. It was in many ways the most ideal situation for getting that kind of research done.

But research institutes are not without their distractions for the scholars in residence; one's time may not be totally one's own. If the institute organizes collegial activities, for instance, a scholar may be torn between the need for solitude and the opportunity to share ideas and work with others.

> One of the things these centers do is give people shelter . . . and a certain frame of mind. . . . Then perhaps at a certain point in the year, they come out of their shells if they really want to. This is difficult to manage because obviously you do want to see these people . . . , [but] if it's really important to a certain person to be monastic, for at least part of the time, they should be allowed to be.

A sabbatical offers a scholar freedom from the routine demands of work, but it is often necessary for the art historian to secure a grant to coincide with this time in order to supplement reduced income and support research abroad (see also "Finances"). Administrative duties too can tax one's energy and leave one unprepared for a sabbatical when it does occur,

> For some years, with the chairman's job, I didn't apply for a grant. I simply stopped because I was too busy. . . . I took one semester during my chairman-

> ship, but when you are chairman you are not in gear. If you are going to make use of a sabbatical, you have got to get out there with your mind in gear.

or can make it impossible for one to be away for a lengthy period of time.

> I got a fellowship from the Deutsche Forschungsgemeinschaft, that would be your National Endowment [for the Arts or for the Humanities], for a [research] stay of three months. . . . I never could really get off for three months, so I split this time . . . [into] three-week [segments].

TIME AND WRITING ▪ For the art historians interviewed, writing, like research, seems to require distinct periods of concentration when the distractions of university or museum work do not intrude.

> I [finished the book] in the time I had off from Christmas to after Easter, but I had done a lot of work before. . . . I had collected a vast amount of information. . . . And the pace was speeded up because I knew that once I got back in here, I hadn't a hope in hell of doing anything except supervise the work, lecture, control the students, examine them. . . . I am teaching postgraduates, supervising Ph.D.s, undergraduates, the lot. We are quite busy, so you can only [write] really when you are out. You can do a bit of collecting [information] at the weekends . . . , but you haven't got much chance [to write].

> I would have maybe six weeks in France in the summer . . . and come up with some interesting ideas. . . . I haven't published it, but I have simply filed it away [because] once I get back . . . the phone is going all the time and there are a thousand problems.

> During the school year you can order your photographs and microfilms, collect bibliography, get things on interlibrary loan, Xerox things. But I can't—and there are people who can—do the kind of sustained thinking that has to go with writing. I find that very difficult, especially time-consuming. . . . So I work my summer research and writing . . . around nonteaching time.

> It's very difficult for me to do any kind of creative thinking without the sense of a long period of time available to me. If I have today off and tomorrow

> there are other things that will absorb me fully (something administrative, . . . lots of meetings, and a class), . . . I have sort of a restless feeling about this free day. . . . I can read some article, not profoundly, but check it out. . . . I can organize my index cards; I can copy a few disks. I can do all kinds of cleanup, mechanical work; I call it "pushing around paper clips." Or I can go to the library and enter the page numbers of certain citations in my footnotes . . . , but I can't really work out the origins of the Venetian palace plan or take the first step toward that. I want elbowroom in terms of time.

Different writing projects demand varying amounts of time, and the scholars often had to define their projects pragmatically to meet long- or short-term goals. The pressure of time can even determine whether a certain type of research will be pursued.

> I think the reason why so few idiots get into this kind of [transcription] work is because it is enormously time-consuming. With the tenure system the way it is, you can't afford to take on a project of this kind because you could get . . . to the tenure [decision] before your big book gets out. The academic system doesn't encourage people to go into this kind of project.

At the same time the nature of the material can determine the duration of effort.

> One sees a lot of things when one's on the road that look curious, interesting, peculiar, that look as if they aren't really quite what the guidebook says they are. But one passes them by anyway. And then one sees other things that look interesting and peculiar and doesn't pass them by. On one hand, . . . you recognize the merit of a question inherently [as demanding book-length treatment]. . . . A big book has a softer schedule [than an article]. . . . It's going to be a work of years. But on the other hand also, you may recognize that the subject has merit as an article, that this is a subject . . . you can make a well-rounded piece out of, that fills a void . . . in the literature.

PRIORITIES ▪ The scholars acknowledged that the priorities they established in their lives influenced their ability to meet the schedules they set for their work. They reflected on the apportioning of their energies during the hours of the day,

> [For] the last four or five years I [have] tried to produce every day something that brings me a step further in [my] research. I'm unsatisfied in the evenings if I have not got the feeling that I [did] something new. The result of that is that I try to do all the [administrative work in my museum] as quickly as possible to be free for what I really want to do. I usually develop my plans early in the morning when I walk to [work].

as well as over the courses of their careers.

> One of the great things about teaching at [my college] is that . . . I have no office. My theory is: no office, no office hours. [When] students want to see me, they can. . . . I think that's the kind of decision one has to make early on, whether you're going to have this big commitment to a university or not. . . . I wanted to start my own magazine, I wanted to do these other projects, and I just didn't want to sit around holding the hands of . . . undergraduates.

From those art historians who teach, administrative tasks often received harsh criticism as a waste of valuable time.

> We set ourselves up with far too many committees . . . constantly reevaluating and reconsidering and wondering whether this is the right way to do it and justifying and self-evaluating—surveys on this and reviews on that. It isn't a very profitable way to spend your time. . . . I think that [we] really should just get to the library and read and write—that is really what is important—and teach.

Teaching itself, however demanding of time, is for many art historians an activity that enriches their work,

> I find teaching is really a very full-time job. . . . Sometimes you've got to keep a distance between what you're working on, researching on, writing on, and your teaching. I've found that a big problem. But of course teaching the stuff is very valuable. It's a way of discovering what you really do and can articulate, what works, what flops.

or keeps them on track.

> I always thought that if I had had three years off to go to Paris to work, I would have published [my last book] ten years earlier. . . . But on the other hand, what I did was good for my academic career. . . . Freedom is a very complicated thing. If you're not pushed, if you're not in a situation where you have responsibility, it's difficult to be responsible to oneself. For myself it's necessary to be in the [university] environment, to teach.

The specter of an annual review is for some an impetus to achievement.

> I have a kind of annual conscience, which is due to the fact that we do publish annual reports in which we all say what we are doing. That acts as a tremendous spur to me. . . . I like to have done two or three things. . . . You might say that is a very public statement about what you have and have not been doing. . . . In fact we will be given more money the more research we do. . . . But this is fairly recent.

The art historians shared descriptions of their work habits. Time and place could have important impact on their productivity.

> I had a key to the Warburg Institute; that's when I got into my habit of working nights. I would come back after dinner, at nine at night, and I would let myself in. I would stay until dawn.

> I can't work at home. . . . I don't have good enough willpower, between the refrigerator and the television—the bad conflicts of life.

Most important, perhaps, is the need to define and focus on the project at hand in order to make the best use of one's time. Self-awareness may guard one against distractions, whether external or internal to one's work.

> I'm restless. I move in too many circles, and I have too many interests. [Sometimes] it's necessary to force myself [to stick to] one subject. As I'm interested in so many fields, I can spend days and days working without any result. . . .

> It's [a] pleasure, but on the other hand, it's [a] pleasure to produce something of worth.

> The traditional argument in our field is that it is good for you to go through thousands of photographs to find what [you] are looking for. You will find a lot of stuff you didn't know along the way. It will put the problem in perspective. . . . Shortcuts are bound to result in simplistic findings that don't take full account of the richness in the material. . . . Well, take it from me, the gain from serendipity is nothing compared to the incredible loss . . . of time. . . . I am not going to be able to do it.

> My problem was that I had been very perfectionist. I knew every Dante commentary known to man but hadn't had quite the time to get myself into the sixteenth century. . . . The Courtauld had given me this exaggerated idea of scholarly perfection, of completeness. . . . It was inhibiting for the young; it was an unrealistic standard. . . . I thought it was very wicked to think about . . . things superficially.

Finally, although the group of art historians whom we interviewed are "high achievers," they weigh carefully the human cost of overwork and the benefits of leisure.

> The years I was at Yale were amongst my most productive years and terrific. [I was] teaching, . . . publishing articles, doing exhibitions—that stuff was great. But I felt like a drone. I felt like my life was primarily just beavering away and working, and the quality of life wasn't good.

> I made it a point to take a month off every summer and have an actual vacation. . . . And that worked very well. That improved both the character and quality of my writing and working.

SUMMARY ▪ Research and writing are best undertaken during uninterrupted blocks of time. For art historians who teach, the long breaks in the academic year provide time both for travel to conduct research and for writing. Time spent in research abroad is best used when preliminary work is done at home, with work in the library alternating with work in the field. Photocopying and word-processing technologies make possible the efficient transport of essential materials between home and research sites at the same time that they multiply the quantity of material to be handled. While fellowships at research institutes offer the luxury of time uninterrupted by the responsibilities of a job, the distraction of critical discourse with colleagues in residence can be tempting. Sabbaticals may free one's time as well, but winning a supplemental grant that will help finance research abroad can be time-consuming. Some aspects of the research effort, such as creating bibliographies, taking notes, organizing materials, and securing reproductions, lend themselves to the fragments of time available during a workaday routine. The duration of a research project may be determined not only by the nature of the inquiry but also by competing activities. Priorities are necessary to ensure that short- and long-term goals are met and to protect against the erosion of time by the administrative tasks that are part of both museum and academic work. Teaching, although it drains time and energy, is seen as contributing to research. Periods of relaxation can enhance the quality of work as well as the quality of life.

WISH LIST

We asked the art historians what, if they could make any task easier, would most facilitate their work. One scholar quipped,

> I'd like to have a better memory.

Those scholars who had some experience with automation responded with suggestions specifically directed at information technology (see also "Organization of Information," especially "Information Technology and the Future" and "Information Needs of the Present"). The data banks they described belonged largely to the realm of imagination. Their visions nevertheless showed a concentration of interest in the areas of bibliography, images, and subject matter.

> Bibliographical research in general is very difficult. We would love to be able to call forth and look at the table of contents of the new periodicals and the old ones. I'd love to be able to punch a button and get the table of contents of *Pantheon*, 1929, for instance, and just go through them.

> For me the great dream is images indexed by a reasonably efficient subject index. . . . Imagine my task, if you please. I have images I need scattered

> in among ten thousand books and at least that number of periodical volumes, and in thousands of boxes aggregating several millions of photographs at the Rijksbureau voor Kunsthistorische Documentatie. . . . That is my tool, and it is a clumsy . . . tool. . . . So I would love to be able to have a big bank of images to search. I would love a reasonably sophisticated catalogue, and I am aware of how complex that is. . . . I would love to have any and all systems that can index and make accessible these . . . textual and iconographic traditions. . . . Some [existing indexes] are better than others, and some are more useful than others. Most of them, unfortunately, have very strong built-in limitations, either of subject matter or coverage or utility.

> I would like to spend less time in getting books. Library problems are still time-consuming in a certain way. . . . If I spend time getting information, I lose time to concentrate on the object. . . . Access to libraries should be as automatic as possible. If I had a computer on my desk where I could read the [catalogue of the] whole library system, that would help me a lot.

For the scholars who work with material on their own computers, the wish was for a connection to a broad world of information from their office or home,

> I'd also like to learn UNIX because . . . I'm interested in working at home and having that kind of connect[ion] to sources. I'd like to have it connected to all kinds of publishers' sources.

or for a word-processing program that would sort and relate information in complex ways.

> What I wanted to be able to do ideally is . . . flag or mark things to go into the index, and at the end I'll have it all there. . . . I want to index incipits alphabetically . . . and then . . . according to subject matter. The number of subject matters is much more than four. I want to also be indexing from the same documents representations, miniatures, [and] types of manuscript. I need a dozen or two dozen [indexes].

For many of the scholars, however, our question about what tools they would wish for provoked pointed reflection on their personal needs, hopes, and desires far beyond the realm of technological intervention.

> I do need my own Nikon [camera] and all that stuff, that would help a great deal. But oddly enough I don't consider . . . the mechanical aid as being the be-all and end-all. Even when I have got my computer, I don't think I am going to talk to colleagues enthusiastically about megabytes, etc. I am not terribly interested. It doesn't turn me on at all; I view them as a means to an end. What I want more than anything is to get back and be involved in a major project and feel again as I did.

> I want as much personal empathy with [and] cathexis of the objects of research as I possibly can [have]. It's better to have discovered them yourself. . . . It's actually built into the process of writing. . . . It would be much nicer if you didn't need to have [any intermediary] access. I mean, I'd much rather have the time to do it myself.

The previous sections have touched on a variety of problems that art historians face, and in some instances have included the scholars' suggestions of remedies. In what follows we turn back to those issues in order to illustrate the changes—both realistic and ideal—that the art historians imagine would have profound impact on their practice of the discipline. Many responses brought up the problem of cost (see also "Finances," especially "Grants" and "Costs of Travel").

> The major thing is really . . . open access . . . to different kinds of information—free, if possible. Internecine academic rivalry could be gotten around if people had equal access to books, because access is power. And the power has been contained in compartmentalized ways . . . , which depends on who you know, or if you're at the right school at exactly the right time, and [the number of] fellowships.

If money were more available to them, the scholars could afford to expand their libraries and hire research assistants.

> If I could be given unlimited money, I would be buying myself a lot more books . . . , source material that is being republished. I own quite a lot of these already, but . . . my salary doesn't stretch [easily] to that sort of thing.

> I'd like a team of slaves, who would go to the library and Xerox material, gather [and] bring to me the material I'm looking for. . . . [My former research assistant] would go to this place and that place and the other place, and she would find it. The next time I saw her, there it was. And that's just great. And she also was somebody who's very interested in feminist theory. She had done a lot of work already in pulling together a lot of material, psychoanalytical material and whatever, that was very useful to me.

They described information aids that they believed would help in the research process. One scholar remembered a helpful index that is defunct.

> I would like our periodicals index to be restarted. Ours was a very detailed account of what was in an article, and it [was] done by our own librarians of our own material. I used *RILA* once, and . . . it didn't suit what I wanted to know. . . . Ceasing to keep this index was an act of great stupidity, and now they have stopped and will never start again.

Another conceived an international guide that she thought would be of great use to both new and experienced researchers.

> I . . . imagine . . . some sort of publication. . . . Let's say you pick[ed] ten major libraries in Europe, and you just said how they worked, how they were set up. It probably takes a graduate student some weeks to do [anything]. If you at least knew what to ask when you walked in the door, you would be probably several weeks ahead of yourself. I think that would be a very valuable thing. You don't even have to be a graduate student [to need it]; if I went to Berlin, I wouldn't know where to go. . . . You might . . . commission people to write it . . . [who] really knew the ropes.

The scholars also expressed ideas about how the publication process could be made less expensive for them in terms of both time and money (see also "Writing and Publishing," especially "Illustrations and Art-historical Texts," and "Finances," especially "Costs of Publication").

> I think that the copyright laws [should be changed], the way in which one writes to a museum [for permission to publish an illustration]. . . . I think that

> the museum should put their house in order and simplify the [reproduction] process. . . . When I ask for a photograph, they should give me the copyright [permission].

Wishing for greater collegial interaction, the scholars envisioned new academic communities and arenas that would foster critical debate and broaden their intellectual horizons (see also "Personal Factors in Art-historical Research," especially "Colleagues").

> I would like a group of colleagues. I mean it would be wonderful to be allied to a kind of research center or . . . a group of working scholars who were congenial, . . . intellectually congenial, to have that kind of mutual support.

> [With the support of my university] I was developing the idea for an institute [for advanced study in art history], which would be modeled more like the Institute for the Humanities at Cornell, which brings scholars in, has them teach a seminar and involves them, gives funding to produce a major conference. . . . We hope that'll make an impact on the field.

> [The ideal conference] would have to be established as an academic event. . . . It would have to be some kind of series. . . . Nothing is achieved by just doing it once. The format would have to be thought about very carefully in order to escape from the [traditional format of a] presentation, plus desultory question time. . . . I would strongly favor what is normal in literary criticism: precirculated papers [followed by] a discussion of the papers. . . . It should be possible. I think it would have to be thematic, and there would have to be continuity. In other words, if we decided we'd have a conference on patronage and the determination of meaning in the visual arts, . . . we'd have the same people coming back [for five or six years]. This is all very idealistic, but it does seem a really hard-driving attempt [is needed] to yank into being this culture of argument and discussion that ought to exist naturally but just doesn't. . . . A conference ought to [have] rather hard-edged, provocative, complicated questions articulated beforehand.

One art historian mused at length on the future of the discipline, hoping that it would become more highly integrated into the world of humanistic studies at large (see also "Cultural and Social History").

> It's my sense that art historians as a special, a particular breed will probably become less important as time goes by, become smaller in number. There will be fewer and fewer people who actually specialize in art history. This may be also a wish . . . too that really they'll be historians, who deal with different periods and times and places, who use visual data. . . . I guess it comes to be a matter of how historians and art historians can begin to work together.

The same scholar continued to ponder the ways in which interdisciplinary research might affect the future of art-historical inquiry.

> The object of [art-historical] study itself is changing in interesting ways, which then allows access to visual material on the part of others, historians, social scientists, psychologists. So there really are a whole series of very closely and complexly interwoven changes which are not reflected yet in institutions, or very slightly. The problem of how you then design archival systems to handle this is a very interesting, a very serious problem.

Finally, one scholar wished for more sophisticated drafting tools and even computer-enhanced graphics that would help him analyze the buildings he studied. But with his conclusion that what he needed most was the time and money to do research abroad as well as a talent for synthesizing information creatively, he perhaps spoke for most art historians.

> [I would like] a decent drafting table. I work on a drawing board with a T-square, and it would be wonderful to have a proper surface and a straightedge that rolled up and down on a rail at the edge and all that. . . . What I would like to do . . . is axionometric viewpoints. . . . Just in working with this [draughtsman who was] doing preliminary [axionometric] sketches and just to force yourself to think [three-dimensionally] . . . was terrific. I could conceive of computer imagery in thinking of the building in three-dimensional terms. But if you wanted to ask me, "Is that essential to [your] mission?" I would say probably that it would be a very stimulating and interesting thing to have but not actually essential. . . . Central to my mission is the ability to spend prolonged periods in the field in France, and then a better ability to put [it all] together.

SUMMARY ▪ Electronic catalogues, indexes, and data banks could enhance research if they were affordable to the user. Free and ready access to the electronic catalogues of major libraries and research institutions was a major concern. Subject indexes to data banks of both verbal and visual materials are particularly desirable. Those who worked with data-processing programs wanted to be able to index their own research materials according to a larger number of information fields than provided by currently available software. Outside the electronic sphere the wishes touched on time, assistance, and better access to information and materials of various kinds. More critical debate within the profession and more integration of the discipline into the larger world of humanistic studies were dreams yet to be realized.

Art-historical Points of View

ANALYTICAL TECHNIQUES

The history of art has long been seen as divided into methodologies, approaches that emphasize one or several aspects of the work of art and the information surrounding it. This study found no sharp delineation between one approach and another; indeed quotations below that are found under different categories may sometimes belong to the same person. Moreover, although the variety of points of view offers a rich sampling, it represents only that: a sampling rather than a systematic or comprehensive summation of the field. The following discussion, then, is simply intended to organize a set of subjects touched on by one group of scholars with strongly held beliefs about what is important when confronting works of art.

Once collected and organized, research materials are marshaled to produce many kinds of results. Some of the approaches mentioned, such as iconography, connoisseurship, or formal analysis, can be isolated and are discussed later in this section. The most common pattern, however, seemed to be that of pragmatism: the use of whatever evidence would answer the questions being asked.

The questions took many forms. Sometimes they arose from the doubting of conventional wisdom:

> Calvinism became the great label to put on virtually every meaning in Dutch art, . . . [a] cliché . . . about the spirit of sparseness and economy. So I was very pleased as a young researcher to find that the picture was richer than that, that there were controversies going on about imagery which you could analyze in ways that other people hadn't.

> In the time of Berenson the three great centers of painting in Italy in the fourteenth century were Florence and Siena and the Veneto. . . . [In the 1950s] we began to see there were many centers.

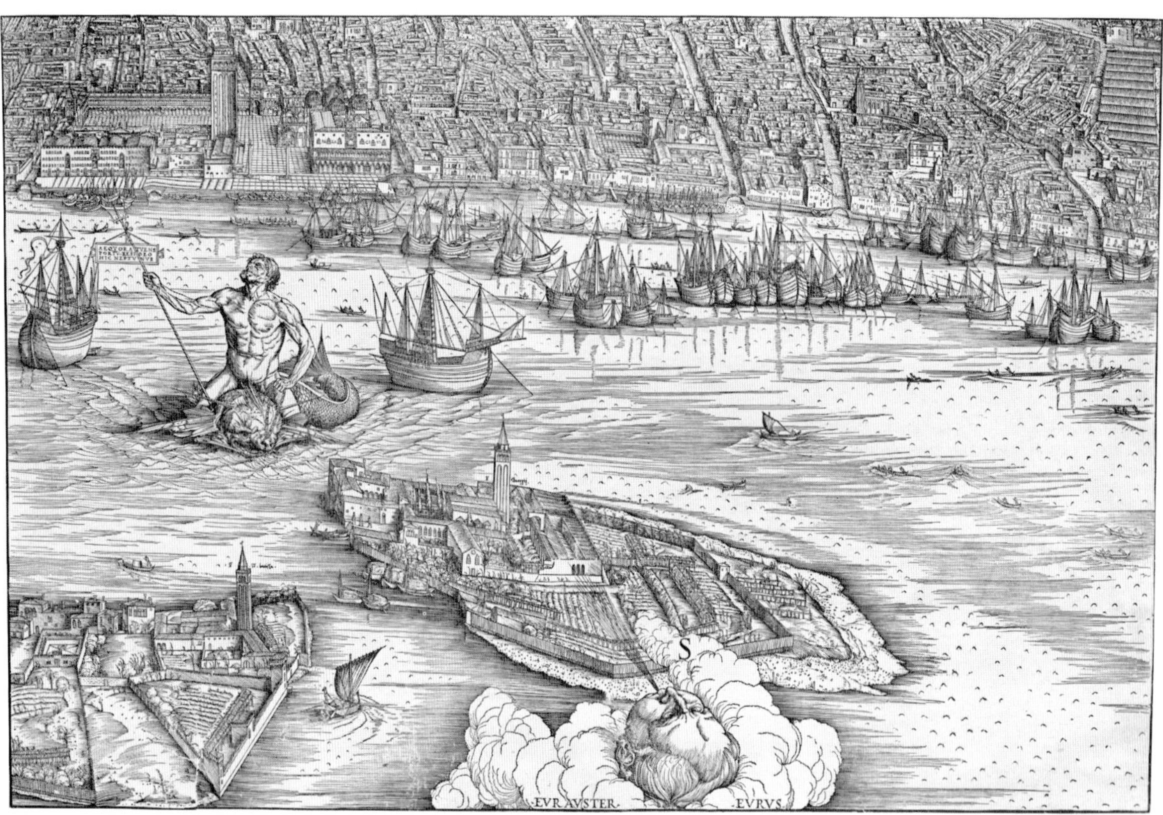

10. JACOPO DE' BARBARI, *View of Venice* (detail), 1500, lower center block of a six-block print, Kunsthalle, Hamburg, photo by Ralph Kleinhempel, courtesy Juergen Schulz

Other questions pushed beyond what had already been discovered:

> I wasn't the first person to notice the spikeblock [see fig. 22, p. 146], or even to catalogue it. But I was the first person to say I was going to find out what it is and really explain it.

> Everybody has written about [Jacopo de' Barbari's view of Venice; fig. 10], but no one's ever asked, "How was it made?" Because how do you make an aerial view in the days before airplanes and balloons? Again nobody ever asked, "What does it signify?" Why would you make an aerial view in the first place in the year 1500?

> Nobody ever said, "What did [Mondrian's studio; fig. 11] look like? What did it represent? What was its relationship to his art?"

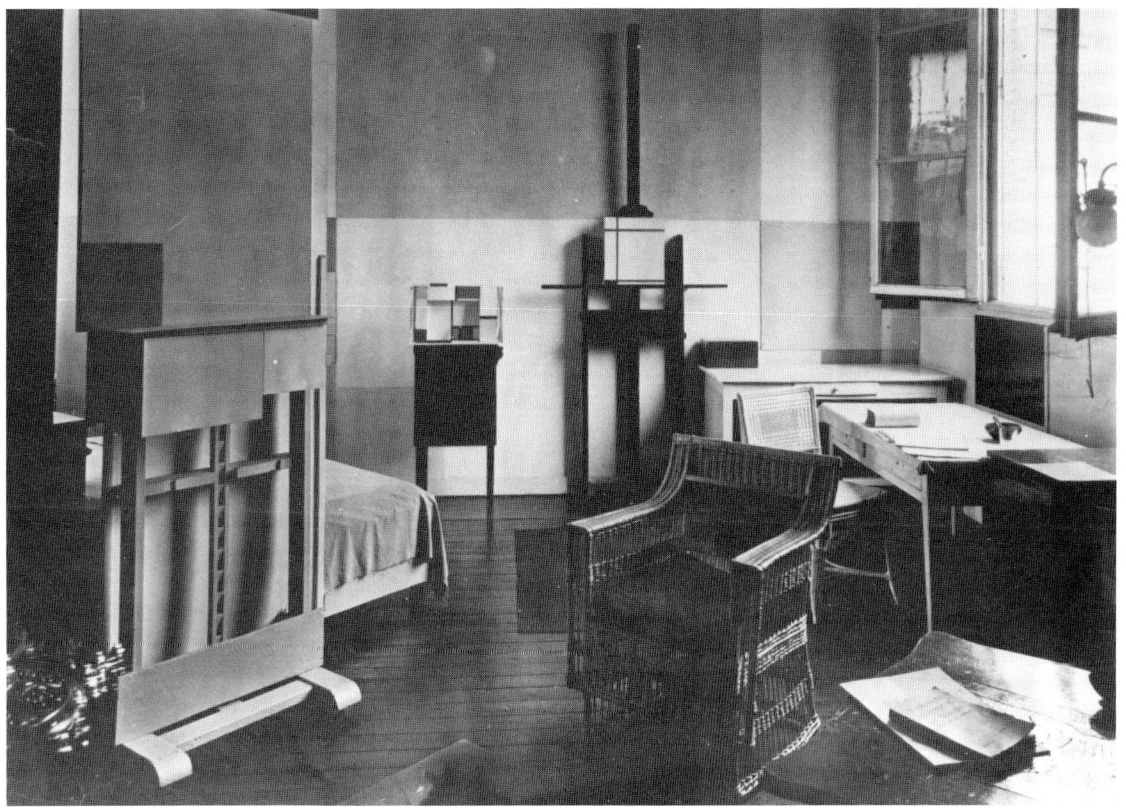

11. INTERIOR OF PIET MONDRIAN'S STUDIO, rue du Départ, Paris, 1926, Documentation Archive, Gemeentemuseum, The Hague, photo by B. Frequin, Voorburg, courtesy Nancy Troy

Still others asked unconventional questions about standard works:

> There were two incongruous aspects about [the *Isenheim Altarpiece*; fig. 12] that were asking for explanation. One is that the two fixed wings at the outermost left- and right-hand sides don't move, whereas the other double wings can be moved. And they show Saint Anthony and Saint Sebastian of a vastly differing scale. Why would Saint Anthony be so much larger than Saint Sebastian?

> These [Impressionist] paintings and this moment in French history remain as somehow powerful symbols [of] modernity and the emergence of [a kind of] life we recognize as more difficult. . . . America cannot stop putting on Impressionist art exhibitions. . . . What view of modernity does [Impressionism] give that proves so attractive to us? And is there a way of criticizing

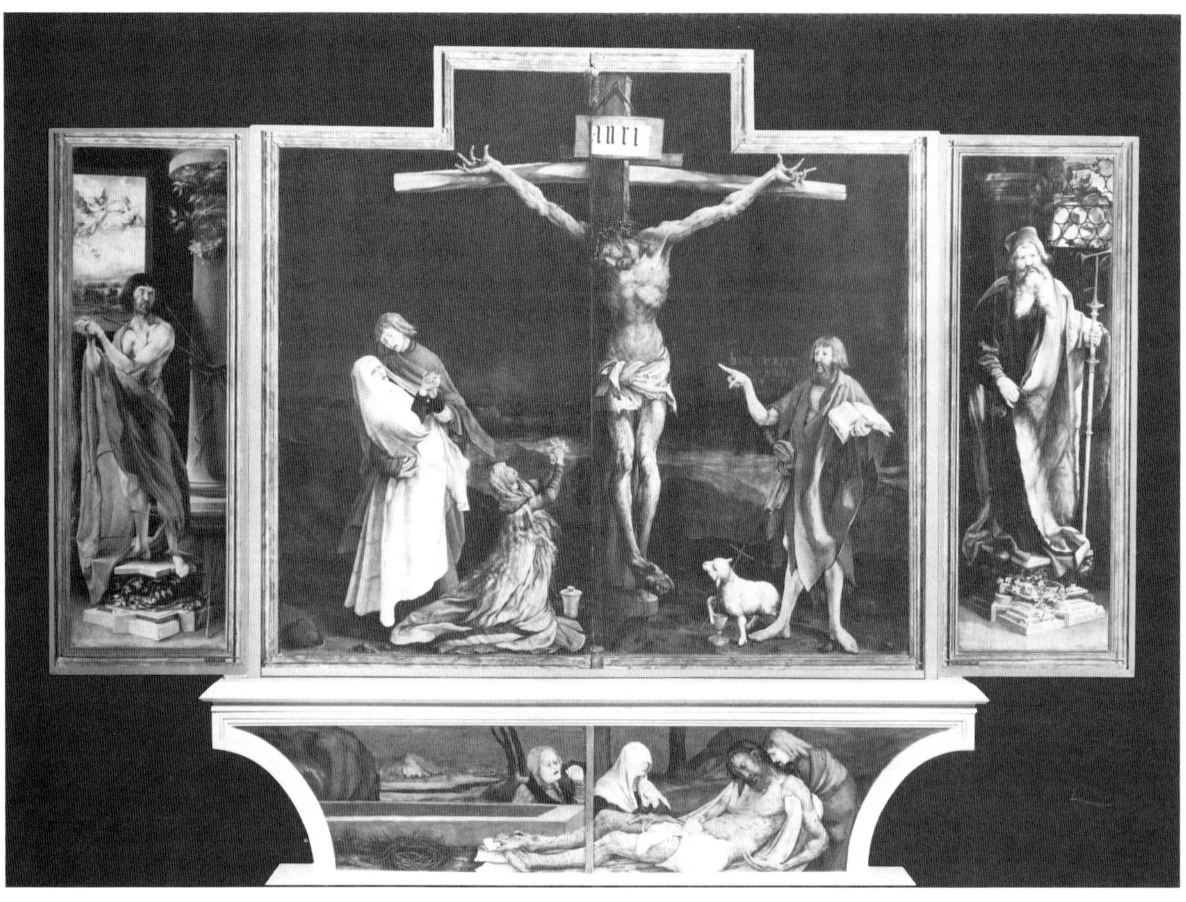

12. MATTHIAS GRÜNEWALD, *Isenheim Altarpiece*, circa 1510, Musée d'Unterlinden, Colmar, photo courtesy Giraudon/Art Resource, New York

that view without being absolute and puritanical about it, but getting a distance from that account?

There were problems for me, paradoxes let's say, in Surrealist practice that I'd always been curious about—one of them being in the photographs in *L'Amour fou* [see fig. 13]. Why would André Breton, king of Surrealism and the dream [and] all of those things that are supposed to be a reproach to the merely real, have . . . illustrated his book with photographs?

In the Adoration of the Magi [window in the west facade at Chartres] the three kings come with coins in their hands. . . . They are exact copies of gold coins minted in Almoravid Spain. . . . Why did [the artists] represent such a detail, and how did they get such a coin?

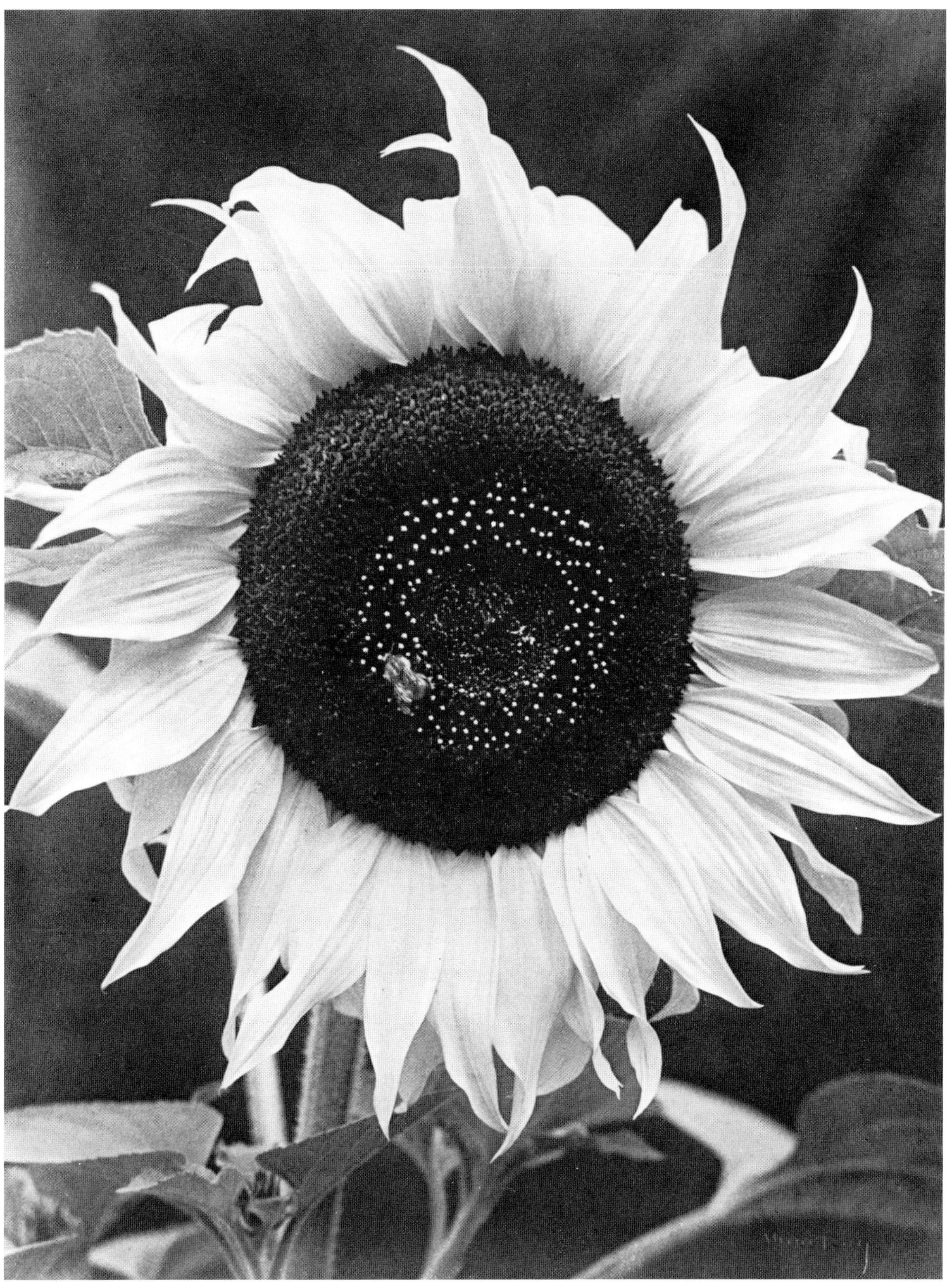

13. MAN RAY, *Sunflower with Bee*, 1925, reproduced in *L'Amour fou*, by André Breton (Lagny-sur-Marne, 1937), The J. Paul Getty Museum, Malibu, © 1988 Man Ray Trust/ADAGP—Paris, ARS—USA

Once the questioning process begins, it can lead almost anywhere. The connections between the art object and the world around it might be entirely within the bounds of art-historical materials:

> You cannot study stained glass without studying every other medium [or] technique. You need to know a lot [about] architecture, . . . all the types of painting, what is going on in sculpture. . . . Stained glass is the synthesis.

> My interest is in the connections between Italian Gothic art and French Gothic art, . . . between Venetian and Austrian art, . . . in the art of the borders.

Or they might send one into other academic disciplines:

> Pietro Aretino, playwright, pornographer, courtier, was a friend of Giulio Romano. In two of [his comedies], Giulio Romano is mentioned; he wanted to boost him. Now these plays (that had not been observed) were reprinted in London in 1589. That makes a gap between Shakespeare and Giulio Romano much shorter. "That rare Italian master" is what Shakespeare called Giulio Romano, and I [proposed] this hypothesis about why Shakespeare could have known about him.

> That's a drawing which is so famous. . . . Nobody recognized before that [it shows] two different varieties of the same flower, . . . a cultivated garden form and the wildflower; they can't grow together [on the same stalk]. It was called, up to now, a Dürer. I think not.

> Everything I would read about western photography had to do with . . . ideas taken from nineteenth-century American studies about Transcendentalism. . . . The whole notion that what [early photographers] were after was the beauty or the presence of the divine began to collapse under the weight of evidence that this was a scientific expedition. . . . I was then, of course, confronted with learning the history of geology.

In recent years connections have extended into many more fields. In just one project, involving a set of fourteenth-century wall paintings, the scholar recounted a search that began where we might expect, with the paintings' relationship to contemporary works and to vanished sources, but continued in an exploration of the following categories: the architectural setting of the murals,

> I stayed in the place some time, just to understand the connection between the paintings and the walls and the windows. . . . The room is in a tower [some distance from] the castle. . . . I don't know if it was [a private room] just for the bishop himself. . . . In the sixteenth century it was a room for guests of the cardinal.

the conservation history of the murals,

> It is necessary to have not only a good documentation of today's state of the paintings but, if possible, also a documentation of the paintings at the beginning of this century. . . . I went to see Lionello Tintori, who restored the cycle. . . . [But] these frescoes were restored the first time in the sixteenth century.

the background and interests of the patron,

> [What was the] meaning of the frescoes for the patron, . . . who was a German aristocrat with many agrarian possessions in Bohemia and Moravia? . . . Why did Bishop [George] of Liechtenstein choose the subject of the Labors of the Months? We are aware he was interested in nature. . . . But in this cycle we find not only the activities of an aristocratic society, hunting [and] snowball fighting, [but also] an interest in the everyday life of the peasants.

the agricultural technology of the period,

> Just to understand if the painter used models, drawings, or also keen observation, . . . I discussed [the frescoes] with a friend who is interested in the history of material civilization, and he told me about a wonderful book . . . on the labors of the peasants. [The author] was a linguist. In the 1920s and '30s he collected a treasure of photos of rural activities peculiar to the Tyrol. . . .

> And many [implements] were exactly the same at the beginning of the fifteenth century. . . . Was Bishop George of Liechtenstein interested in new techniques in the agricultural field?

the literary background of the subject matter.

> In the [representation of the] month of May, for example, there are the struggle of a man with a lion and a fountain [with] a crack in the stone. I need the collaboration of a Romance philologist, of a medieval archaeologist, [and] of an agrarian historian.

One area of investigation that has drawn increasing interest is what is called the "fortune" of a work of art: not just issues of provenance or restoration—although these figure in the study—but a history of that work's life and its effect on its changing environment.

> I was able to prove where [the painting] had been soon after it was painted [by Rubens]. . . . I found it belonged to Boswell . . . ; Wordsworth knew this picture; Constable knew; everybody knew. . . . You could write a whole essay on the taste for this in England in the nineteenth century. Constable died with a print of this on the end of the bed with his feet touching it.

> [The] long-term life of [a] building brings about all these later interventions. Instead of looking at these as negative interventions, I look at them as an integral part of the real history of the building. . . . [Every work] of art ought to be looked at that way, . . . by seeing it not as an object datable to the moment of its first varnishing, and thereafter it is merely a passive rider, a kind of stowaway on the boat of history. . . . [If you have] interest only in those things which belong to the original moment, you have a very impoverished picture.

> [The seventeenth-century Roman collector Francesco Angeloni] describes the hanging order precisely . . . of the Aldobrandini collection in Rome, of which he was a curator, . . . about 1620 . . . at a period when the regionalization of Italian art is accelerating and there is a new idea on the various schools of

> painting—Bologna, Venice, Lombardy. . . . And these pictures were the formative influence on Bellori, who is one of the most important theoretical writers of the seventeenth century.

If all these (and many more) issues external to the work of art preoccupy the art historian, it must be said that the problem of how far afield the art historian should go in the search is a subject of controversy.

> You have a whole panorama of positions in art history, from . . . what I would call vulgar Marxist art history to higher Marxist art history, through non-Marxist sociological art history, through various attitudes—the iconographers will be in there somewhere—to people who are basically interested in style only, connoisseurship.

Various categories in that spectrum will be discussed separately below. Nevertheless even the most convinced "connoisseurs" spoke of the value of pursuing the external relationships of the work of art.

> Part of the kick . . . comes from . . . locking onto some single work of art that has real richness, is complex, is difficult to account for, has lots of threads leading in . . . different directions.

> To me art history opens out into cultural history. But I try to stay always very closely attached to the object. . . . I start with the pictorial fact and try never to lose touch with that. But I think when it's relevant, there's no area that can't or should not be explored.

At the same time one of those who investigates the context wondered,

> Does knowing about patronage [enhance] our ability to give an account of the work and its historical life, or are we just adding anecdotal detail, contextual details, to the history of art?

We heard many comments about the relationship of art history to other disciplines, for instance,

> whether art history is one of the humanities, one of the social sciences, whether it's entirely anomalous, whether it has correlations with music history or with anthropology.

One scholar argued that the apparent "new" move to link works of art to the content and methodologies of other disciplines is in fact a return to a breadth that typified the history of art from its origins and even until recently.

> Charles Eliot Norton, in the late 1870s [at Harvard], was a professor of the history of art in its relationship to literature; that was his actual university title.
>
> People at the turn of the century and into the twenties and thirties were really much more literate in philosophy and psychology than postwar people. . . . Aesthetics, even anthropology, all these things were seriously important to the education of those who dealt with art in, say, the first half of the century.

He and others decried the process by which

> the very success of the discipline . . . led to becoming increasingly isolated, increasingly specialized.
>
> Art history, which after all was born of complex involvement with philosophies, . . . got insulated from these wider questions. It seemed to will itself into an empiricist slumber.

Nevertheless there was considerable suspicion of any imposition of theoretical or ideological determinism on the work of art. One scholar had a historical explanation of the trend.

> There are art historians who, like some of the great German art historians, try to make embracing theories for the history of modern art. This took place at the moment when the vanguard movement was conceptual art [in the 1960s and 1970s]. . . . The counterpart to . . . conceptual art was a kind of conceptual

> art history, in which . . . certain art historians were trying to give their art history the qualities of completeness which I associate with the work of art but not with the discussion of the work of art. . . . The things that we retain from [the German theorists] are the great insights they had, not the systems.

Another scholar warned of the art-historical preconceptions being brought to bear on new fields in the discipline:

> The history of photography is being constructed on the model of the history of art. You've got to get authors together, you've got to get careers, aesthetic principles, you've got to organize the whole thing on the model of . . . the history of post-Renaissance Western art, . . . canons of beauty, canons of taste and judgment, and also a set of meanings that are recognizable to humanists.

The differences over what art history "should" do extend to the area of gathering evidence too. Interest in the provocative question and the ingenious connection has not dimmed the allure of exhaustive research.

> In a way I have a higher regard for the catalogue raisonné than I have for the political, social stuff that I do, as the top of the tree of art-historical endeavor. . . . What I admire most is the proper sort of rehabilitation of a major artist and the finding out about that person, the describing of the creative development, the changing appearance, provenance.

One scholar, however, provided an argument against both the exhaustive search for evidence and the mechanization of the scholarly process:

> It is sometimes more interesting, or more important, to throw out an idea than to go and prove it to the hilt. I really worry about the future. . . . This is what I call a kind of misunderstanding of . . . science. . . . To write a corpus of all neo-Gothic sculpture [for example], why should one? . . . Data are useful for testing hypotheses, [but] the hypotheses come first and the confirmation is never final.

He continued to muse about the state of the discipline:

> You can be a "very good" art historian and never have troubled your mind about any explanation: there is a drawing by so-and-so here, [and] another drawing there, and it's later, and this painting is [done] for this man, and so on.

None of the scholars with whom we spoke seemed in any danger of such ossification, however. All were involved in a passionate search for a better understanding of the work of art. The multitude of paths by which they arrive at that understanding reflects not a mechanical uniformity but, on the contrary, a healthy variety.

CONNOISSEURSHIP

As is well known, one approach that dominated the history of art in America, England, and Italy earlier in this century is called connoisseurship. In its narrowest meaning,

> the term *connoisseurship* means . . . making qualitative judgments based purely upon aesthetic significance, not being involved with extras. . . . Every picture, to some extent, reaches out into an extra-aesthetic world, but connoisseurship should be strictly quality judgments.

Given this definition, connoisseurship can be said to be the least "historical" branch of art history, but to require the greatest visual sensitivity to the object.

> First, you look at the [stained] glass very closely with binoculars. . . . Then you look at the glass itself at the same time [that] you go around . . . the building. You see if the panels really fit the window in which you see them because very often they have been moved.

> If an artist draws free[ly] and [is] a good draughtsman, then he's relatively quick and sure in his line. Somebody who copies is not as quick, [is more labored,] because he tries to do exactly the same as the model. . . . Very often the whole appearance [of the copy] is convincing, but in detail things sometimes are less convincing.

There is currently open debate in the profession about the value of connoisseurship as an analytical tool. Some scholars would like to emphasize less aesthetic, and more historical, lines of questioning. Other scholars believe that connoisseurship provides an essential basis for all other art-historical inquiry.

> The differences among those groups [with varied methodologies] come into a political level . . . , so if you are a connoisseur, you are a "conservative" or "reactionary." . . . The introductions to every article by [the "progressive"] group will start with what art history did in the last fifty years, [saying that] connoisseurship . . . didn't lead us to the right questions, so this is what old-fashioned and reactionary people do. *Reactionary* is a political term that has nothing to do with art history. . . . If I want to have ideas about a painting, . . . I should have some very basic and fundamental answers before going into ideas. If I don't have the answer to the question[s], "By whom is this painting?" and "When was it painted?" then this probably would [affect] my going [further].

In the historiography of the discipline, connoisseurship is intimately bound to the concept of attribution. The assignment of works to artists has made the central preoccupation of connoisseurship the artist's oeuvre, the definition of artistic personality through the identification and analysis of the works and the writing of catalogues raisonnés.

> Berenson and Longhi . . . reflected an art history that was concentrated on the individual artist as the saint and the hero, the corpus of the work, and the catalogue. That's what art history was . . . before the First World War.

Increasingly, however, scholars have evaluated artists' oeuvres in the light of biographical facts as well as other historical data to place works of art within historical contexts.

> Mondrian . . . was—except for a brief time in Holland—virtually unknown wherever he was. In Paris he saw other people, but they didn't see him. And when he was in New York at the end of his life people knew who he was, but nobody was being influenced by him. It doesn't tell you very much to put a Mondrian in with Pop [art], however interesting that juxtaposition might be. But it tells you an awful lot to put a late Mondrian [together] with a middle and an early Mondrian.

> [Rubens] used as a prototype the Elsheimer *Flight into Egypt* about four or five times previous to this [painting], as a young man. This is a picture of old

> age, of the last five years of his life, when he was living in the Château Steen in the summer months and beginning to even paint (not just draw) outside.

But "major" works are only the beginning of the quest. In the reconstruction of the artist's oeuvre, the scholar may be called upon to sift through copies, engraved reproductions, and all manner of related works.

> Such famous masters as, for instance, Rogier van der Weyden or the brothers van Eyck or the Master of Flémalle produced much more than survived. On the other hand, many more pictures of fifteenth-century Netherlandish art survived than can be attributed. . . . You finally can create an oeuvre by surviving originals and by reflections of later copies. . . . And that was fascinating to me, to see [the importance of putting] even bad pictures in the right position.

> There is a drawing in the British Museum which nobody had related to this [painting] but which was probably a study for this. . . . It was engraved, so I had to cope with contemporary engravings after it.

> Dürer, on his second trip to Venice, asked the Signoria to give him a copyright for his engravings, because at that time Marcanton[io Raimondi] was . . . reproducing Dürer's woodcuts and engravings and selling them. And Dürer asked . . . [for an injunction] that [he] not use the monogram AD. [Marcantonio] was later the reproducer of Raphael. [During] his early period in Venice, he reproduced nearly all Dürers. That means that at [about 1500 Dürer prints] were so famous in Italy that one could make money by reproducing [them]. . . . One knows that Dürer himself had agents traveling around . . . selling his prints. We have one letter in which he mentions that one of his agents died during his stay in Rome, and he had a loss because after the death of that agent, people took away his prints.

The ascertaining of date, of relative position in a chronology, is often the next most important task, after attribution.

> It's necessary to get an idea how early [something] is possible. . . . It helps you to understand the time, the development, and the level on which an artist

> was able to work, . . . whether he is the creator of all these things, or [whether] he himself copied.

> I was interested in the [internal] chronology, the sequence in which buildings were built. I wanted to be able to get a sense of where they started to build, . . . which walls came first, how they divided up space, how they remodeled buildings, how they changed them over time. . . . So I didn't really deal with the [external] chronological controversies.

The intimate relationship between connoisseurship and documents contemporary with the works of art was made clear in the work of several scholars.

> I was able to discover in one of the most famous sixteenth-century buildings everybody has written about, a whole bathroom, which nobody knew existed. . . . Moreover virtually everybody thought that the mosaic floors—because they matched the ceiling patterns so nicely—were the work of the sixteenth century. I found out, on archival evidence, following up a kind of gut suspicion that I had about them, that they were done in the eighteenth century. They are part of the restoration campaign. . . . [These discoveries and] many other aspects of the building, . . . in combination with the archival and literary and other evidence, allowed you to come to understand [that the building] wasn't at all what [was] said in the literature, and it wasn't at all what it looks like today.

> The way in which that west end . . . was conceived, and the unearthing of a lost master mason whose name was Bleuet—I had been aware or conscious of that master before the texts came up. . . . I knew he was there simply on the basis of style.

> By pure chance I found in a German archive some letters by Marsden Hartley addressed to Franz Marc and to Kandinsky. . . . And now I'm doing some research. . . . The material is growing [out of Hartley's] European [sojourn] . . . in Paris, Munich, and . . . Berlin: . . . three different [centers] of European modernism and an American artist. The idea is not only to show his personal development but also to analyze Hartley with his background of . . . [the]

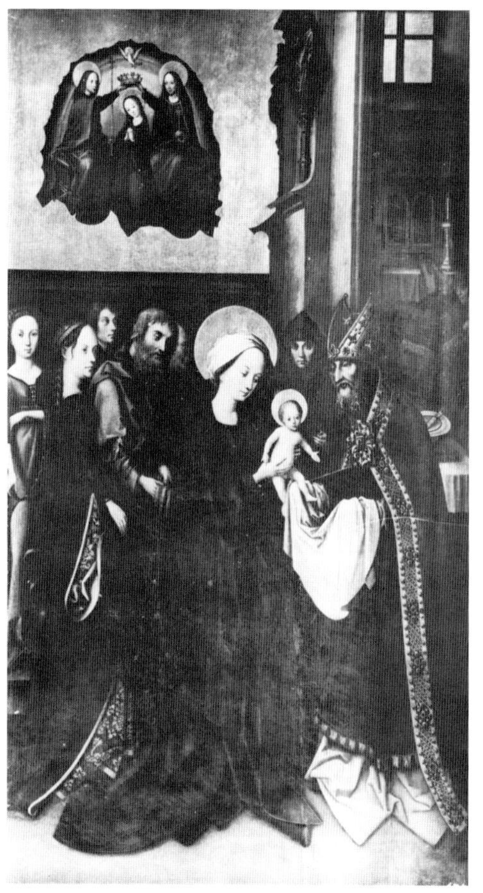

14. HANS HOLBEIN THE ELDER, *Presentation in the Temple*, from the *Weingartener Altarpiece*, Augsburg Cathedral, 1493, photo courtesy Marburg/Art Resource, New York

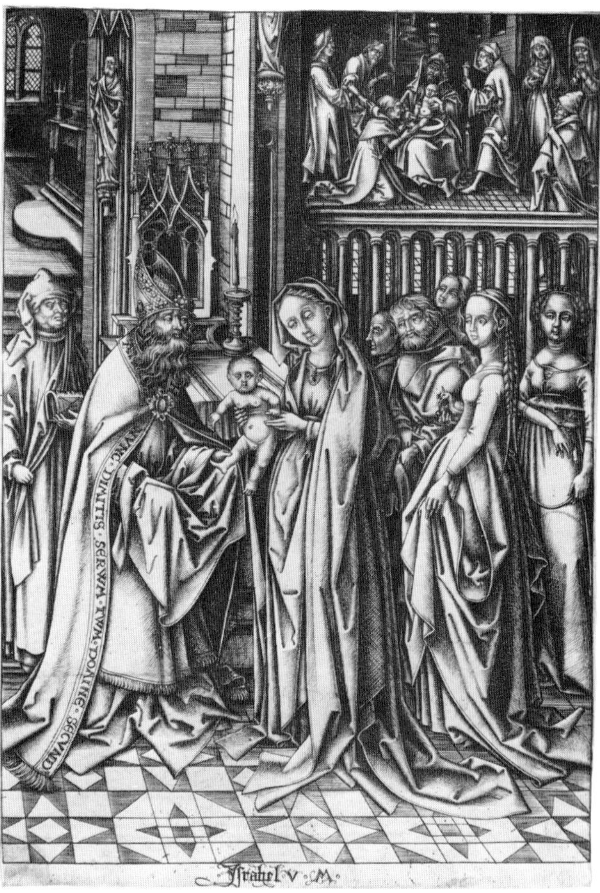

15. ISRAHEL VAN MECKENEM, *Presentation and Circumcision*, from the Life of the Virgin series, circa 1501, National Gallery of Art, Washington, D.C. (Rosenwald Collection)

> neoromantic American tradition. He thought Paris was terrible, . . . didn't stay in Munich . . . , and then went to Berlin [where] he was very happy even though very poor. Then he went back to America; the whole [story] is a very interesting moment in his life, . . . a kind of self-discovery.

All this apparatus can be brought to bear in intricate ways.

> I showed that . . . engravings by Israhel van Meckenem were reproductions after lost drawings by Hans Holbein the Elder, which he made to be engraved. . . . I . . . explained this stylistically. . . . The . . . differences between

> Holbein's *Weingartener Altarpiece* [of 1493] and the engravings by Meckenem [see figs. 14 and 15] . . . cannot go back to Meckenem because they show clearly the development of Holbein. . . . They were produced exactly at that point of Holbein's development in the *Frankfurt Altarpiece* of 1501. And in that period Meckenem also made the famous double portrait [which] represents a Swabian type . . . absolutely unknown to the region where Meckenem lived. But Holbein used that type, . . . and he came from Swabia. And there are other drawings by Holbein [of] 1501 [that] show exactly the same type of representation. So one can stylistically show that [everything] in the Meckenem print is exactly that state reached by Holbein in 1501.

> The most effective connoisseurs, the most knowledgeable judges of works of art, seem to proceed a long way on intuition. . . . Then there is a whole range of investigations that are often a process of playing between instinct and what you can verify: what class of object that thing belongs to, how it relates to the class, what its brothers and sisters are, and how it looks in comparison, what the function of the thing was meant to be, and whether what you are looking at reflects accurately what you were intended to see.

That accurate reflection of what the artist intended sometimes depends on the art historian's awareness of issues related to the physical conservation of the work of art. One scholar who works in a museum lamented the fact that few art historians or curators are able to take advantage of the information that conservation technology can provide.

> Curators are not generally knowledgeable about conservation problems. Neither are they trained nor do they have the right attitude about their responsibilities. They are not trained because there are few opportunities, and their attitudes are wrong because they are the victims of a kind of mistaken notion of the division of labor between art historians on the one hand and technical people on the other, as though in medicine there were doctors who cut and doctors who made the diagnoses.

Consultations with specialists in conservation provided the same scholar important insights when he conducted research.

> Modern technical photographs can also be very valuable in understanding better how pictures were painted, and I have often used them. In certain of the work I have done, I have needed both a restorer and a photographer.

Most art historians, however, must depend on whatever conservation reports are available when they study an object. If one's research happens to coincide with the conservation or restoration of a work of art, one may be in an especially advantageous position.

> I worked on the [stained-glass] panels [of Saint-Ouen de Rouen] . . . in workshops in the process of being restored. I could go to the church to see the architecture and the rest of the decorations, but I could study the glass itself on tables, which is far easier, because you can see [more] details [than] when it's in situ.

One exemplary interaction between art historian and conservator involved a Rubens landscape.

> We have a marvelous Rubens . . . in our collection called the *Landscape by Moonlight* [fig. 16], which belonged to Joshua Reynolds, and it has been x-rayed. . . . There are amazing things going on under the surface. . . . The whole subject matter or non-subject matter in this landscape depends upon this technical evidence. . . . Under here are hidden figures which Rubens painted out, and there was a fire [here]. The x-ray showed more figures going right over these additions made by Rubens. . . . It is famous for its shooting star, and that is all original. . . . Why did he change his mind, . . . at what point [did] he cancel the figures? . . . [The conservators] do the technical, descriptive part, but it is for me to [make] sense of it. . . . They could tell me which brushes, what size of brush he was using in different areas. . . . There is one of these fresh bits of wood that is still embedded . . . from when the panels were being joined together, . . . and this [added] side is just sketchy, . . . whereas this [original] area is dense with activity.

Not only the luxurious forms of cultural production—like Rubens's *Landscape by Moonlight*—but also the utilitarian forms reveal some of the secrets of their histories in the light of modern scientific analysis, as with dendrochronology, for example.

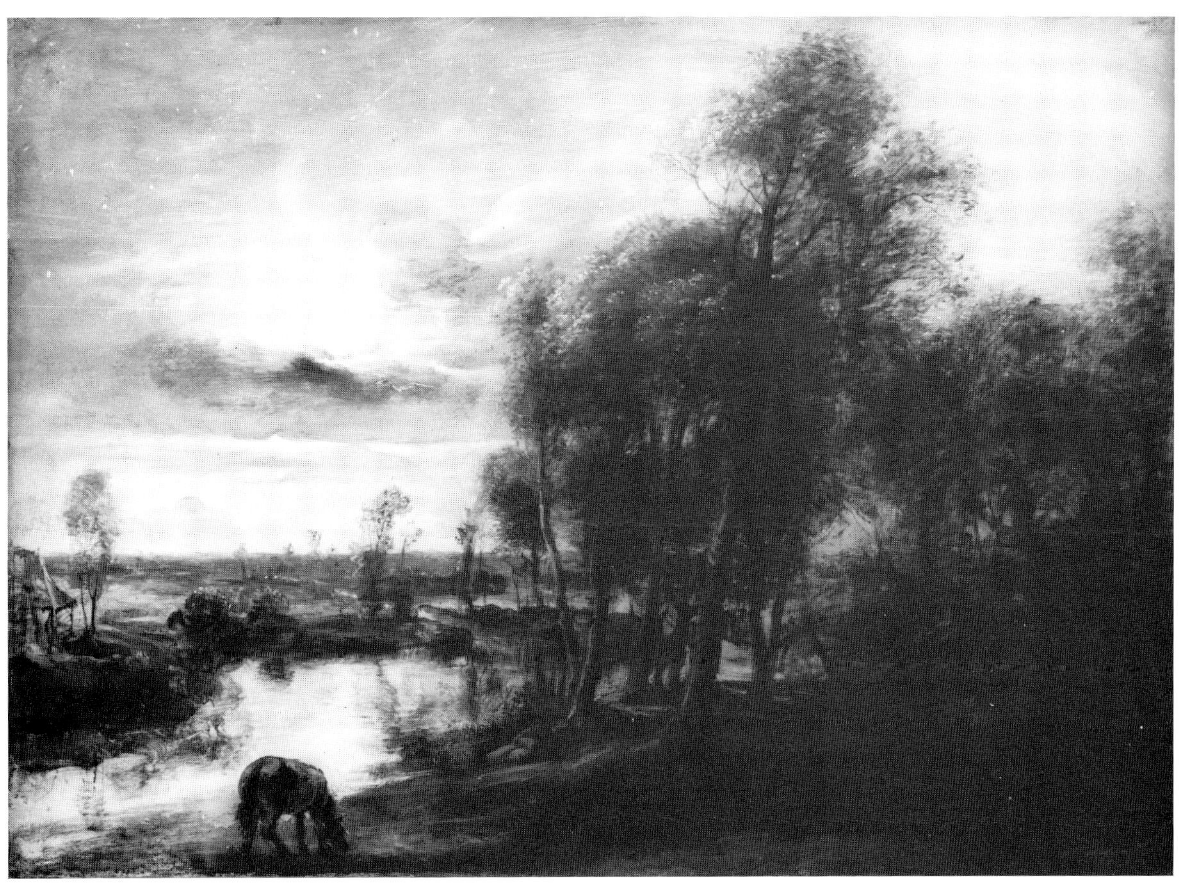

16. PETER PAUL RUBENS, *Landscape by Moonlight*, circa 1635, Courtauld Institute Galleries, London (Princes Gate Collection)

> A very major enterprise somewhere out in the country—a magnificent barn—will leave absolutely no [written] record because this is a category of building . . . that simply relegates this object out of the range of historical records. And then you can do completely different things: you can date the beams because of the growth of the wood, which is irregular. There are computerized charts which allow you . . . to line up for hundreds of years the growth patterns of trees in a particular region.

A possible career path for an art historian is that of historical adviser for restoration surveys or projects. While none of the scholars interviewed now works full-time in such a capacity, several have acted as restoration consultants. Like museum work (see "Personal Factors in Art-historical Research: Choices within the Discipline"), the field of restoration allows scholars direct contact with works of art, which can be especially satisfying.

> [My first] job [in the national historic monuments office] gave me a chance to work day by day with originals in a very creative way. I had to travel to [investigate] recently discovered things and to decide what would happen [to them]. . . . You wouldn't believe what you can find. . . . [For example, on] a wall that is a little bit uneven you [might uncover] old frescoes. . . . And that makes you very aware. . . . You can find in the dust [of a monastery] a bundle of Dürer prints or fifteenth-century bookbindings with the arms of Frederick the Third. . . . Those were the highlights that I appreciated.

The same scholar, however, initially felt somewhat ill equipped to advise on certain practical aspects of restoration procedure.

> There is a law in Austria that says that no alterations may be made to a historic building belonging to a local or the national government without informing the Bundesdenkmalamt. . . . For instance, in the case of a church, all the people who are [involved]—the landowners, the mayor, the monks or the abbot, priest, or whoever, and the representative of the Bundesdenkmalamt—come together and discuss how the work will be done. . . . And you as an art historian have to discuss how to keep the church dry. Nobody taught you *that* in your education!

Nevertheless, acting as a government representative, one may feel that one can make significant contributions toward preserving for the public—as well as for future generations—the national artistic heritage.

> I'm an expert for the Musée du Louvre, which keeps its eye on customs. When they see stained glass [about to leave the country], they ask me to go and have a look. I have found quite a few things. . . . Quite frequently dealers [consult me. One] had three panels—decorative grisaille— from the fourteenth century, and he asked me if he could sell them [to] an American collector. I said, "Yes," because these three panels were from different [places], restored, and would not have added anything to our patrimony. You cannot keep everything, but a few things are really important and [of] very high quality. We had better keep them!

An art historian can bring the analysis of content and meaning to restoration efforts. In a situation where a number of participants have special skills and particular concerns, the art historian may have to be persuasive.

> I've worked . . . with architects from the Monuments Historiques. . . . There was a [church] window in which only fragments were left. The architects said, "Maybe we could try to make two windows of the pieces." . . . They wanted to [separate] two scenes. So I tried to reconstruct the [narrative] sequence to give them the clue that they had to leave the whole thing the way it was—together.

One Italian scholar described a project in which the detailed study of the monument is part of the restoration.

> [A group of researchers] is working together [on] the problem of the Campo Santo of Pisa. . . . This wonderful monument is in very bad condition. . . . A bombshell set fire to the ceiling, . . . and the heat had a terrible effect on the frescoes. Restoration followed the war, [but] this group . . . [is] studying different [aspects] . . . not only of the . . . building and the decoration, not only the problems concerning the iconography of the cycles of frescoes but also the history of the Campo Santo. When it was built, it was a religious monument, but it became at the beginning of the nineteenth century a wonderful museum of antiquities: . . . new sculptures, Romanesque and classic sculpture were carried into the Campo Santo. The [comprehensive] history of the monument is now the subject [for] research not only by art historians, [but] also for . . . archaeologists. . . . A good, complete project for [the] . . . restoration of the Campo Santo, . . . there is nothing [in Italy] comparable to this enterprise.

An art historian may also be called upon to serve as a consultant to those involved in the buying and selling of works of art. One scholar cautioned against offering advice based on connoisseurship or aesthetic judgments alone.

> Everybody wants to know as exactly as possible what he acquires, and even the auction house is interested in having the right attribution. . . . [Our]

aim [as art historians] is to get insights. . . . When opinions are created without arguments, . . . that's wrong.

The research that art historians do can have significant implications for the valuation of objects on the art market. Our scholars spoke of that connection with varying degrees of interest.

> When I started working on [the painter], one of [his] paintings, which is on sale right now in New York, was available for thirty thousand [French francs]. . . . And now it's close to a million. . . . I'm a big part in all that.

> The status of those prints is very freaky. [A photographer] made the prints [for Juliet Man Ray], and on the back he had written, "This is a print from an original negative by Man Ray. The print was made by [the photographer] on such and such a date. Two prints were pulled at that time, and this was done with the authorization of Juliet Man Ray." And [they both] signed it. So it's very clear . . . that this is a modern print made not by [the artist], but from [his] negative. Now the value of such an object—you know, a collector isn't going to buy [such] a print.

> Pictures that were selling for ten or twelve thousand are now selling for around one hundred thousand. . . . In the case of the better and [the] better-preserved pictures, [their value increased by] multiples of three and four and five . . . after publication.

If there were complaints about the connoisseur's ties to the art market and about the reliability of the connoisseur's attributions, the scholars with whom we spoke understood the joy of solving the endless puzzle of where, and to whom, things belong.

> All these things derive from other things, so that nothing is completely alone. Everything is connected with something before and after. And that means it has a long historical dimension, and . . . a relatively broad dimension in its time. . . . It's very interesting to find the position of the object.

FORMAL AND STYLISTIC ANALYSIS

To the extent that it limits itself to a description and visual analysis of the work of art, formal analysis would appear to be closely aligned with connoisseurship. Formal analysis too limits itself to the work of art but emphasizes visual analysis and verbal description.

> David Smith's sculpture tended to be rather frontal and two-dimensional. . . . But even the more planar sculpture was constructed in such a way that different views would produce shockingly different senses of what it was you were looking at. At a certain point [Smith] began to make sculpture in which the front view and the side view contradict each other.

> [In] the Cameroon problem the head is conceived of as [having] a protective shield that slides over it [and that provides] both revelation and protection for the head as [the layers] cascade down.

> You can't just talk about the robe or the figure or the way that the folds work. You have to think of the robe in terms of an instrument that expresses stylistic intention, which is, in Giotto's case, to make extremely weighty monumental figures that are plastic. And everything he does, drapery, modeling of faces, is in the service of this ideal.

The insights that derive from formal analysis, the conventions to which it adheres, and its relationship to other kinds of information were illustrated by a wry anecdote about a fellow student's presentation in graduate school:

> Many of the [paintings] are . . . divided into a lower story . . . and an upper story in which somebody . . . is raising something to the upper story. For instance, . . . [in an Adoration of the Shepherds] the Virgin and Child are up in a kind of hayloft, and the shepherds are offering the presents with their hands raised. . . . The Devil tempting Christ is also raising the stone that [Christ] is supposed to turn into bread. . . . So the nature of the gesture is ambiguous, whether it's good or evil, . . . giving or somehow tempting. It's a new ambiguity of gesture that is not characteristic of High Renaissance painting. [The] ambi-

> guity . . . is also there . . . because [the artist] cheated his way into getting the commission, and then . . . he did the whole thing for nothing [as] an act of charity. But it made his career, made him famous. . . . [The professor] said, "That's very interesting, but you haven't proved anything."

The term *stylistic analysis* appears to be at once less clearly defined and more pervasive in art-historical research. While it may involve intense concentration on the image, its use appeared to blend with other areas of investigation.

> What [the professor] did was teach you how to see, teach you the possibilities of visual analysis, not on the level of some abstract series of questions; it had nothing to do with simply formalistic concerns in and of themselves. Just the centrality of visual analysis and the range of possible questions you could address through visual analysis, ranging from expressive ones, [to] human ones, [to] contextual ones.

> [A lecturer might have said,] "It's a Baroque picture full of swarming figures organized into a series of serpentines, emphasizing the central role of the man in red." [But this professor would say,] "Who's the man in red?" And I'd say, "Moses!" Terrific. . . . "So why show Moses? What is this?" I'd realize . . . that there were dozens of threads leading in all directions that I had not ever recognized, let alone picked up in the way of classroom lectures on the history of art. . . . It drew me gradually away from a view of the history of art as a kind of illustrated history of ideas to . . . individual works of great interest, complexity, and beauty that could . . . lead me to a fuller understanding of what was around them.

> [In] the thirties people were all agog about Mannerism . . . because of the alleged parallel with modern art. . . . The great conversation point was, "There's Mannerist painting and sculpture. Is there Mannerist architecture?" [Traveling in Italy,] I came across [Giulio Romano's] Palazzo del Te in Mantua. I thought, "Here it is, Mannerist architecture." I came home and said to Schlosser, "I wonder whether you would accept a thesis on Giulio Romano's architecture?" . . . My main task, as I thought of it, was the interpretation of this strange [monument]. . . . I formed a psychological theory. . . . I moved

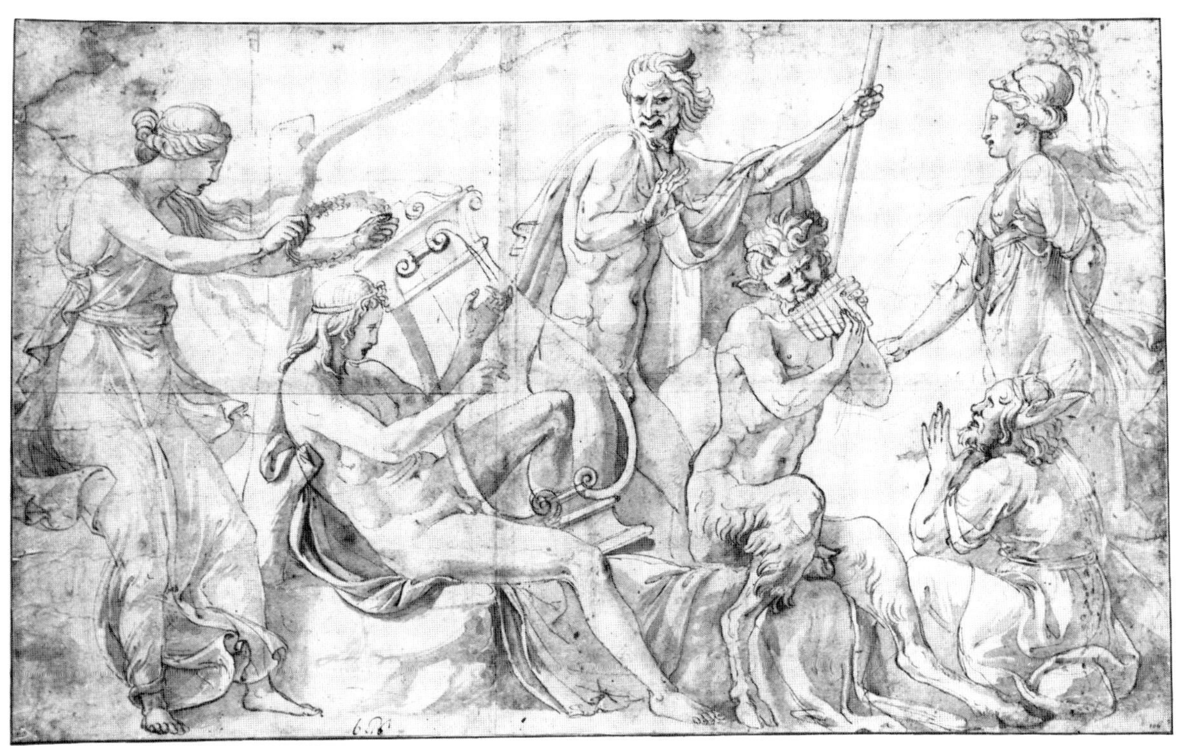

17. GIULIO ROMANO, *Contest of Apollo and Marsyas*, *modello* for a fresco in the Sala delle Metamorfosi, circa 1527, Palazzo del Te, Mantua, Graphische Sammlung Albertina, Vienna

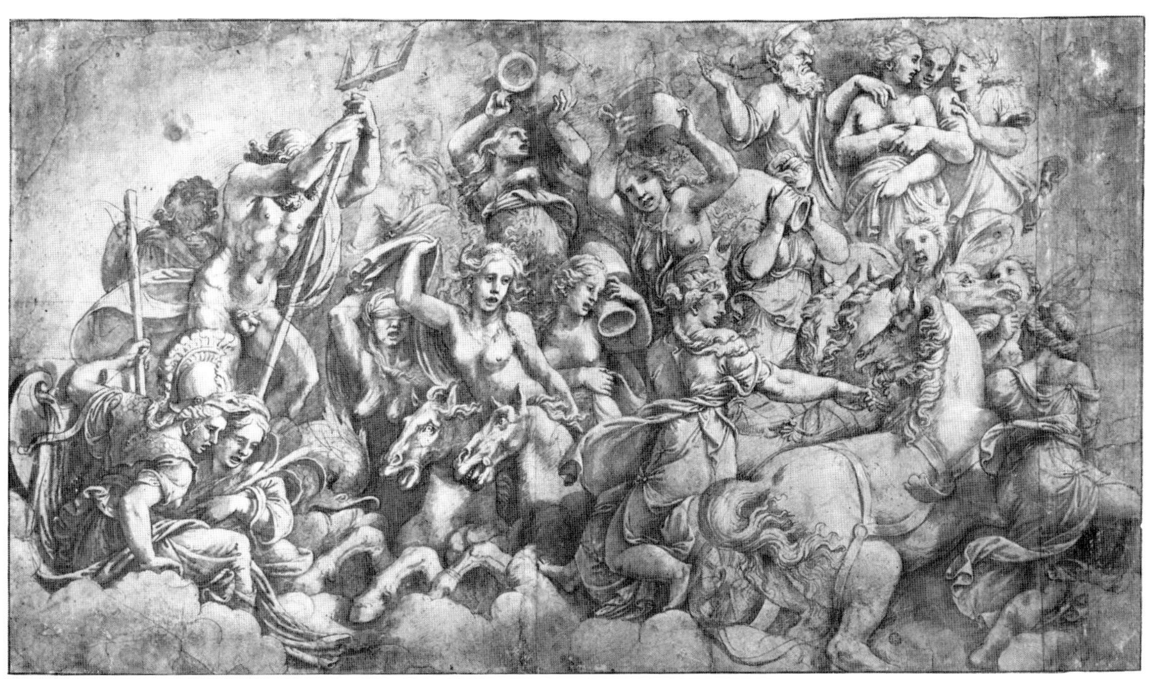

18. GIULIO ROMANO, *Olympus*, *modello* for a portion of a fresco in the Sala dei Giganti, circa 1532, Palazzo del Te, Mantua, Cabinet des Dessins, Musée du Louvre, Paris

> away from [the] interpretation of style as a reflection of the age. . . . I became convinced that Giulio Romano had, as it were, two [styles or modes]. He could be very Mannerist or extremely Classicist [see figs. 17 and 18]. And both of these he could change at will. . . . However, the main thrust of my thesis was I believed that this work [stemmed from] anxieties, nightmares, and that these were personal to Giulio Romano.

> I did a lecture about Napoleon and the arts. And I became more and more interested in . . . the relationship of art and politics. . . . What I wanted to say . . . about the Arc de Triomphe had to do with how a monument which was started in a certain political situation changed in style in another political situation [see figs. 19 and 20].

Perhaps the most familiar model for stylistic analysis is the comparison of two works of art in the classroom. The value and the limitation of this comparative method were best illustrated through more stories from graduate school:

> [His] formula was that . . . the Florentine paints what he knows is there; a Venetian paints what he sees is there. . . . The whole substratum on which Florentine painting is built is . . . the intellectual knowledge of how things functioned: anatomy, perspective, color theory. . . . Michelangelo . . . dissects, and he begins to understand the skeleton, the attachment of muscles, and the overlaying epidermis, and how he grasps the figure. Titian never dissected anything in his life. Titian paints what he sees. His understanding is optical rather than intellectual. . . . In a sense, that is more pragmatic.

> He would put up two pieces of art . . . and just ask students to comment on the differences and the similarities between them. And we would do this with complete surrender. "Well, that's a sculpture, and that's an etching. And that one has monumentality, and that one has intimacy; that one is plastic, and that one is graphic. . . ." He took it completely seriously, but . . . he told us this anecdote about Hamburg in the early thirties, when a group of students got together and, after having gone through these dualities, . . . came up with the theory that every artist was basically either a tailor or a carpenter. . . . But

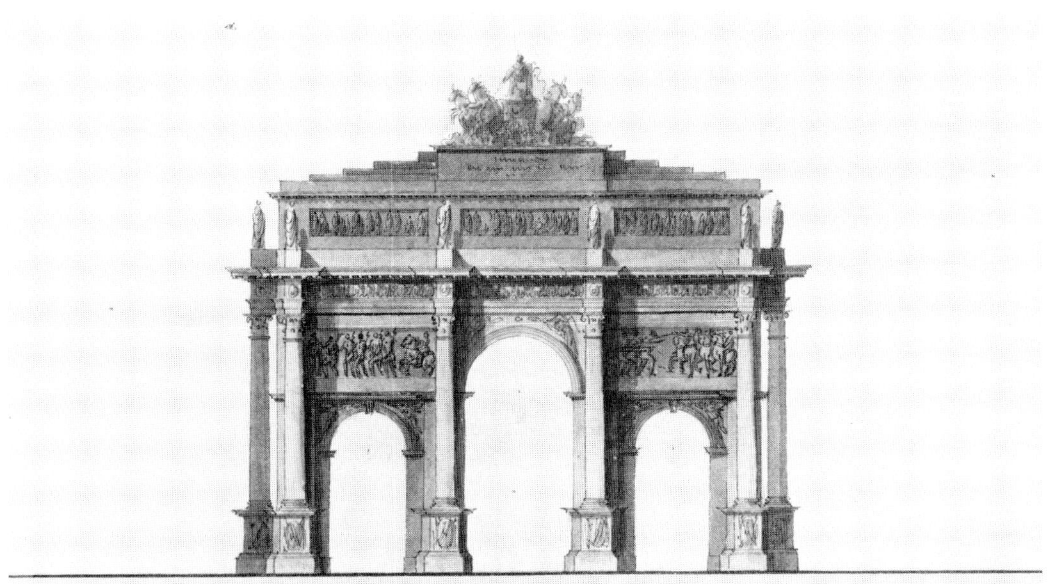

19. JEAN-FRANÇOIS CHALGRIN, *Triumphal Arch*, 1806(?), Bibliothèque Historique de la Ville de Paris, Paris, photo courtesy Jean-Loup Charmet

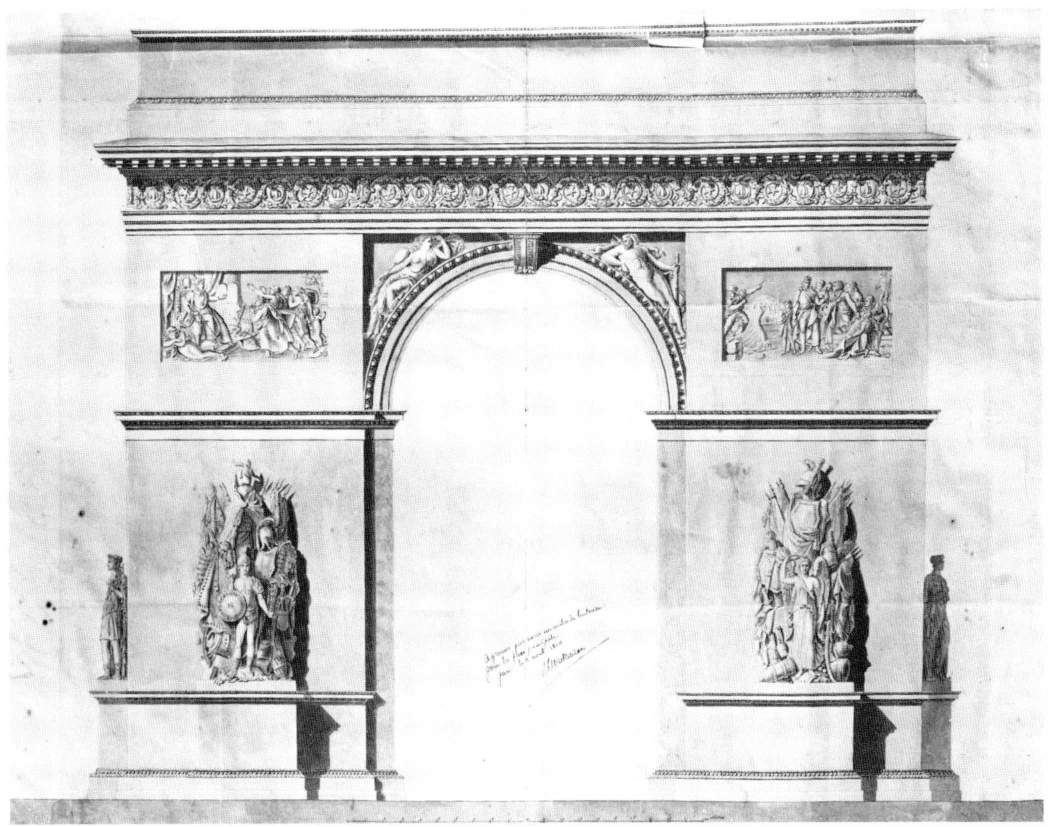

20. JEAN-FRANÇOIS CHALGRIN, *Arc de Triomphe*, 1810, Cabinet des Dessins, Musée du Louvre, Paris

> even if they could make fun of it, they were trapped in a dualistic way of thinking and a dualistic way of looking.

A nonverbal but very influential form of visual and stylistic analysis can be found in the installation of works of art in an exhibition space.

> There are unspoken messages that are given by the arrangements of things that . . . are just harmonious, that look happy and natural together. The biggest challenge, and the least visible, is to arrange works of art so that . . . it looks as though they were fated to hang in such a combination. . . . And to embed . . . observations, unspoken commentary, to allow the works of art to, in a sense, comment on each other. It's different from writing an essay, it's different from arranging plates in a book. It's a skill unto itself.

The debate over how strong a commentary to make in the hanging of works can be heated.

> What you see on the side walls of the room prior to [Picasso's] *Three Musicians* [is] the first big step beyond anything that Braque participated in, Picasso's *Harlequin* of 1915. It was a major picture . . . [as] Picasso knew, and he wrote a letter in which he mentions this. That picture introduces the very big flat areas that are the first step in the direction of *Three Musicians*. So that what you're seeing is step one and the conclusion of the development. . . . If I could call upon every collection of modern art in the world, I would do that . . . with the whole of modern art history.

> My standard is to make [didactic] comments . . . work in balance with the absolute obligation to make the individual works of art look beautiful and at home. . . . I cannot bear . . . [to] abuse individual works of art in service of the themes [one is] trying to exemplify with them. . . . You want things that are good neighbors aesthetically and, if possible, good neighbors historically, . . . reminding you of something you might have known, or encourag[ing] you to think about some relationship—historical or aesthetic.

CRITICISM

The ambiguous position of criticism within the history of art seems to be especially strong in the United States. The alienation the critic feels vis-à-vis the history of art was striking, as was the implied disapproval on both sides that results from the strained relationship:

> Literary critics . . . feel perfectly secure in the center of their discipline, . . . that is, as people who are involved in an analysis of a text, which presupposes a lot of historical knowledge and precision but does not necessarily involve itself in doing primary historical research. So it's perfectly acceptable to be a literary critic, [but] it's not acceptable to be an art historian as critic.

> There was a . . . gulf between what I thought was interesting as a question and what most art historians thought was interesting as a question. . . . For me criticism immediately asks the question, "Why should we be interested in this? What's good about this?" . . . [In] art history it goes without saying that we should be accumulating information, and it doesn't matter whether it's interesting or not.

In Europe, however, the distinction seemed less strong. In some countries art historians may regularly write criticism in both the public and the academic press, and an objective approach to the history of art may well merge smoothly with the more subjective critical response as it is applied to historical material. One description of a "critical" study formed a seamless unity with art-historical concerns:

> The idea of the exhibition was that . . . the history of painting in the thirteenth century . . . arrive[d] without a problem at Giotto. . . . Longhi . . . wrote against this evolutionistic view. . . . He tried to demonstrate that central Italian painting before Giotto was in great part provincial Byzantine painting, not of interest for the future. . . . For understanding Giotto, it was more important to understand [Northern Gothic] art of the thirteenth century.

The use of criticism from recent modern periods has gained increasing favor as a means not just of gauging "reaction" to the modern movement but also of understanding the art itself.

> There were previous people who'd written very well about Salon criticism, [but this involved] a more systematic effort to confront Salon criticism as a thing in its own right, which might give us crucial information about meaning, rather than . . . whether or not critics got it right—you know, were or were not hostile.

If all these approaches forge an intimate bond between words and the work of art, one scholar reminded us that the word and the object are not equivalent:

> My belief is that the essential experience is incommunicable through words and that there is no way to express it. . . . The areas which we can verbalize are not the most important areas. . . . [Even] formal[ism] is quantitative; you can say a lot of things about style which are provable. . . . What you can't say is why [of] two Rembrandts [with] the same kind of subject, in the same style, at the same moment, why one is full of deep meaning and the other may be rather dead.

STRUCTURALISM AND SEMIOTICS

Structuralism and semiotics have entered the realm of art history and have been subject to considerable controversy. As presented to us, the structuralist methodologies offer the scholar the possibility of finding unity and coherence in material that is otherwise disparate.

> What is Surrealist photography? . . . Was there any way to understand this rather disunified field as having some hidden coherence? . . . I began to realize that it was [in] the structure of the photographic sign that I would start finding something that would unify this variety. These things that didn't necessarily look alike, or involve the same apparatus, . . . all seemed to have some similarity of structure. I was finding this at the level of the description of the sign.

> [Minoan] architecture . . . seemed so bizarrely irregular and haphazard, . . . and yet they obviously planned these things to look this way. . . . A lot of rooms are cubic . . . which means that all three dimensions are identical. . . . So our thought was, then, would this cube be a unit? . . . We were doing a very

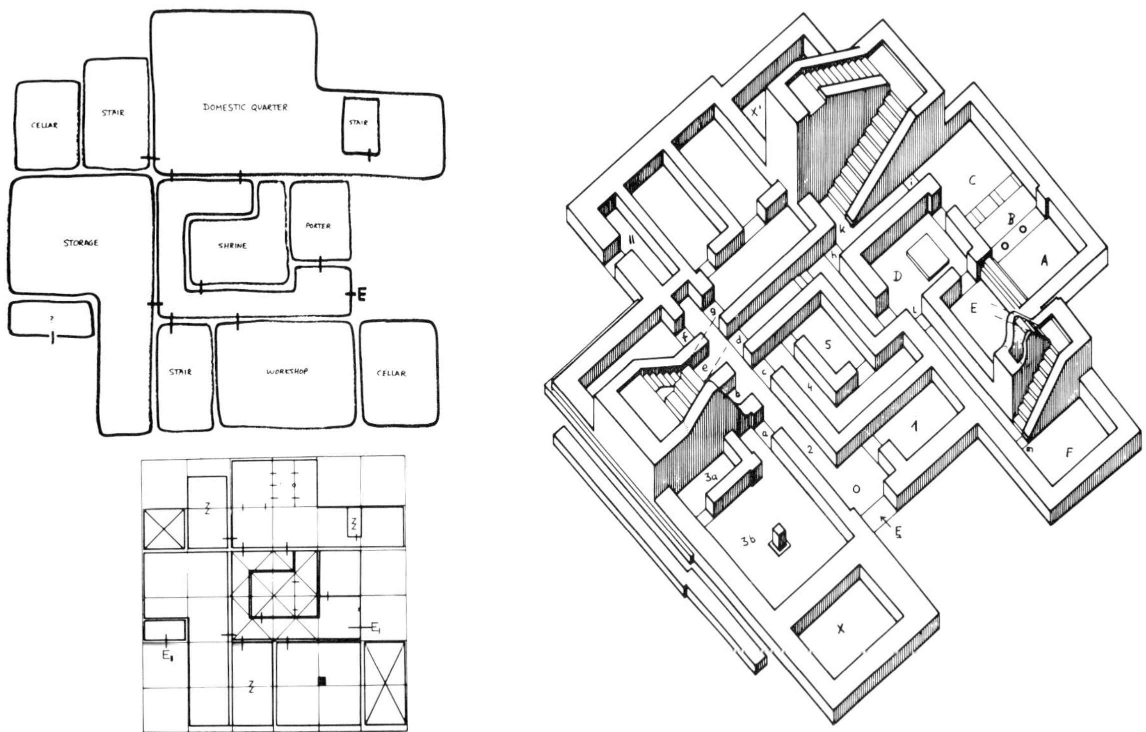

21. TYLISSOS, House C; above, functional zoning; below, areal proportions, and right, isometric view; illustrations from Donald Preziosi, *Minoan Architectural Design* (Berlin, 1983)

simple kind of combinatory analysis. What we did was tabulate the instances to get a sense of what was grammatical for the architecture [see fig. 21].

These new approaches to art-historical study have looked to a new set of authorities. In place of Berenson, Burckhardt, Panofsky, and Riegl, another set of authors was continually cited:

I started reading Barthes.

I had just been reading a lot of Lévi-Strauss, about his analysis of myth. I thought, "This works just the same way."

I started reading Peirce.

Mostly we were reading Chomsky.

> I started reading Walter Benjamin.

> That chart, in its clumsy way, . . . did have, obviously, something to do with Lévi-Strauss. [I thought,] "Is there a way of putting this material down in order?" [and thought] about binary oppositions and such.

The scholars were mindful of the opportunities and problems posed by the new methodologies.

> We need to sew the study of the arts back into the study of history and society and culture. The methodologies . . . to do that are coming from parallel disciplines which have already done that in their own way: anthropology, literary studies, history.

> Insofar as I've been interested in using structuralism as a tool in my own approach to certain problems, structuralism puts in question certain ideas about history. So I've had a problematic relationship to what you could say are the normal views of what it is that historians do.

Most of all, the need for a theoretical construct beyond examination of the material seemed necessary for a full understanding of the material.

> I knew a lot about the material as material, but I really didn't know how to think about it.

The contrast between such theoretical models and the traditional ways that art historians have approached the discipline was highlighted by another story from graduate school.

> [In the English literature department] they were in the midst of pre-Deconstructionism. It was all a question of critical method, of hammering out your relationship with the world of language, all sorts of fancy theoretical stuff. . . . I was training myself . . . to deal with visual facts, to compare them, to connect them with cultural facts, to build hypotheses based on them. And [my friend in the English department] was telling me that I had the soul of an archivist.

The greatest skepticism of the structuralist approach came from those who have rejected the incorporation of new approaches from other disciplines.

> I find much of my own discipline now engaged in what I call, disparagingly, intellectual ambulance chasing. . . . These people are reading Derrida, and we must read Foucault and . . . Geertz. . . . It tends to breed . . . a kind of slavish imitation, without, to my mind, sufficiently reflective or sensitive [understanding].

Doubts were raised even by some of the enthusiasts.

> Yes, one could say that you're creating a theoretical superstructure which has no necessary reflex in the art itself, . . . which is utterly divorced from the actual artistic object.

> I thought that the whole structuralist and semiotic adventure had sort of floundered in many ways. . . . It was ironical for someone like me, who'd drunk in all this . . . stuff. . . . To see it finally used [to] guarantee philosophical and critical solipsism, ambiguity, indeterminacy, and . . . cynicism . . . was distasteful to me.

ICONOGRAPHY

Iconography, the study of the meaning of works of art, has in the twentieth century constituted one of the primary art-historical methods for placing art in its context. Much iconographic study centers on the matching of images to texts—literary, theological, or historical—that explain the literal or symbolic meaning of the image.

> [About an object carried by Christ during the Passion, the professor said,] "What is that? Is it a book? Is it a symbol of something?" And I wanted to know what that was. . . . I started studying texts, assuming that if I just started reading texts, I would find the answer.

> A famous world map destroyed in World War II showed the orb with a head on the top, hands on the sides, and feet below, and the head was clearly

> that of Christ. What is the significance of such a diagram? Well, you will find that there are early medieval and high medieval authors who speak of the created world as Christ's body.

From such beginnings, however, most of these scholars had gone to deeper levels of investigation.

> If literature and art are, in a sense, both symptoms, then the ultimate question is, what is it that they are symptoms of?

> I wanted [to show] that the artist was inspired by more than aesthetic motives, that the meaning of the painting is more than just the object of visual delectation, that the role of the patron was essential to the genesis of the work, [and] that this complex of patron, subject, and artists was of greater importance and interest as an object of study than standing in front of just the piece of paint and canvas. . . . [I wanted not only] concrete historical things but . . . more. I also wanted a spiritual, metaphysical dimension, which was always the bottom line in iconographical, iconological art history.

They expressed doubts about a purely textual approach, finding it too narrow, even mechanical.

> It's the fault of those who adapted Panofsky[1] to the art history curriculum. That almost mechanized the study of iconology. . . . You know, if Saint Anne raises her right hand, that's related to chastity or avarice, and there are twenty-five other instances. It was a kind of amateurish pattern recognition, . . . a kind of mechanical process.

> [A teacher] spoke with scorn of iconographers who pick a subject and just go through the material applying the method, . . . just stamping out, . . . a cookie-cutting exercise.

---

1. See Erwin Panofsky's *Studies in Iconology: Humanistic Themes in the Art of the Renaissance* (New York, 1939), in which he distinguishes between iconographical and iconological analysis.

> Art historians had been in the habit of saying, "We want to understand the image; we find a text, we call it a 'prooftext,' and now we explain the image." [A colleague] said, "This is passing the buck. You don't explain an image by citing a text [and] explain a text by citing an image."

From asking the questions "What does it illustrate?" and "Who is depicted?" one scholar, inspired by a colleague, moved on to the questions "Why was it done this way?" and "How does it fit with its time?"

> When I first came across [the spikeblock], I knew it was an instrument of torture [see fig. 22]. I just assumed that by looking at medieval Dutch texts I would find out what it was, what function it had. . . . I didn't think there was necessarily any deeper historiographical issue there, except the one of invention. . . . I started reading Dutch Passion tracts, and I had a giant collection of texts about the spikeblock. . . . I was motif-hunting. When I met [F. P.] Pickering, he was already on the level beyond the motif-hunting: the same motifs have a history in common, are the result of a specific historical and literary process. . . . He opened my eyes to . . . certain kinds of texts as being root sources that were transformed in history to create narrative elaborations.

For this person the very concept of meaning was dependent on historical change.

> A text is not a discrete object or a discrete piece of evidence; a text is something which has its own history and has its own complex processes in historical transformation. And symbolism [and] iconography are living traditions. You can't isolate one object or one moment and make sense of it in itself; any object or moment is part of an ongoing tradition in which conventions of representation [and] systems of thought are in flux.

While no scholar interviewed expressed an inflexible position on the use of iconographic method, one argued especially for better communication between differing schools of thought.

> Right now in our discipline we are having a discussion about the social history approach and the iconographical approach. I am a German, and coming

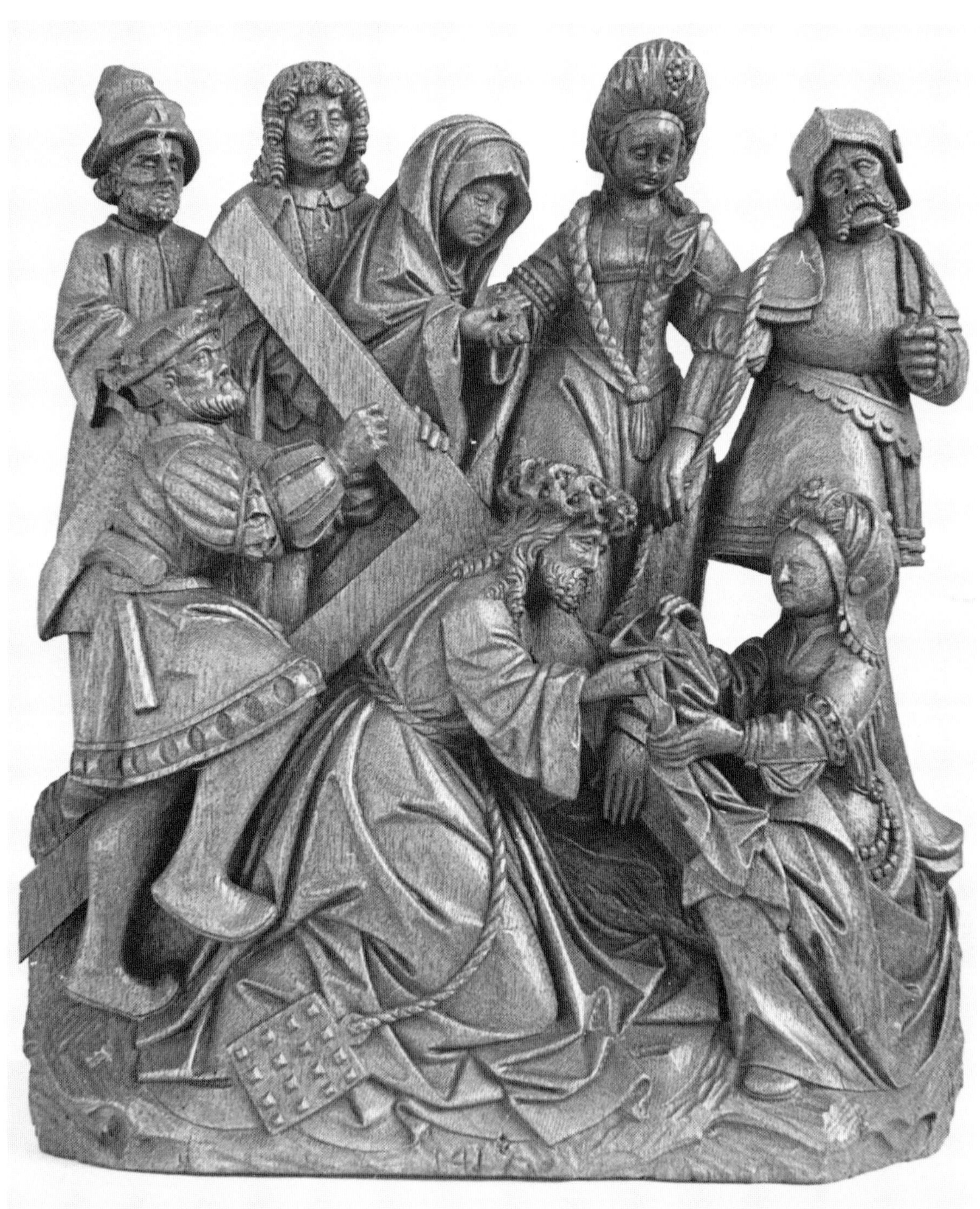

22. NORTHERN NETHERLANDS, *Bearing of the Cross*, circa 1525, Rijksmuseum het Catharijneconvent, Utrecht, photo courtesy James Marrow

> to this country [the United States], it's very interesting to see the difference between the . . . camps who have problems speaking to each other. [Some say] our approach has to be social because art . . . has a background in . . . society, and others . . . do iconographical work, [which] they say is the basic and still interesting approach. And there is no communication between them. . . . I think one should combine them.

The iconography of seventeenth-century Dutch painting, an area currently under revision, received especially close attention from this group of scholars.

> We overlooked, until very recently, the really cardinal and central importance of history painting in the Netherlands. We had a myth that the Dutch didn't need that anymore, [that] they had kicked religious art out, that public art was a small matter for them, and that the real creativity of Dutch artists was focused largely on the rendering of real-world pictures. . . . We now take Dutch history painting much more seriously. Furthermore we now know how to classify genre paintings more knowledgeably than we used to, . . . not simply to find all the pictures with dogs in them, or portrait sitters who hold flowers in their left hand. . . . [For instance] a woman feeding sweetmeat to a dog is in fact an emblem of enslavement to love. . . . That is a whole line of thought in Calvinist and, in fact, humanistic thought.

> Saenredam wasn't just painting this church because it had such an interesting structure and such interesting light [see fig. 23]. And certainly Huygens wasn't buying it for that reason. . . . Huygens wanted a painting of the Mariakerk, and this inscription on the relief [in the painting] had special meaning to the patron [see fig. 24]. I deduced [from] Huygens's own poem . . . that this was the case; it was in the front of his mind when thinking about the church.

Iconographic research poses its own problems for the researcher, for art is seldom catalogued by its subject matter. The lack of helpful resources was a common complaint.

> [The difficulty of searching for subject matter] almost forces me to do monographic work, to deal with one artist at a time.

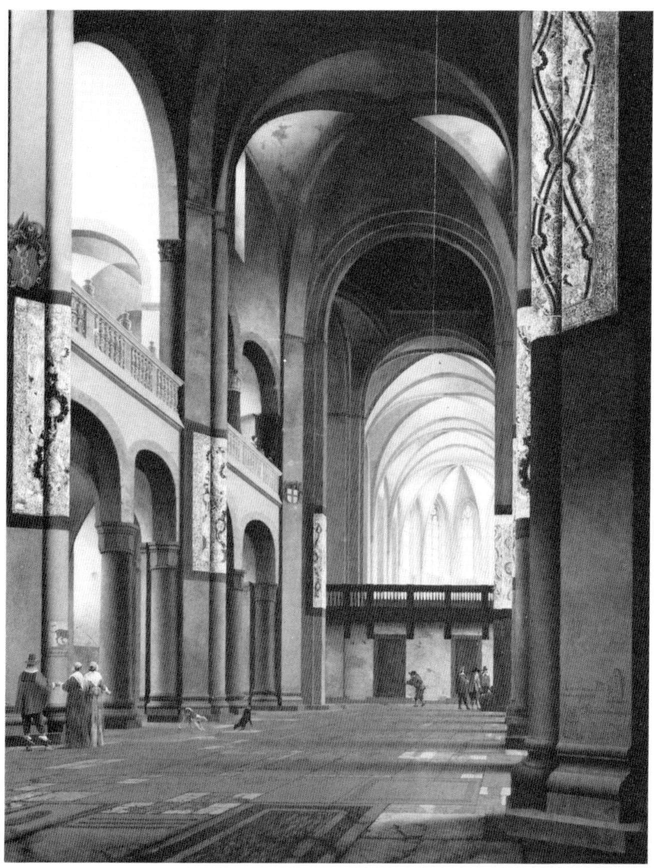

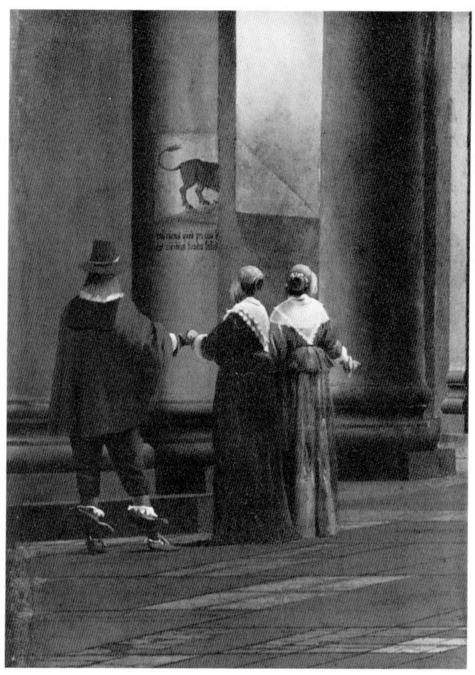

24. Detail of fig. 23

23. PIETER JANSZ. SAENREDAM, *Saint Mary's Church, Utrecht*, view of nave and choir, 1641, Rijksmuseum, Amsterdam

> The number of instances in which we have authoritative books or articles on the tradition of the Flight into Egypt in Northern art is very small. . . . There is no index that will give you a list of all of the articles on John the Baptist.

> In museums [she] would yell [from another room] . . . , "There's a lantern here!" and I would go running. . . . And sure enough, there was a John the Baptist with the lantern I'd never seen before. Practically every day I'd come across unknown examples of some of these things.

Even more than standard motifs or themes, it was the odd representation of a subject that excited the scholars' curiosity and pointed up the difficulties of their search.

> There was a picture of Christ led before the judges. And it had two people sitting on a bench who were both bishops. . . . [I] said, "I don't recall ever

> seeing Christ led before two bishops." But I had no way of checking that, short of stopping and going through my entire library again.

Iconographic problems from each era require their own means of solution. One hears of a very different search for meaning in twentieth-century art.

> In Surrealist art, . . . two ideas that were very important were the Labyrinth and the inhabitant of the Labyrinth, who was the Minotaur. The Labyrinth is this place of darkness; it's underground; it's horizontal; it's also the space where one could say art was born, that is, in cave painting. . . . The *Documents* group was absolutely involved in speculations about cave art, about the Labyrinth, about a certain kind of development of art out of practices of violence and mutilation, and about this underground, groping-in-the-dark kind of experience. I think that's very much what's going on in the sculptures of Giacometti.

One story concerning twentieth-century art brought into sharp relief the difficulties of iconographic interpretation, highlighted especially by the intervention of a living artist.

> [Joan Miró] had talked about how important poets were for him, . . . much more important than other painters. . . . He would always mention Alfred Jarry. Sometimes he would even say *Ubu Roi*. And so [my colleague] began to discover in these paintings the personages of Jarry's world. She found a painting where there was a representation of Ubu and Mère Ubu [see fig. 25], and this constellation of figures seemed to relate to [a certain point in the play]. . . . So when she interviewed Miró—Miró of course was quite old at the time—she showed him the picture of this painting, and she said, "C'est Ubu, n'est-ce pas?" And he said, "No. It's a dog, in fact." So she called me, very upset. She said, "What am I going to do? He says it's a dog." I said, "We are honor-bound to record that he says it's a dog."

Even such daunting experiences, however, could not diminish the fascination produced by the search for meaning in a visual image. The notion that a single image can hold a universe of themes and references permeated many remarks.

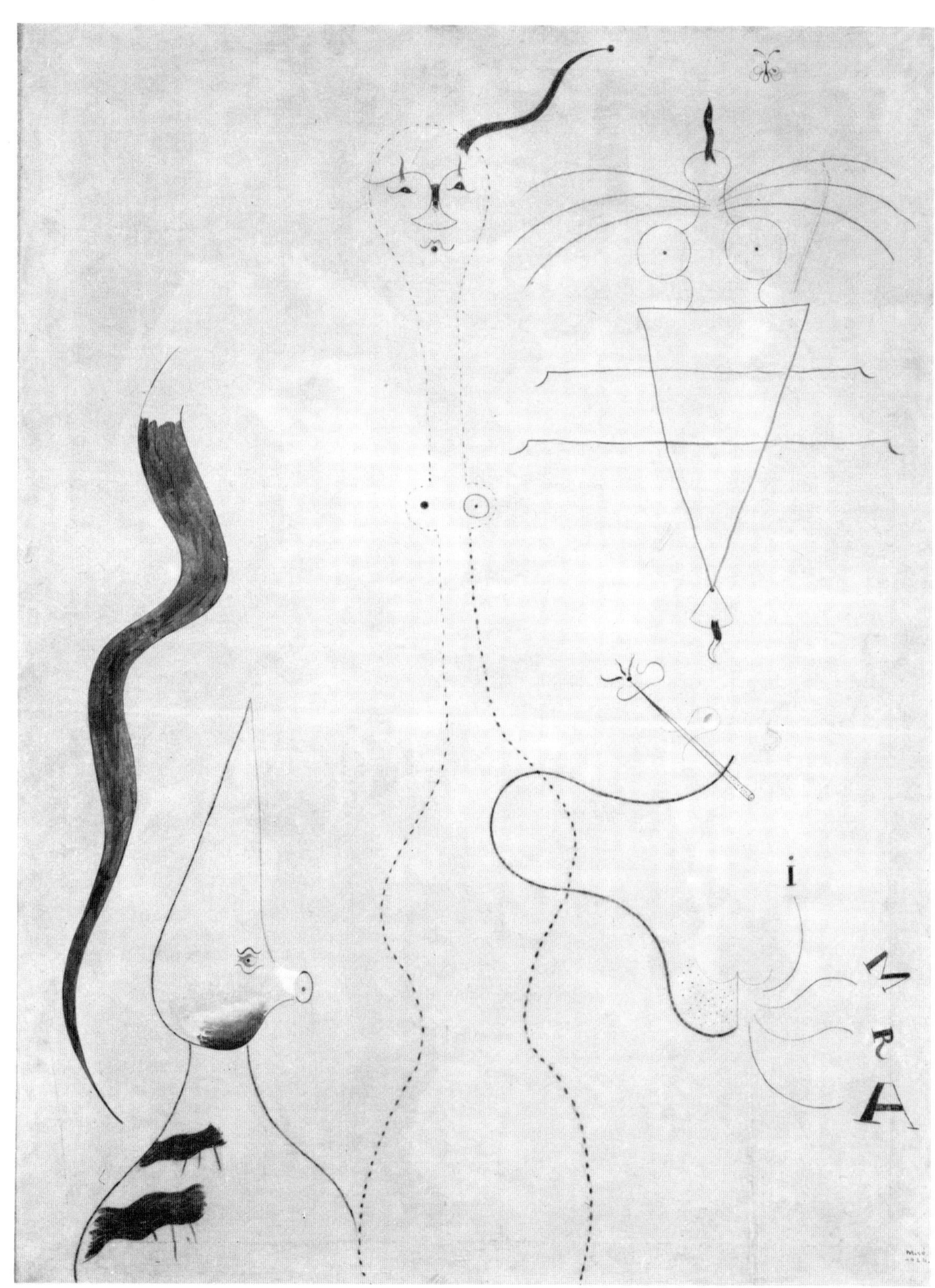

25. JOAN MIRÓ, *Portrait of Madame B.*, 1924, Berry-Hill Galleries, New York, photo courtesy Nathan Rabin.

> You take a medieval world map which shows the world as it is conceived to look. But if you look at it closely it has on it diagrams or inscriptions or little pictures of all the monsters of the earth, of paradise, of Adam and Eve and the tree, of the missionaries converting the heathen, or the old man in the mountain, the ostrich that lays jewels rather than eggs in Arabia, and on and on. And what is the meaning of such a document, . . . just a geographical diagram? It is a summa, a syncretistic diagram, that tries to represent all that is known in diagrammatic form.

CULTURAL AND SOCIAL HISTORY

Many art historians treat works of art as an integral part of the cultural activity and production of the society to which artists belong. To understand the meaning of works of art, these "cultural" historians insist, it is essential to look beyond factors intrinsic to their visual form and to interpret them in relation to the cultural factors that shape art and are in turn shaped by art. Since culture encompasses all forms of human expression, including religion, society, politics, economics, and a range of activities from spiritual, intellectual, and artistic thought to the production of material artifacts, cultural historians of art generally address all or some part of this panoply in an effort to explain the function of art within the society that produced it.

> There's a greater . . . appreciation that art is not simply another visual document, is not simply a passive reflection of history, but rather an active shaper of it, as much as other components of society. . . . The definition of the subject of art-historical study is changing too, so that there's more of a tendency not to privilege the hierarchical, fine-art object quite as much . . . and to see it as part of a larger material culture and its relationship to other kinds of practices, social practices.

Those scholars who are committed to studying the cultural context of works of art generally see their work as revisionist, as a reaction to formalism, connoisseurship, and iconography, which were dominant in the discipline well into the 1950s and 1960s.

> When we were young students at the University of Florence, we were interested . . . not only in connoisseurship . . . [but also] in exploring the field of

art history, not only looking at the artist but looking at the patrons, at the public, and so on. This kind of reflection was not so easy to do in Italy immediately after the war, because [emphasis] was on the artist, or the reconstruction of the corpus, or . . . on influences—very little on the patrons [and none] at all on the public. . . . There was a little more interest in art criticism and the history of art criticism, . . . but the pieces were not put together. . . . Our generation began to discover that it was more important . . . to see the connections between the patrons and artists, patrons and critics, critics and artists, marketers and artists, marketers and collectors . . . to put together . . . a more global history of art.

In a [Dutch] literary monthly . . . , [I published] an open attack on the principles of connoisseurship applied to the establishment of autograph quality or authenticity. That had been bothering me for a long time; part of it was just a feeling of antipathy in art history between the connoisseurs and the historians. I've always felt myself on the more historical side. And I'd been struggling with concepts to try to demonstrate what's wrong with connoisseurship. . . . Why is the quality of the argument so inadequate for the purpose to which you want to apply it?

[My] previous books were entirely cavalier about the crucial question of the internal order of the picture and the way in which the form of the picture connected with the historical circumstances. They were basically studies in iconography, historical iconography. [When it came to] the pictures [they] were all right, but they were naive. . . . I wanted [later] to devise a way of talking about the pictures which tried to deal with this difficult business of how circumstances become form.

Among these scholars tensions are evident between the respective roles of art and culture, and their relationships to each.

[My mentor Roberto] Longhi was very intelligent and a very good connoisseur, [but] he was always a little troubled with the problem of society. He told us, "Pay attention first of all to the work of art. From the work of art, from the picture, from the sculpture, from the architecture, you can arrive at the

> culture, at the society. But if you begin with the society [and move to the work of art], you are in danger of taking what you find in the society and putting it in the work of art." . . . For him it was more interesting to study pictures than patrons, but for me . . . it was impossible to study painters without studying patrons.

> I shift [in my work]. Sometimes you are closer to the work itself . . . , and sometimes you are more theoretical. Looking back, I would say that I started very close to the [work. Later] I wanted more history and history of ideas, but I have the feeling that now I'm going back to works of art.

> [In] the Saenredam article the object was still the center of attention. The painter and . . . the patron were still performing an autonomous act. In [my work on] Rembrandt I had really come to doubt the autonomy of the artist. . . . But I got guilty feelings about this . . . that [I was] betraying the essence of the field the way I was taught it. . . . By the time I finished the Rembrandt book, I had abandoned that [guilt].

Historians who are interested in art and culture reconstruct the relationships among different cultural products and groups in various ways. In general they move their attention from the individual work of art in ever-widening circles to the world with which the art and artist interacted.

> Who was this Timothy O'Sullivan [see fig. 26]? . . . The history of photography tries to give a certain amount of ballast to its contention that photography has to do with Transcendentalist experience, a sense of the divine speaking through nature. They have more and more been involved in trying to prove their case . . . through an analysis of [the geologist] Clarence King. In other words saying [that] Timothy O'Sullivan [the photographer] is just sort of the manipulated . . . puppet on the end of the strings of the geologist. . . . So then I [started] doing research about Clarence King, which . . . meant trying to figure out where Clarence King stood in relationship to the various debates that were going on in the 1850s and '60s. Mostly these debates had to do with Darwin . . . , because Darwin had to establish a kind of time frame that was long enough and gradualist enough to support his notions of evolution. The

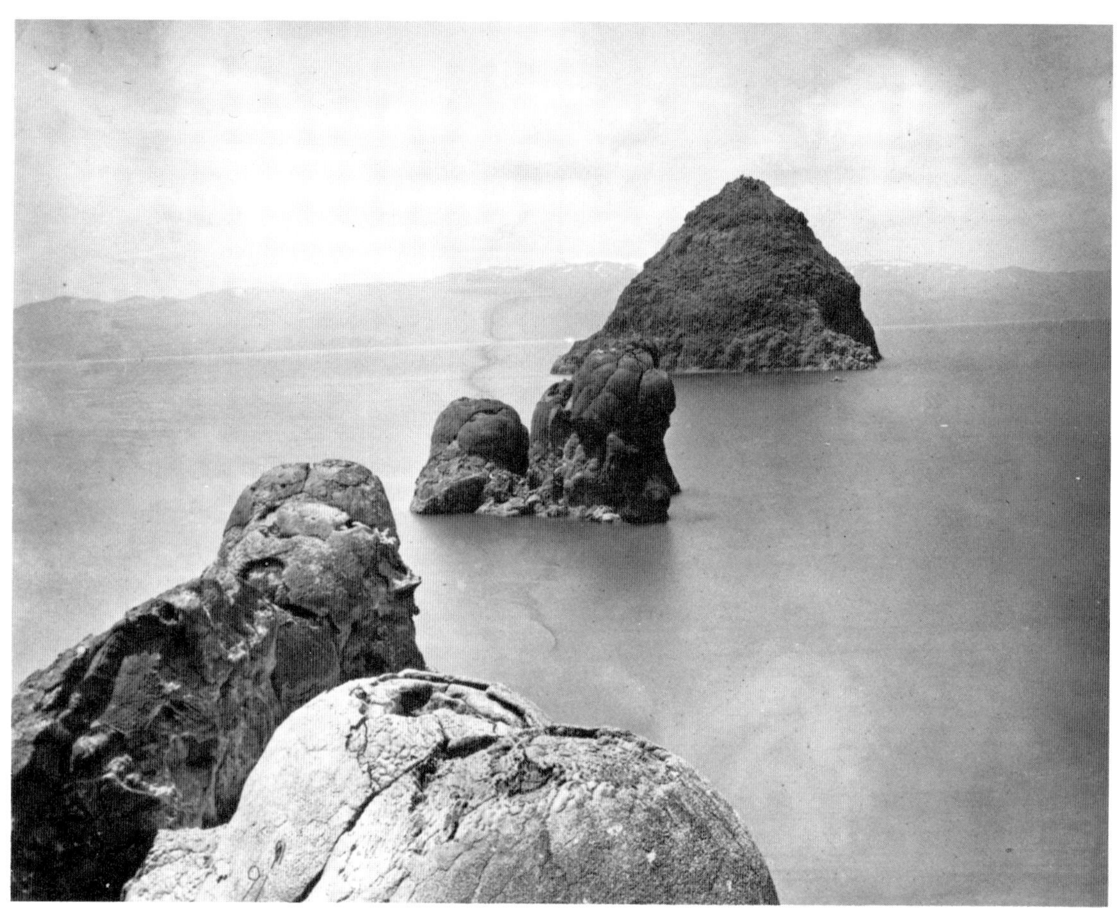

26. TIMOTHY O'SULLIVAN, *Tufa Domes, Pyramid Lake, Nevada*, 1867, National Archives, Washington, D.C. (photo no. 77-KS-3-147)

biological dimension had to be, in a sense, floated on this historical frame, this geological frame.

[For the Rembrandt book] I thought all I needed to do was to produce a more up-to-date biography . . . with more attention to this question of patrons and the outside world. . . . My expectation still was that it was Rembrandt who caused his own development . . . , and there were people who responded. . . . But then . . . something totally opposite happened. I found groups of people who were related much more directly to each other than they were related to Rembrandt. So this nexus began developing of people with mutual connections, which were much more significant and interesting than their taste in art. . . . These burgomasters of Amsterdam and merchants had very little to do

> with art otherwise, but a lot to do with Mennonitism or Remonstrantism or politics. . . . [I found] a shift in values . . . away from aesthetic to social values.

For earlier artistic periods, in which information about individual artists' lives or contributions is scarce, a scholar may find it fruitful to look at artists collectively or to study the groups for whom artists worked.

> We have been so excessively concerned with the . . . powerful master mason['s] vision of the cathedral, . . . there has been no concern whatsoever with the clergy, with the organization of construction, and with the role of the fabric [the church officials in charge of the building]. These are the people that hired the masons and purchased the materials and made the decisions on the construction process.

The consideration of the artistic tastes and values of those who wield power in a society may lead one to study the larger cultural impact of the art associated with the dominant group.

> My [approach] to [medieval] stained glass . . . [is to] see how [it] can be connected with the representation of royal power in the fourteenth century. . . . How did [they] use this type of image? . . . It's monumental; it's set in a church [and] can be seen by everybody. . . . Is there really a difference in the representations in churches and in private chapels?

The works of art commissioned by religious or political leaders can have effects over a wide geographical area on those who are related to them through a variety of social networks.

> I remember Panofsky said that Avignon was not of great interest . . . for the history of European painting. In my view . . . Avignon was . . . really a very important cultural center [because of the presence of the popes], an international center [where] . . . ambassadors and princes and the Emperor and the King of France and so on [came, bringing] painters with them. The architect of Prague Cathedral was a Frenchman, Matthieu d'Arras. The Emperor found him in Avignon. Sometimes [a] king, emperor, or prince asked for an architect,

> a painter, or a sculptor [from Avignon]. . . . Documents [also] show that some bishop or cardinal asked for drawings from the paintings in Avignon for a petty king in the beginning of the fifteenth century. And the paintings [dated to] the middle fourteenth century.

An art historian asking questions about transmission of artistic values across space may also wonder about cultural transfers through time, or the recovery of the arts of the past. How and why does a patron come to appreciate works of art commissioned by previous generations?

> Why was [the patron] interested [in] fourteenth-century art? For iconographic reasons? For historical reasons? [Probably not] for artistic reasons, because in the beginning of the seventeenth century, I don't think the interest in fourteenth-century painting was so strong as in the nineteenth century, for example. He was not Ruskin. It was for historical and religious reasons. . . . We have some ideas about the trends of culture in the eighteenth century, but it is very difficult to understand the trends of culture of the seventeenth century. We have on the one side science and Galileo and so on, but [on the other] the erudition, the interest in antiquity, in the classical world, and in the medieval world. But why medieval?

Some historians look beyond patrons to the audiences for whom works of art are intended. They may even study the changing public reception of art objects through time, their cultural fortunes.

> We speak of the public, of the publics: . . . you have the public of the time when the painting was painted, but after, the painting is [still] there, or not there but in a collection in a museum. . . . And the public is not always the same public.

When a work of art such as a palace becomes a national symbol over the centuries, the public's reaction to it at different historical moments may have significant cultural implications.

> I discovered there was nothing about nineteenth-century Versailles [in the literature]. There are interesting, fascinating, problematic parts of [the palace

> of] Versailles's history, which were completely [overlooked]. . . . What I think is original in [my] approach is not to try to find out what events were represented [in the Versailles paintings]; that you could just check in any history book. But what I tried to figure out was what people in the 1830s thought about certain historic events [represented in the seventeenth and eighteenth centuries at Versailles]. . . . You could see the changes in political interpretations . . . from the literature of Henry IV [1553–1610] through the seventeenth to the nineteenth centuries.

One scholar described a study that began with the concrete question of patronage but evolved into a consideration of more fundamental issues involving art and culture. Although his goal was the interpretation of works of art, he achieved that end by contemplating an abstract model of cultural processes.

> I [went] to Paris thinking that I would have a good, solid, empirical Ph.D. topic there, the Second Republic's patronage. It didn't work out at all. . . . [I] realized that it wasn't going to be a neat and tidy package about patronage, [which was an] empirical nugget [that] was just very limited, just wasn't rich enough, just wasn't going to adjudicate on the questions which seemed to me to be the really interesting ones. . . . I realized that [I] was going to be circling around, . . . gradually forming the picture of what I saw as the nature of a certain historical moment—the key issues, the key instances within it—and feeling about for constant connection between the historical totality and the paintings. . . . I was always on the lookout, because that's a terrifyingly vague prospect, for *condensers*; I mean particular bodies of evidence in which the connection between the totality and a certain painting might really be readable. But I really didn't have an a priori view of what those condensers would be and where the focus would be, what kind of material would really divulge the connections.

While the art historians whom we interviewed may have developed strong theoretical and philosophical preferences for certain approaches to cultural history in their published works, their biases did not emerge in this study as fixed, hierarchical patterns. Instead, in retrospective glimpses of their scholarly activities, they described responses to various problems and revealed rather fluid ways of investigating the concept of art within culture.

What follows is a kaleidoscopic presentation of varied points of view as to which lines of questioning shed the most light on the function and meaning of art in society.

One scholar found political events that tempered cultural exchanges at the intersection between artistic and political geography.

> Isabella d'Este liked a picture she had seen in the palace of the Bembo [family] in Venice, a Flemish picture. They graciously said . . . , "We will loan it to you," and then they immediately start[ed] asking for Mantuan horses to take Pietro Bembo on his first journey to Rome to make a very splendid entry. (That is one thing the Venetians weren't too good on, horses, but the Gonzagas were great horse breeders. . . .) There were times when no Mantuan could set foot in Venice. . . . There couldn't be any art ordered at certain points; all commissions were suspended because they were at war. It is a simple fact which historians knew, but art historians had somehow forgotten about [it].

An understanding of the economics of production and trade sometimes offers insight into the practical and material factors that affect both appearance and dissemination.

> The high-grade hardwood for construction [in Renaissance buildings] came from the Tyrol . . . and from even further away. It is very interesting to look into those aspects because . . . they tell you a lot. . . . I think the proportionate calibration of rooms . . . , like in Palladio's buildings, has much to do with the lumber supply, the beam lengths.

> The first [copper engravings] that we have are playing cards. [Their role in the history of printing] makes sense if you consider what you do with playing cards. . . . You consume them relatively quickly, and they have to be equal. . . . To play with cards was so in fashion in the fifteenth century that monks in monasteries [did it, although] their laws forbade them to. . . . Playing cards were exported to far away places. We know that about 1470 . . . Venetian playing-card makers asked for restrictions against imported cards from Germany.

In the work of an architectural historian, political history seemed to illuminate the economic constraints that restricted the patron's activity and to explain the visual evidence of two different building campaigns of vastly different character.

> In 1232 there was a great riot, and the bourgeoisie rose up against the bishop. . . . One of the chronicle sources tells us that they were especially angry at the bishop for exacting taxes that were too heavy. And the riot took place . . . seven years after the start of the construction work. . . . The king intervened and ended up confiscating the bishop's income. And these . . . details suggest that the work was heavily financed by the bishop at the beginning, a crisis ensued, and then when work resumed again, it was much less fully supported. And I . . . see in the sequence of construction . . . [one] part of the building which is lavish and massive masonry and a very ambitious program [with] a very sculptural approach to the walls, and a[nother] part of the building which is clearly cost-cutting, where there are obviously shortcuts in terms of production of ornamentation and so on.

Some art historians find insights in the analysis of the stratigraphy of social and economic classes. They may investigate the habits and activities of certain classes in a specific cultural milieu. For one scholar the investigation of political and socioeconomic attitudes and conditions revealed links between an artist's subject matter and contemporary culture.

> I was going to . . . reconstruct the circumstances of Courbet's production 1848–51 and, in particular, look at what it could possibly have meant to be doing the pictures he did in '49, '50 [see fig. 27]. How did those pictures connect with that historical moment? . . . I began to work on . . . the history of the Second Republic in very much more detail, trying to tie down exactly what was happening to the peasantry and so on. . . . It must have been when I was reading the Courbet criticism that [I began to see] the business of social identity in the countryside, whether or not the people in [a certain district] were specifically and safely bourgeoisie, . . . as an issue from my general historical reading. And then I began to realize that, time and again, this indeed *was* the issue. How were [these critics] to describe these people?

The search can take in a broad range of evidence.

> I started to look at [the] wonderful wealth of antiquarian local investigation. . . . I went to the departmental archives at Besançon and did some work there. And I also worked in the Archives Nationales [in Paris with] very

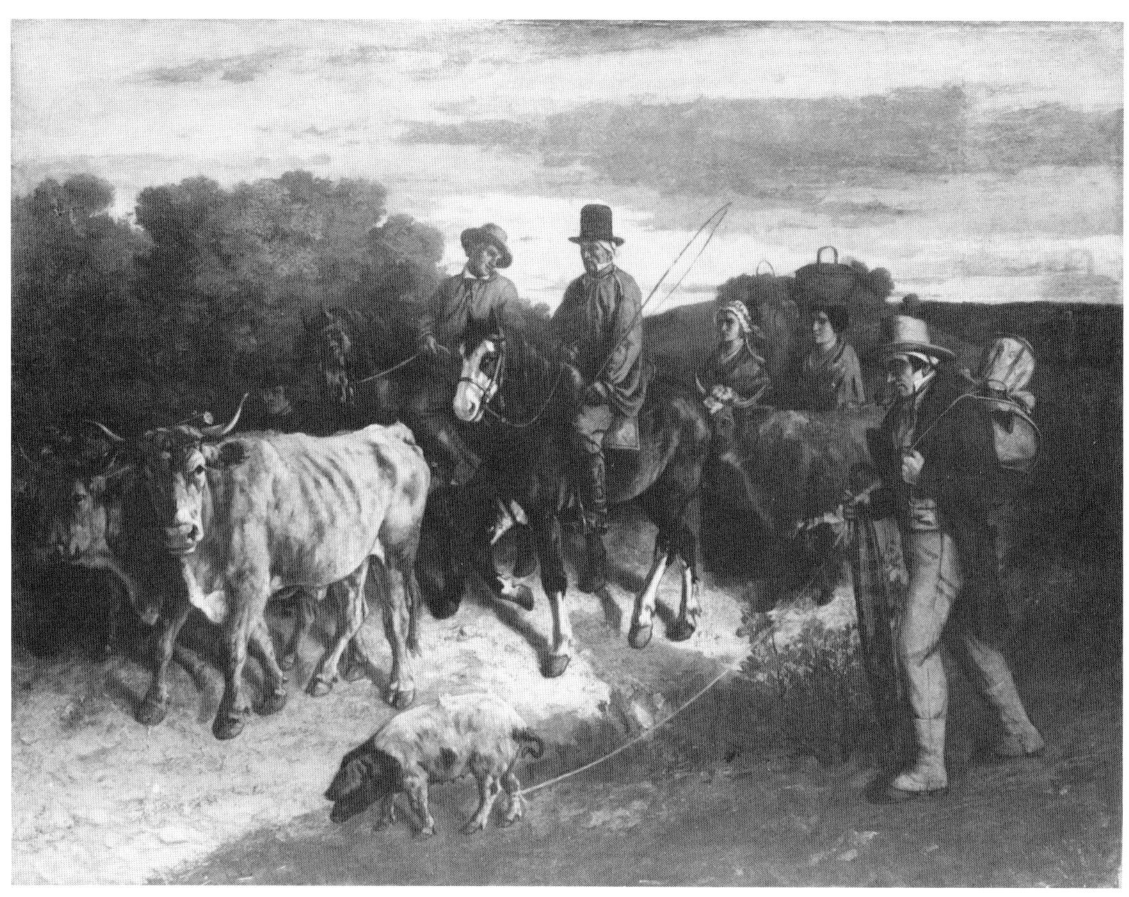

27. GUSTAVE COURBET, *Peasants of Flagey Returning from the Fair*, 1850, Musée des Beaux-Arts et d'Archéologie, Besançon, photo courtesy Charles Choffet

> standard sources like the procurer general's reports, [which] are a marvelous source. . . . [I eventually realized] how extraordinarily rich Salon criticism and newspaper response was as a resource for the kind of things I wanted to know. . . . This was the "eureka" moment, [to think] "Oh God, this reponse to Courbet in 1851 is extraordinary! People are blurting out things which really give the game away, what's at stake. So I've really got to read all this stuff . . . treat it as a discourse, comprehend it in its own right."

Yet the conduct of bibliographic research outside the history of art may be handicapped by the unfamiliar literature and indexes. It is difficult to know where to look for source material, how to organize one's search, and on what to focus one's attention.

> [Art-historical documentation] is easy for an art historian. It is more difficult when you look for documentation on the side of history—political, ecclesiastical, or economic history—because we know our libraries, and our libraries, like the Hertziana, are specialized in the history of art but not open to different fields of history.

> When I was studying about the problem of art and the Industrial Revolution, I found a wonderful paper on Wedgewood and the politics of advertising, very interesting for the kind of pictures he bought or [ordered] and also for the form of his pottery. I found this article in an economic history review; it [would have been] impossible for me to find [such an] article in an art-historical bibliography.

Working outside art history, scholars may also rely on colleagues for information.

> I'm in touch mainly with historians, [one of whom] is the best specialist on the history of war.

> I . . . met up with people at the Bibliothèque Nationale and the Archives Nationales, . . . mainly historians. . . . I learned a lot about history from them. They were all working on nineteenth-century French topics, and they were terrifically helpful.

> I talked constantly to people. . . . My discussions with art historians I found less fruitful for what I was doing than my discussions with the archivists and historians and book people.

Two scholars used archaeological models to argue for the breadth and depth of evidence that the art historian should consider.

> The notion of archaeology is one of the mental strategies that have long left their home turf and have been applied to a whole range of other investigative purposes. Just as in a sense the Second World War army button that is under the gravel of a classical site in Sicily is part of the total record of that site,

which—at some particular point in an imaginary future—might be as crucial for an understanding of twentieth-century history as is some little potsherd that is five feet further down and tells you that they at one point had Persian import pottery. . . . I think in that sense history is a continuum of discontinuities, and if the continuum gets artifically collapsed back to an interest only in those things which belong to the original moment, then you have a very impoverished picture.

Schliemann was interested in the discovery of . . . the Troy of Homer, and . . . treasures. . . . All the rest was of no interest for him. Now many archaeologists are digging in a completely different manner. They are interested in all they find, because the problem [at hand] is not [the] only thing, but [rather] . . . the story of the earth, the story of this place. And it is not so interesting to find treasure but the hidden history of the place. The same thing is perhaps possible in historical research. . . . Our manner [of reading] the sources, the documents, [should be] more . . . global.

THE CASE STUDIES

Introduction

The case studies supplied the AHIP-IRIS team with data complementary to that gathered in the interviews. While the interviews provided retrospective glimpses of diverse personal experiences, the case studies allowed us to observe two research projects over the course of six months.

SELECTION OF PARTICIPANTS ▪ To ensure the close observation and frequent contact necessary for the case-study project, the selection of participants was made from the art history faculty of Brown University. Professors Rolf Winkes and Juergen Schulz agreed to begin new research projects under the observation of IRIS's Office of Program Analysis.

THE CASE-STUDY PROCESS ▪ Each professor was given the use of a half-time research assistant whose primary responsibility was to carry out whatever tasks would facilitate the research process. The assistants were further responsible for maintaining daily records in the form of task sheets (see appendix 5) detailing the separate steps of the research process as they occurred. The art historians too agreed to use these task sheets, since the isolated nature of the work did not allow their activity to be observed by a second party.

The task sheets were submitted to the Office of Program Analysis approximately every three weeks, at which time the Bakewell-Beeman-Schmitt team interviewed the scholars and the research assistants. The participants were free to describe their activities on the task sheets as they saw fit, with no controlled vocabulary imposed prior to the beginning of the study. The interviews, however, helped to establish some level of consistency in the recording of information, as well as to clarify and deepen our understanding of the day-to-day details of the work. As was intended, the task sheets and the triweekly interviews documented details that are often forgotten as soon as they occur because of their repetitive and prosaic nature.

TREATMENT OF THE MATERIAL ▪ To help organize this material at the end of the project, the information on the task sheets was coded and put into a statistical software package called

Statview (Calabasas, Calif.: Brainpower, Inc.), which was then queried as a data base and which produced the charts in appendixes 6–10. In addition we excerpted and filed narrative passages from the task sheets. The following report is thus drawn from both quantitative and qualitative description.

NATURE OF THE PROJECTS ▪ The two projects investigated very different types of problems in different fields of art-historical specialization. Professor Winkes undertook to plan an exhibition of Roman portraiture as it appears on Roman coins, while Professor Schulz traced the evidence of a medieval building that had disappeared. Aside from the dissimilarity of content, the two projects differed in four other ways that had important consequences for the gathering, organization, and use of information.

First, they had dissimilar goals. On the one hand, Winkes's Roman portraiture and numismatics project was to lead to a museum exhibition, an exhibition catalogue, and an automated data base of information on Roman coins. Schulz's architectural research, on the other hand, was to contribute to a larger study for a publication on thirteenth-century Venetian palaces. Exhibitions, catalogues of works of art, and interpretive monographs are all principal products of art-historical research; thus the two projects offered a cross section of concerns important to the field as a whole. It should be noted that both projects were parts of long-term endeavors continuing far beyond the case-study period.

Second, the research teams assembled for each project functioned differently, allowing us to observe contrasting interaction and divisions of labor among the participants. Winkes chose to divide the half-time position and hired two quarter-time research assistants. He structured the work of his team as a collaborative operation, in which each member was responsible for distinct areas of research that were eventually integrated. Communication facilitated by frequent meetings formed an important base for the project's accomplishments. In contrast, Schulz hired one research assistant, whose combination of strong linguistic skills and inexperience with art-historical research required a more hierarchical structure. Directed to materials chosen by Schulz, the assistant collected all possible references to the subject, which were then screened by Schulz. Thus the operation was two-tiered, with a "gross" filter at the primary level and a "fine" filter at the expert level.

Third, the projects relied on different kinds of sources. The participants in Winkes's project gathered information from readily available—for the most part—secondary sources such as museum catalogues and other standard references that they collectively identified. This process relied heavily on communication with librarians and professional colleagues. Schulz's project turned to more esoteric sources, specifically primary documents published in transcription in relatively obscure collections and in the notes and appendixes of historical studies. Schulz himself had previously identified these through indexes of many types, bibliographies, and secondary sources. Schulz's mastery of bibliographic searching techniques obviated the use of intermediaries, giving him the role of reference librarian in his own project (see appendix 8, which tabulates the involvement of others in Schulz's research activities).

Fourth, Winkes's team was involved in the automation of information, while Schulz processed information manually. While the participants in the Roman portraiture and numismatics project recorded some information manually, they gradually assembled data in established cataloguing categories to create an automated "neutral" data base for general access. They entered on disks the classified material according to a preexisting bibliographic data-base program, which they modified to conform to categories that fit the project (see "Roman Portraiture and Numismatics: Use of Computer Technology," for details). In addition Winkes relied on BITNET, an electronic network to which Brown University belongs, to communicate with his exhibition collaborators in Belgium. Therefore, in its use of electronic communications and data-base tools for data entry, Winkes's project was comparatively sophisticated for a research effort in the humanities, although data gathering still followed traditional library research methods. More typical of standard practice, Schulz used photocopies extensively and traveled regularly to other libraries in search of elusive documents. Because the final product, a book, was to be the sole point of general access to the research results, Schulz filed his photocopies as well as handwritten bibliographic and research notes in his personal library according to his own classification scheme.

Roman Portraiture and Numismatics

THE SUBJECT OF INQUIRY ▪ Rolf Winkes, professor of classical art and archaeology at Brown University,[1] undertook a research project to develop an exhibition on Roman portraiture and its relationship to numismatics (see figs. 28 and 29). Scheduled to open in the Bell Gallery on the Brown campus in Providence, Rhode Island, in 1989, the exhibition will travel to Brussels, Belgium, and São Paulo, Brazil. Two publications will accompany the exhibition: a handbook for the public and a scholarly catalogue. Anthony Hackens, a numismatist at the Institut Supérieur in Louvain la Neuve, near Brussels, will be in charge of publishing these works, while Brown University faculty and students will be responsible for the organization of the exhibition.

The purposes of the exhibition and the publications are threefold: first, to document and reproduce unpublished Roman coins from the collections of Brown University and the Royal Cabinet in Brussels as well as from various collections in São Paolo; second, to bring together geographically dispersed coins and to publicize through scholarly analysis the latest methods of identification, classification, and analysis of Roman portraits; and third, to provide museological training for graduate students in both classics and art history at Brown University.

PERSONNEL ▪ Winkes chose Nina Duncan and Kelly Kamborian to share the half-time research position provided him through the AHIP-IRIS study. Both Duncan and Kamborian were first-year graduate students in the classics department and brought to the project indispensable language skills in German, Ancient Greek, and Latin. Their enrollment in Professor R. Ross Holloway's concurrent numismatics course helped them develop ancillary bibliography and understanding of the field during the course of the project.

Nevertheless the assistantship of twenty hours per week (January to June 1986) allowed only enough time to begin work on the exhibition. Such a complex undertaking,

1. Winkes is director of the Center for Old-World Archaeology and Art (COWAA). While the AHIP-IRIS study was under way, he served as acting director of COWAA.

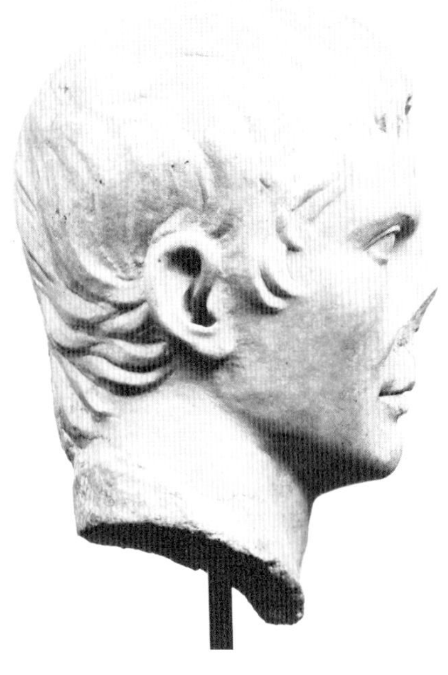

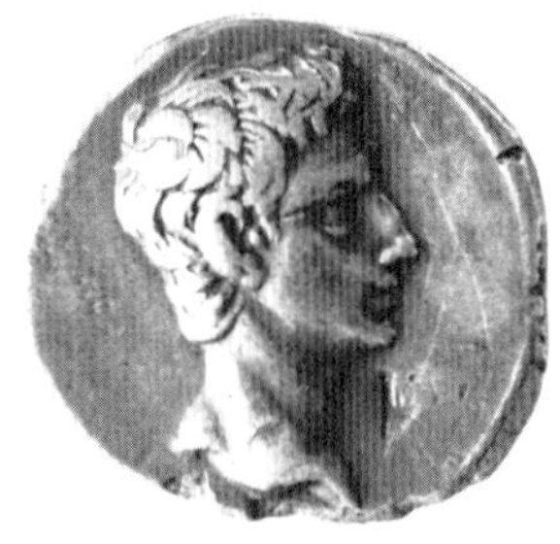

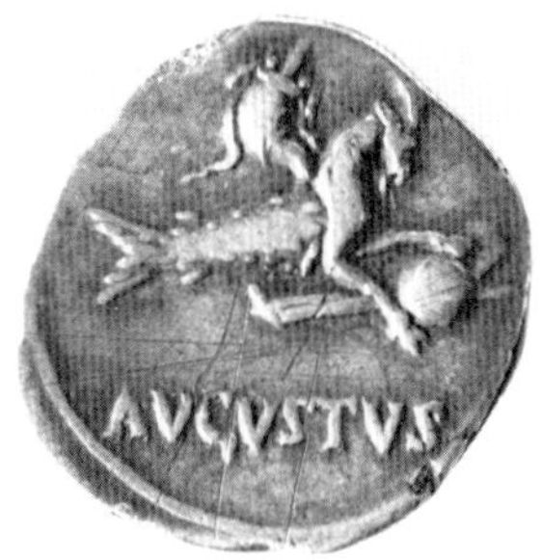

29. SILVER DENARIUS (obverse left and reverse right), mint of Emerita, Spain, circa 22–19 B.C., Brown University, Providence, Rhode Island (Harkness Collection)

28. PORTRAIT HEAD OF AUGUSTUS, early first century A.D., The J. Paul Getty Museum, Malibu

which involves the study of unpublished material as well as the cooperation of institutions in different countries, requires a significant investment of time. Winkes's master plan scheduled an organizational lead time of three years from the inception of the project under the aegis of the AHIP-IRIS study to the opening of the exhibition in Providence (February 1989). Moreover he factored into the project's calendar the participation of other graduate students for two additional semesters during the academic year 1988–89. These students would see the project through its later phases as they fulfilled the requirements for a yearlong museum methods course required of all candidates seeking a master's degree in the history of art at Brown University.

RESEARCH ACTIVITIES: THE ASSISTANTS[2] ▪ For her part Duncan worked to develop a list of commemorative coins to include in the exhibition, specifically coins with portraits that dated from the first century B.C. through the fourth century A.D. (Augustan to Constantinian periods) and that came from collections in Belgium, Brazil, and the eastern United States

2. See appendix 6, "Participants' Activities," and appendix 7, "Purposes of Activities." These tables analyze the number of times each activity was performed and length of time each took in terms of the participants' total contributions to the project. See also the graphs in appendix 10, "Analysis of Hours by Month," which show the periods of occurrence and durations of the participants' activities between January and May 1986.

and Canada (the Philadelphia-to-Montreal corridor). At the same time she prepared a general index of Roman portraits in order to choose comparative material for exhibition with the coins.

To develop the exhibition checklist and comparative index, Duncan first searched for collections of Roman coins in museums worldwide. She found it difficult to locate such holdings because published guides such as the *International Directory of Arts*, *Museums of the World*, and *The Official Museum Directory* did not consistently use "coins" as a subdivision under the subject heading "classical art." While the detailed appendix in Cornelius Vermeule's *Greek and Roman Portraits in North American Collections Open to the Public* (Philadelphia, 1964) was useful in compiling comparative portraiture material, it neglected numismatic portraits altogether. Therefore Duncan listed classical collections in general as possible sources. Then she indexed information on portraits in these collections by consulting whatever museum catalogues were available.

Concurrently Duncan undertook a preliminary selection of coins for the exhibition from Brown's Harkness and Bishop collections. Former graduate students had catalogued these coins, indicating moneyer, weight, and reference number from Edward Allen Sydenham's *The Coinage of the Roman Republic* (London, 1952). Although Roman coins were handmade and are therefore unique objects, they were produced in series, so that information about a single coin applies to a group. Duncan used a second catalogue, Michael H. Crawford's *Roman Republican Coinage* (London, 1974), to corroborate the references from Sydenham and as a source of more recent scholarly opinions about controversial aspects of coin classification, namely dating. The identification of the subjects of numismatic portraits on the coins in Brown's collections posed occasional problems for Duncan as well, for some portraits that seemed to represent historical figures in fact represented mythological characters.

Duncan was able to supplement her work with the Brown coins through trips to see the displayed coin collections of Harvard's Fogg Art Museum and Boston's Museum of Fine Arts. These institutions were close to where she lived and worked, and thus travel to them was not costly in terms of time or money. Finally, it should be noted that none of the three participants traveled further from Providence than Boston to perform the activities documented for the AHIP-IRIS study,[3] although Winkes planned research trips to Brazil and Europe in conjunction with his role as organizer of the exhibition (see below).

---

3. See appendix 9, "Locations of Activities."

Kamborian meanwhile assembled a comprehensive general bibliography of secondary source material that complemented Duncan's index.[4] The bibliography was to address not only issues of numismatic classification—such as denomination, material, mint, and date—but also questions of the analysis of portraits, such as the sitter's identification and attributes, inscription, and the relationship of the portrait on the obverse of the coin to the image on the reverse. Convinced as he was that portraits on coins cannot be studied in isolation, Winkes charged Kamborian with identifying a broad range of bibliographic sources. Because coins are an integral part of the abundant legacy of Roman portraits produced in widely varied media, such as marbles, bronzes, gemstones, cameos, and architectural reliefs in stone, Winkes asked Kamborian to consider as potential sources of information any studies dealing with late Republican and Imperial portraiture.

Kamborian first turned to the syllabus of Dr. Holloway's numismatics course for references and added to them references from the *Bibliographie zum Jahrbuch des deutschen archäologischen Instituts*, a thorough guide to literature in old-world archaeology. Winkes's research for a book on the portraiture of the women of the Augustan house provided her with further sources, and as she delved into the material, she amplified the bibliography with other promising citations. For both research assistants meetings with Winkes provided opportunities not only to coordinate efforts but also to learn more about the nature and conduct of art-historical research.

RESEARCH ACTIVITIES: THE PRINCIPAL SCHOLAR[5] ▪ While Kamborian compiled bibliographic data, Winkes read and evaluated the secondary sources that she identified. The relationship between their activities can perhaps best be described as reciprocal. Since Winkes was especially interested in recent articles and books that emphasized such methodological

---

4. In appendix 6 the searches for specific articles and books are listed as "bibliographic searching 1," and less specific searches for material on given topics as "bibliographic searching 2." Although Winkes delegated the task of building a bibliography to Kamborian, both research assistants contributed to the activity, as the data presented in appendixes 6 and 7 makes clear. Duncan and Kamborian also compiled the bibliography, index, and checklist through activities designated as "searching for works of art" in appendix 6. The activities in this category included the visual study of materials such as slides, published reproductions, and objects on display.

5. See appendix 6, "Participants' Activities"; appendix 7, "Purposes of Activities"; and appendix 10, "Analysis of Hours by Month."

strategies for the study of portraits as iconography, typology, and symbolic content, he pursued these studies himself, adding to the bibliography.[6] Often his research in the source material led him to change his instructions to Kamborian about the kind of material that she was to gather. For example, a number of articles on portrait types suggested that the key to deciphering typological meaning might be found in studies of Roman society.

Winkes's research also affected the direction of Duncan's work. Initially he asked her to compile a corpus that would include only numismatic and freestanding marble portraits. Readings on the role of medallions in Roman portraiture and on the relationship between imperial images on coins and in sculptures, however, convinced him to enlarge the search to encompass portraits in other media as well. Thus, in the early stages of the organization of the exhibition, the research process was fluid, and activities were open-ended, requiring regular and frequent communication between Winkes and his research assistants. As the definition of the project broadened, the assistants felt some frustration about revisions in their assignments.

Although Winkes devoted the majority of his time on the project to analyzing and expanding the bibliography that Kamborian developed, he also spent time writing letters and making telephone calls that his role as organizer of the exhibition demanded. Such direct personal communication, however, he saw as a last resort, not to be exploited until research efforts had exhausted generally available information.

ORIGINAL WORKS OF ART ▪ Winkes concluded that the organization of the exhibition would require that he make a trip to Brazil to see collections firsthand. Neither photographic reproductions nor written descriptions, no matter how thorough, could substitute for personal observation. For the same reason it would be necessary that his colleague at the University of São Paulo's Museum for Archaeology and Ethnology, Research Assistant Dr. Maria Beatriz Borba Florenzano, come to Brown as a visiting scholar to work with the university's collections herself.

Winkes also planned to travel to Europe in the summer of 1986 to see two portrait exhibitions in order to familiarize himself with methods for displaying portraits. While in Europe he would study certain Roman portraits in French and German museums that are either unpublished or inadequately published.

---

6. Winkes left searches for specific items to his assistants, participating only in the topical searches.

ORGANIZATION OF INFORMATION ▪ Kamborian wrote bibliographical citations on file cards. Duncan collected data on file cards as well, designating one card for each portrait indexed. The name of the individual portrayed was the primary heading by which she filed these cards. Additional information that she noted included the current location of the portrait and its museum accession number as well as any of the following data that was available: the date and location of manufacture, name of the ruler during whose reign the portrait was made, medium, and function. If the portrait was on a coin, Duncan also listed the subject of the reverse side, the denomination, and the name of the moneyer. Whenever possible she included a detailed description of the image and any inscription. She assigned unidentifiable portraits to a subject heading entitled "varia."

USE OF COMPUTER TECHNOLOGY ▪ During the course of the portraiture project, both Kamborian and Duncan entered the information that they compiled into a data-base program on the mainframe computer at Brown University. The software that they used was the Bibliographic Management System for Scholars (BMSS), developed by an English professor at Brown, James Coombs. Because this software was for bibliographic materials, it required revision for use in portrait classification. To enter information on numismatic portraits, for example, the bibliographic categories "year," "author," "title," and "publisher" became "date," "ruler," "obverse image" (identity of sitter), and "reverse image" (iconographic subject matter), respectively. In other words, information fields acquired new definitions. The postfields (repeating fields) of "author," "title," and "publisher" became "date of reign," "mint," and "medium," respectively, while the categories "status" and "call number" translated as "location" and "accession number." The "abstract" field of the BMSS program metamorphosed in the portraiture project as a field devoted to transcriptions of legends and identifications of allegorical figures, which could be searched by key words.

In addition, at an early stage in the project, the participants organized information concerning typologies of portraits in an unusual way, using the graphics program MacPaint. Their typological chart rendered visual, and thus easily accessible, the differences of opinion about the relationships and distinctions among portraits. The MacPaint software also facilitated the retrieval of connections between various authors' opinions and portraits. Later, when this information was incorporated in the data-base program, the MacPaint chart became obsolete.

Computer technology has contributed further to the project through the rapid communications made possible by electronic mail. Brown University participates in BITNET, an electronic communications network used by academic institutions in North America.

When the Institut Supérieur in Belgium was recently connected to BITNET, Winkes and his collaborator Anthony Hackens could relay information about the exhibition informally and quickly. For example, Winkes sent Hackens exhibition data that had been entered on BMSS through electronic mail for his comments. In the same manner Hackens will send Winkes the list of Belgian coins to be included in the exhibition together with the accompanying descriptions.

SECONDARY SOURCES AND LIBRARIES ▪ Kamborian faced a complex and challenging assignment in assembling the wide-ranging bibliography that Winkes desired. Bibliographic searches can be exasperating, especially for a beginning graduate student. A single example serves to illuminate the difficulties that she encountered, especially in searching for information published abroad on foreign collections.

A Brazilian numismatist cited informally in a letter a work by Bernardo Ramos published by the Accademia Nazionale dei Lincei in Rome in 1900. Kamborian consulted the *Union List of Serials* and found a number of Accademia Nazionale dei Lincei publications, but none seemed a logical source. Thinking that the citation might refer to a book, she consulted the pre-1956 author index of the Library of Congress. This provided titles under the name Ramos but no book on Roman coins in Brazil. Returning to the list of Accademia Nazionale dei Lincei publications that she had copied from the *Union List of Serials*, she asked a librarian to help her locate them.[7] Although she then found several of the Accademia's serials in the Brown card catalogue, certain factors frustrated her search for the Ramos article. She found the *Monumenti antichi* in the Science Library but discovered the volume for 1900 missing from the shelf. Other Accademia publications, such as the *Classe di scienze morali, storiche e filologiche: Rendiconti*, lacked tables of contents, so that she had to leaf through volumes to look for the article. Hoping that another source might cite the Ramos article, she consulted the card catalogue under the subject headings "coinage, Brazilian" and "coinage, Roman" but found nothing of help.[8]

---

7. Project participants noted the involvement of others, such as reference librarians, in their research efforts on the task sheets. The frequency and duration of such occurrences formed the basis of calculations tabulated in appendix 8.

8. We were not altogether successful in eliciting responses on the task sheets (see appendix 5) to our request for information in the category "subject heading(s) used for search." We speculated, therefore, that the participants sometimes approached searches intuitively and had difficulty reconstructing the steps that they had taken.

She searched the *Bibliographie zum Jahrbuch des deutschen archäologischen Instituts* for references that might assist her, again without success. A call to a reference librarian at Harvard also proved fruitless. Kamborian ended the search, frustrated. It is likely that she did not exploit all the resources that might have been available to her through Brown's library system because she was relatively inexperienced. Nevertheless it is important to reiterate that the project offered crucial learning experiences to both research assistants.

POSTSCRIPT ▪ Although the exhibition itself will be an ephemeral event, Winkes hopes that the research for it and its accompanying publications will make lasting contributions to the field. The exhibition's emphasis on the iconographic and symbolic content of numismatic portraits is new to the field of Roman numismatic studies. Moreover the data base created on BMSS will enable other scholars to examine further the relationships between portraits, biography, iconography, and allegory.

The Palais du Tau

THE SUBJECT OF INQUIRY ▪ Juergen Schulz, professor of the history of art at Brown University,[1] undertook a project to establish the form and determine the history of the late eleventh- or early twelfth-century archiepiscopal palace of Reims, the residence of the archbishop in a major religious and political center of medieval France. A seventeenth-century archiepiscopal palace had replaced the medieval one (see figs. 30 and 31), and little physical or documentary trace of the so-called Palais du Tau appears to have remained.

Schulz's interest in the Palais du Tau stemmed in part from its possible relationship to thirteenth-century Venetian palaces, which he is studying for a book on the subject. Although the architectural sources, date of construction, general plan, and detailed functional aspects of the Palais du Tau are unknown, a T-shaped hall is believed to have formed a portion of the building. T-shaped halls are common to Venetian palaces of the thirteenth century, but their source and meaning remain unexplained. The Palais du Tau may thus have served as a precedent for later Venetian palaces, together with a second twelfth-century palace in France, the Palace of Angers, a monument that has been investigated.

Schulz joined our project having read extensively in the secondary literature on medieval Reims and the architecture of the city. This literature mentioned the Palais du Tau, but only briefly and without bibliographic citations. From secondary sources Schulz gleaned these facts: the building was first mentioned under its present name in a charter of Louis VII of 1138; the main hall was T-shaped; the residential portion was partly rebuilt in the Renaissance and entirely rebuilt in 1690; and, finally, a medieval chapel survived, the upper portion of which dated to the thirteenth century, while the crypt was somewhat earlier.

Notwithstanding these sparse, repetitive, and undocumented references, Schulz hoped to reconstruct the history and form of the Palais du Tau through published and unpublished archival documents. He determined to comb charters, deeds, acts, and chronicles for references to the building. In particular he wanted to read such documents as charters

1. During the AHIP-IRIS study Schulz was art history director in the art department.

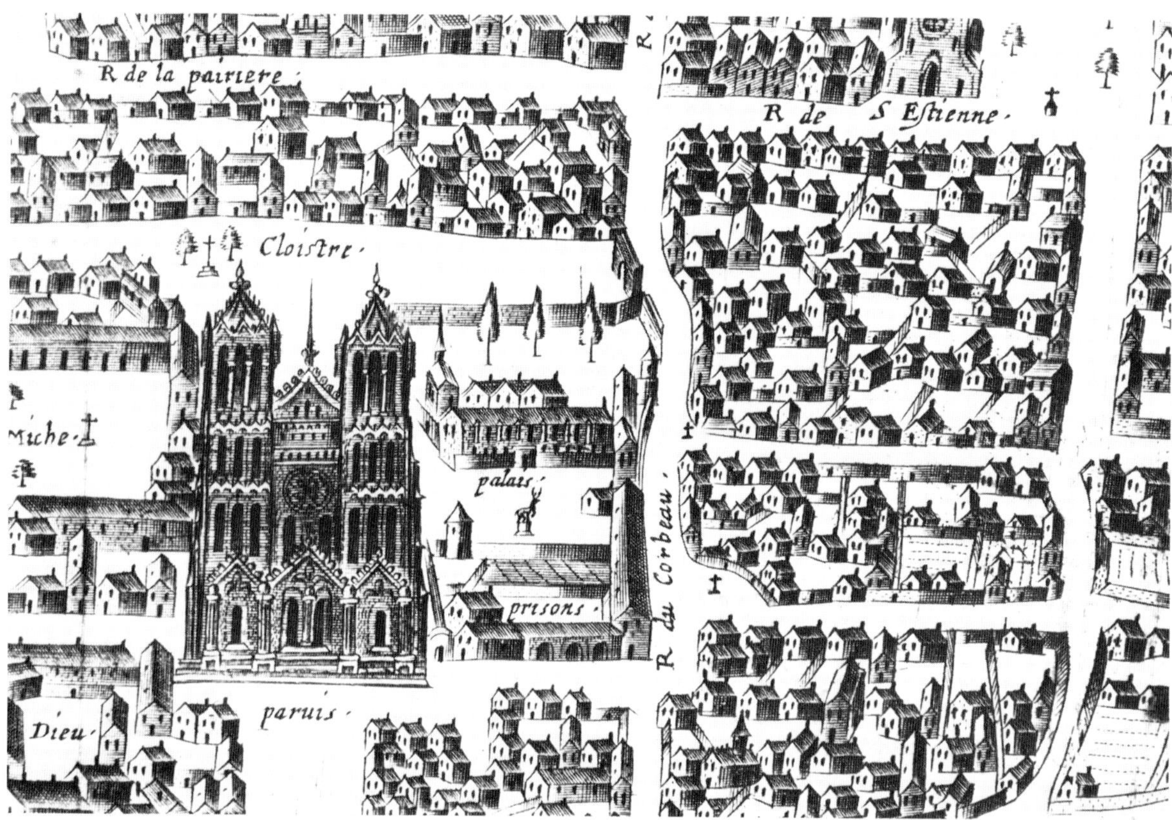

30. JACQUES CELLIER, *Portrait of the City Center and University of Reims* (detail), 1618–19, Bibliothèque Municipale, Reims, photo courtesy Juergen Schulz

issued at Reims, especially by the archbishops and members of their household; records of church councils and synods as well as descriptions of royal coronations and visits in Reims that might have involved the Palais du Tau; narrative histories of medieval Reims; and biographies of early Remois notables.

PERSONNEL ▪ Schulz chose as his research assistant Robert Mitchell, a graduate student in classics. Mitchell's knowledge of Latin and French was appropriate for the textual focus of the project, although he had not worked specifically in medieval documents, art history, or history.

RESEARCH ACTIVITIES: THE ASSISTANT[2] ▪ To introduce Mitchell to the art-historical problem, Schulz spent a session summarizing his research to date on the Palais du Tau and showing

2. See appendix 6, "Participants' Activities"; appendix 7, "Purposes of Activities"; and appendix 10, "Analysis of Hours by Month," for information on the types of tasks that Mitchell performed and their frequency and duration.

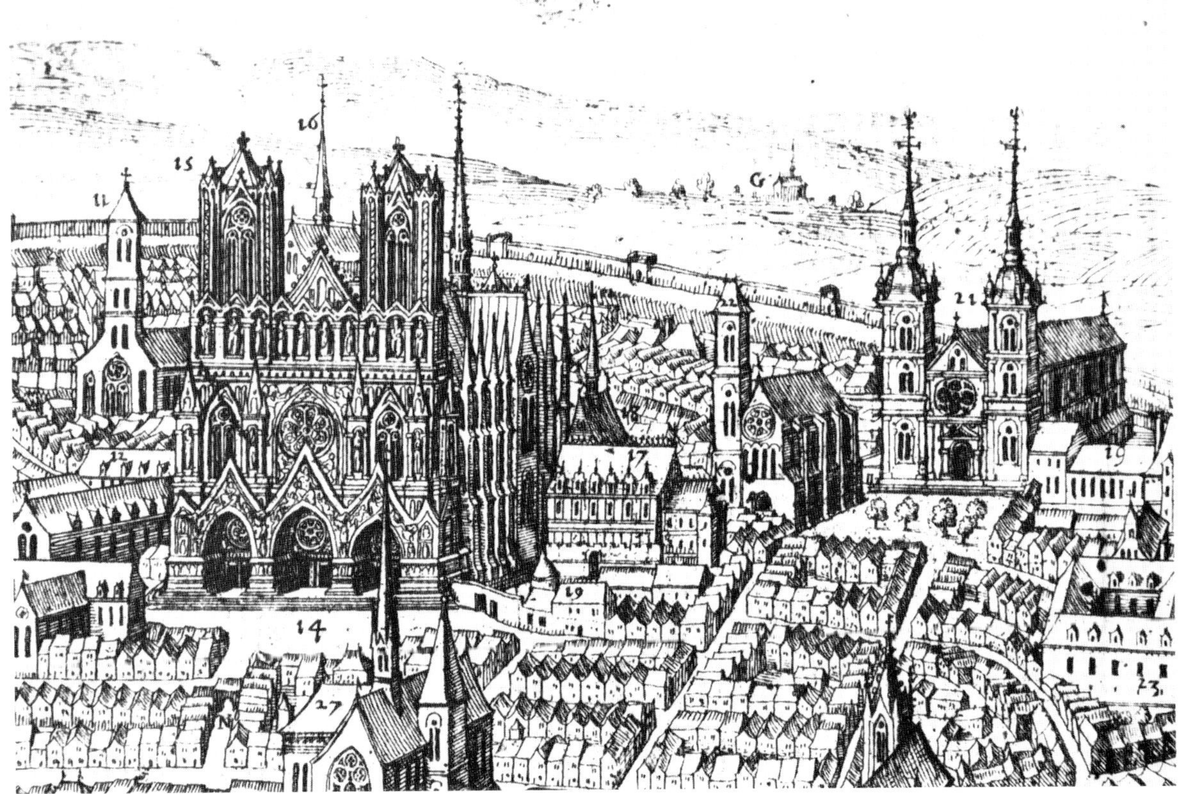

31. EDNE. MOREAU, *Accurate Portrait of the City Center and University of Reims* (detail), 1622, Bibliothèque Municipale, Reims, photo courtesy Juergen Schulz

slides of the existing seventeenth-century palace. Schulz then gave Mitchell a preliminary bibliography that he had prepared before this study began (see below). Mitchell's primary task was to read systematically through published transcriptions of acts and charters (included in four corpuses comprising nineteen volumes), from which he was to extract references to the palace, archiepiscopal palace, or Palais du Tau in Reims. Mitchell then was to photocopy pertinent passages and submit them to Schulz for review and filing.

RESEARCH ACTIVITIES: THE PRINCIPAL SCHOLAR[3] ▪ To prepare the bibliography given Mitchell, Schulz had worked in several American libraries, notably the Rockefeller Library at Brown University, the New York Public Library, the Widener Library at Harvard University, and the Sterling Memorial Library at Yale University. Schulz began at his own institution, where

3. See appendix 6, "Participants' Activities"; appendix 7, "Purposes of Activities"; and appendix 10, "Analysis of Hours by Month," for information on the types of tasks that Schulz performed and their frequency and duration.

he was fortunate to have access to an excellent collection of materials on Reims collected by Burr Litchfield, professor of history at Brown, during his studies of the history of the city's population.

PRIMARY AND SECONDARY SOURCES ▪ In the reference section of the Brown library, Schulz consulted a variety of sources, searching under various categories: in Eugene Paul Sheehy's *Guide to Reference Books*, under the heading "France"; in the printed library catalogues of the British Museum and the Bibliothèque Nationale, under both "Reims" and "Rheims"; and in the *National Union Catalogue*, where he found Reims in a separate volume devoted to the heading "Catholic Church." In addition he searched the general card catalogue of the Rockefeller Library. Traveling to New York, Cambridge, and New Haven, he conducted similar searches in the card catalogues of the New York Public Library and the libraries of Harvard and Yale universities, under the subject heading "Reims." References that Schulz found in all these libraries led him not only to specific histories of Reims and its monuments but also to more general histories of the Catholic church, northern European urbanism, medieval France, and French architecture, widening the search for primary and secondary materials.

ORGANIZATION OF INFORMATION ▪ Under the aegis of the AHIP-IRIS collaborative study, which began in January of 1986, Schulz continued his search for references through the spring semester and into the summer. As he worked, he recorded information manually, following a system that he had developed early in his career. He listed bibliographic citations on three-by-five-inch cards, which he then filed in cardboard boxes. He interfiled notes, photocopies, and some photographs in larger, letter-sized boxes. A common set of headings, developed by Schulz and periodically revised and reordered, classified materials in both files. Duplicate cards facilitated cross-referencing.

SECONDARY SOURCES AND LIBRARIES ▪ Digging deeper, Schulz extended his bibliography through the indexes, bibliographies, and footnotes of volumes whose citations seemed particularly promising. In one session (documented on a task sheet) at the New York Public Library, for example, he located and read three such references, with fairly disappointing results. He found that (1) an inventory of monuments in Reims dealt with churches only; (2) a history of the Reims Cathedral chapter contained no mention of the Palais du Tau; and (3) a history of the topography of Reims offered only one new bibliographic citation.

A single example illustrates both the investigative expertise that Schulz brought to the project and the complex problem posed by the necessity of tracking widely scattered materials. (See appendix 9, "Locations of Activities," for information about the places where Mitchell and Schulz worked; of 109 works consulted, 74 were unavailable at Brown; these were dispersed among libraries at Harvard, Princeton, and Yale and the New York Public Library, showing that no single library in this group would have served as a comprehensive source.) At Brown, in the catalogue of the Bibliothèque Nationale of Paris, he checked the citations listed for authors whom he knew had written on Remois history. Under Henri Jadart (a prolific writer on the subject), Schulz discovered the title of a book on the Palais du Tau, *Le palais archiépiscopal du Reims* (1908), which had not appeared in the literature that he had previously investigated. Since the *National Union Catalogue* contained no listing of this title, Schulz expected that it would not be readily accessible. Brown's interlibrary loan office, however, found the title in the catalogue of the Metropolitan Museum Library in New York. A telephone inquiry determined that the book was missing. Schulz picked up the trail of Jadart when he happened upon a complete run of the *Annuaire-bulletin, Société des amis du vieux Reims* in the stacks of the Widener Library at Harvard University. Reading each issue's table of contents, he found an obituary for Jadart, who had died in 1921. Guessing that the death of a local scholar would be noticed by other local learned societies, and perhaps occasion the publication of a bibliography of his writings, Schulz searched for and found such a compilation in the *Travaux, Académie nationale de Reims* of 1921. In this bibliography was the correct description of the elusive work; it had been an article in the same journal's volume for 1905–6. The "book" listed in the Bibliothèque Nationale catalogue turned out to be an offprint of a long article, catalogued in Paris (at the Bibiothèque Nationale) and New York (in the Metropolitan Museum Library) as if it were a book.

PRIMARY DOCUMENTS AND ARCHIVES ▪ In addition to expanding his bibliography and evaluating source materials, Schulz read further in modern histories of medieval Reims. Because the texts of medieval acts are often published in the footnotes and appendixes of secondary sources, Schulz anticipated that he might find helpful transcriptions there. While these published medieval documents varied widely in subject matter—from the archbishops in their unusual role as counts of Reims, to Remois churchmen and church acts, and to the kings of France and their royal acts—they represented only a sampling of the archival material to be consulted on-site in Paris and Reims. In preparation for a research trip abroad, Schulz combed inventories and indexes to collections in Paris and Reims that were available in this country, looking for citations of documents that might be helpful later.

TIME AND RESEARCH ACTIVITIES ▪ Schulz's work was continually interrupted and intermittently pushed aside altogether by administrative responsibilities and teaching demands, especially at the end of the semester. The months of June and July, however, were quite productive despite the university library's short summer hours, which sometimes delayed research.

Letter writing occupied a certain portion of Schulz's research time. He wrote letters to colleagues about the Palais du Tau project. He also made inquiries to the American consul in Paris as well as to archivists and librarians in both Paris and Reims about conducting research in France.

POSTSCRIPT ▪ Armed with his bibliography of primary and secondary sources and excerpted passages that Mitchell compiled, Schulz planned to spend August 1986 in France consulting documents unavailable to him in the United States. In the Bibliothèque Nationale and the Musée Municipal and Bibliothèque Municipale of Reims, he wanted to study topographical paintings, prints, and drawings of Reims and hoped to locate manuscripts relating to the archbishopric of Reims. He intended to review the restoration reports and drawings held by the office of Monuments Historiques in both Paris and Reims and to consult documents and drawings in the Archives Municipales and Archives Départementales at Reims. Finally, he wanted to examine photographs of the existing archiepiscopal palace and chapel as well as the physical remains of the original palace.

APPENDIXES

APPENDIX 1

LIST OF SCHOLARS INTERVIEWED

NAME	PLACE OF WORK	TYPE OF INSTITUTION	SPECIALIZATION
Enrico Castelnuovo	Scuola Normale Superiore, Pisa	University	Medieval through 19th-century art, politics, industrialization
T. J. Clark	Harvard University, Cambridge, Massachusetts (Fall, 1987: University of California, Berkeley)	University	19th- and 20th-century art
Jennifer Fletcher	Courtauld Institute, London	University	16th-century Italian painting and patronage
Kurt W. Forster	The Getty Center for the History of Art and the Humanities, Santa Monica, California	Research center	Architecture, Italian Renaissance painting
Thomas Gaehtgens	Freie Universität, Berlin	University	16th- through 20th-century painting and architecture
Ernst H. Gombrich	Warburg Institute, University of London (emeritus)	Research center	Renaissance art, psychology of art
Fritz Koreny	Graphische Sammlung Albertina, Vienna	Museum	15th- and 16th-century prints, drawings, and paintings
Rosalind Krauss	Hunter College and the Graduate Center, City University of New York	University	20th-century painting and sculpture; criticism
James Marrow	University of California, Berkeley	University	Medieval manuscripts, iconography
Jennifer Montagu	Warburg Institute, University of London	Research center	17th-century Italian sculpture
Stephen Murray	Columbia University, New York (Until 1986: Indiana University, Bloomington)	University	Gothic architecture in France
Françoise Perrot	C.N.R.S., Paris; Center for Study of Stained Glass, Chartres	Research center	Medieval and modern stained glass

APPENDIX 1 *continued*

LIST OF SCHOLARS INTERVIEWED

NAME	PLACE OF WORK	TYPE OF INSTITUTION	SPECIALIZATION
Donald Preziosi	State University of New York, Binghampton (Fall 1986: University of California, Los Angeles)	University	Ancient architecture; semiotics
William Rubin (and Judith Cousins)	Museum of Modern Art, New York	Museum	20th-century painting and sculpture
Juergen Schulz	Brown University, Providence, Rhode Island	University	Italian medieval architecture, Italian Renaissance painting
Gary Schwartz	Maarssen, The Netherlands	Independent scholar; publisher	Patronage of Dutch art
Nancy Troy	Northwestern University, Evanston, Illinois	University	Early 20th-century decorative arts
John Walsh	J. Paul Getty Museum, Malibu, California	Museum	17th-century Dutch painting

APPENDIX 2

SCHEDULE OF INTERVIEWS

(All Dates 1986)

February 12	New York	Stephen Murray
February 15, 16	New York	Donald Preziosi
April 2	New York	William Rubin
April 17, 18	Santa Monica, California	Thomas Gaehtgens
April 18, 19	Santa Monica, California	James Marrow
April 21, 22	Malibu and Santa Monica, California	John Walsh
April 23	Santa Monica, California	Kurt W. Forster
May 19, 20	Cambridge, Massachusetts	T. J. Clark
May 28, 29	Paris	Enrico Castelnuovo
May 28, 29	Paris	Françoise Perrot
May 30	Paris	Rosalind Krauss
June 2	London	Jennifer Montagu
June 3	London	Ernst H. Gombrich
June 4, 5	London	Gary Schwartz
June 5, 6	London	Fritz Koreny
June 6	London	Jennifer Fletcher
July 2, 3	Providence, Rhode Island	Juergen Schulz
July 2, 3	Providence, Rhode Island	Nancy Troy
November 14	New York	Judith Cousins (for William Rubin)

APPENDIX 3

CATEGORIES USED IN CODING INTERVIEW DATA

FORMATIVE EXPERIENCES

Relatives and family influence
Primary school
Secondary school
Other

COLLEGE AND GRADUATE EDUCATION

Undergraduate educational experiences
Graduate educational experiences
Interest in and contact with art history
Seminars and classes
First research/dissertation
Mentors
Other

PERSONAL AND PROFESSIONAL DEVELOPMENT

Contact with original works of art
Professionalism
Career turning points
Travel
Foreign language acquisition
Extradisciplinary studies and experience
Other skills and interests (nonacademic)
Aesthetic experiences
Other

GATHERING OF INFORMATION

Use of archives
Use of library and bibliographic resources
On-site observation of original works of art
Use of primary literature and texts
Use of surrogate materials (photographs, slides, prints, drawings, reproductions in books, microfilm, etc.)
Background to information gathering (atmosphere of the site, etc.)
Use of secondary literature
Use of intermediaries (librarians, archivists, research assistants, executors, etc.)
Use of interviews (with artists and others)
Other

ANALYTICAL TECHNIQUES

Connoisseurship
Formal and stylistic analysis
Criticism
Structuralism and semiotics
Iconography
Cultural history (literary, intellectual, theological, etc.)
Social history (socioeconomic, political)
Graphic analytic techniques
Analysis of materials (pigment, etc.)
Artistic biography, philosophy, theory
Use of computers in analysis
Other

ORGANIZATION AND PUBLICATION

Filing systems
The writing process
Publication
Personal collections of research materials (books, photographs, slides, microfilms, photocopies, etc.)
Other

DISCIPLINARY BACKGROUND AND CONTEXT

Building of career
Scholarly dialogue (including relations with colleagues, critical reviews, and professional meetings)
Interrelationship of work, career, and research (teaching, curatorial work, editing, etc.)
Disciplinary literature
Influence of other scholars and extra-disciplinary literature
Finances
Marriage and family
Administration and bureaucratic work
Management of research time, energy, and work conditions
Other

WISH LIST

OBSERVATIONS AND PHILOSOPHY

Personal characteristics
Development and explanation of scholarly argument

ANECDOTES AND STORIES

APPENDIX 4

CATEGORIES STUDIED FOR THIS REPORT

COLLEGE AND GRADUATE EDUCATION

Interest in and contact with art history
Seminars and classes
Mentors

PERSONAL AND PROFESSIONAL DEVELOPMENT

Contact with original works of art
Travel
Foreign language acquisition
Extradisciplinary studies and experience

GATHERING OF INFORMATION

Use of archives
Use of library and bibliographic resources
On-site observation of original works of art
Use of primary literature and texts
Use of surrogate materials (photographs, slides, prints, drawings, reproductions in books, microfilm, etc.)
Background to information gathering (atmosphere of the site, etc.)
Use of secondary literature
Use of intermediaries (librarians, archivists, research assistants, executors, etc.)
Use of interviews (with artists and others)

ANALYTICAL TECHNIQUES

Connoisseurship
Formal and stylistic analysis
Criticism
Structuralism and semiotics
Iconography
Cultural history (literary, intellectual, theological, etc.)
Social history (socioeconomic, political)
Graphic analytic techniques
Analysis of materials (pigment, etc.)
Artistic biography, philosophy, theory
Use of computers in analysis

ORGANIZATION AND PUBLICATION

Filing systems
The writing process
Publication
Personal collections of research materials (books, photographs, slides, microfilms, photocopies, etc.)

DISCIPLINARY BACKGROUND AND CONTEXT

Scholarly dialogue (including relations with colleagues, critical reviews, and professional meetings)
Interrelationship of work, career, and research (teaching, curatorial work, editing, etc.)
Disciplinary literature
Influence of other scholars and extradisciplinary literature
Finances
Administration and bureaucratic work
Management of research time, energy, and work conditions

WISH LIST

APPENDIX 5

TASK SHEET

AHIP/IRIS JOINT PROJECT: METHODS IN ART-HISTORICAL RESEARCH — INITIALS

DATE	TIME (FROM/TO)	LOCATION	TOTAL TIME ELAPSED

ACTIVITY/RESULT IF PERTINENT

☐ RESULT OR COMMENT ON BACK

SUBJECT OF INQUIRY

PURPOSE

OTHERS INVOLVED

REASON FOR TERMINATION

SUBJECT HEADING(S) USED FOR SEARCH (Photo archive/library/data-base searching)	DEGREE OF SUCCESS (1 = good, 2 = satisfactory, 3 = poor)	PLEASE EXPLAIN

APPENDIX 6

PARTICIPANTS' ACTIVITIES

	CASE STUDY 1, DUNCAN				CASE STUDY 1, KAMBORIAN			
Activity	**Tasks**	**% Tasks**	**Hours**	**% Hours**	**Tasks**	**% Tasks**	**Hours**	**% Hours**
Reading	4	3.7	6.00	3.7	4	4.6	11.50	8.1
Writing (notes, letters)	29	27.1	49.25	30.0	16	18.4	19.50	13.7
Bibliographic searching 1[a]	11	10.3	11.75	7.2	5	5.7	6.00	4.2
Bibliographic searching 2[b]	3	2.8	6.25	3.8	2	2.3	2.25	1.6
Searching for works of art	14	13.1	18.75	11.4	7	8.0	8.50	6.0
Creating a bibliography	1	.9	1.25	.8	3	3.4	5.50	3.9
Creating a list of collections	4	3.7	6.00	3.7	–	–	–	–
Locating materials in library	4	3.7	1.50	.9	6	6.9	7.75	5.4
Checking out library books	–	–	–	–	1	1.1	2.50	1.8
Verifying references	13	12.1	20.75	12.7	–	–	–	–
Photocopying	–	–	–	–	2	2.3	2.00	1.4
Meeting with others	7	6.5	4.75	2.9	23	26.4	24.50	17.2
Making telephone calls	2	1.9	.50	.3	–	–	–	–
Using computer	15	14.0	37.25	22.7	15	17.2	48.25	33.9
Organizing	–	–	–	–	2	2.3	3.00	2.1
Reflecting	–	–	–	–	1	1.1	1.00	.7
Other	–	–	–	–	–	–	–	–
Total	107	99.8	164.00	100.1	87	99.7	142.25	100.0

[a]Searching for a specific article or book
[b]Searching with a topic in mind

Note: The participants' lack of experience in defining and quantifying research activities resulted in occasional discrepancies among appendixes 6, 7, 8, 9, and 10. Mitchell's tables reveal noticeable lacunae.

CASE STUDY 1, WINKES				CASE STUDY 2, MITCHELL				CASE STUDY 2, SCHULZ			
Tasks	**% Tasks**	**Hours**	**% Hours**	**Tasks**	**% Tasks**	**Hours**	**% Hours**	**Tasks**	**% Tasks**	**Hours**	**% Hours**
29	47.5	21.00	47.2	30	88.2	105.00	90.1	6	12.5	6.50	10.2
4	6.6	4.25	9.6	–	–	–	–	5	10.4	5.00	7.9
–	–	–	–	–	–	–	–	14	29.2	22.75	35.8
2	3.3	2.50	5.6	2	5.9	5.50	4.7	12	25.0	21.25	33.5
–	–	–	–	–	–	–	–	–	–	–	–
1	1.6	.25	.6	–	–	–	–	–	–	–	–
–	–	–	–	–	–	–	–	–	–	–	–
–	–	–	–	2	5.9	6.00	5.2	3	6.3	1.00	1.6
–	–	–	–	–	–	–	–	–	–	–	–
–	–	–	–	–	–	–	–	–	–	–	–
–	–	–	–	–	–	–	–	1	2.1	.25	.4
15	24.6	5.75	12.9	–	–	–	–	6	12.5	6.25	9.8
2	3.3	.50	1.1	–	–	–	–	–	–	–	–
5	8.2	8.50	19.1	–	–	–	–	–	–	–	–
1	1.6	.50	1.1	–	–	–	–	–	–	–	–
1	1.6	1.00	2.2	–	–	–	–	–	–	–	–
1	1.6	.25	.6	–	–	–	–	1	2.1	.50	.8
61	99.9	44.50	100.0	34	100.0	116.50	100.0	48	100.1	63.50	100.0

APPENDIX 7

PURPOSES OF ACTIVITIES

Purpose	CASE STUDY 1, DUNCAN				CASE STUDY 1, KAMBORIAN			
	Tasks	**% Tasks**	**Hours**	**% Hours**	**Tasks**	**% Tasks**	**Hours**	**% Hours**
Preparing for meetings	–	–	–	–	–	–	–	–
Discussing organization and research	6	5.6	3.25	2.0	14	16.1	16.75	11.8
Seeking or giving direction	–	–	–	–	7	8.0	7.50	5.3
Seeking opinions of other scholars	–	–	–	–	1	1.1	1.25	.9
Studying methodologies	–	–	–	–	–	–	–	–
Studying typologies	–	–	–	–	–	–	–	–
Building bibliography	2	1.9	1.00	.6	8	9.2	10.50	7.4
Creating reference files	54	50.5	95.00	57.9	39	44.8	87.25	61.3
Seeking Roman portraits in collections	27	25.2	36.75	22.4	9	10.3	8.75	6.2
Determining availability of coins	5	4.7	6.25	3.8	5	5.7	7.50	5.3
Reading for content	1	.9	1.50	.9	2	2.3	.75	.5
Ordering photographs	–	–	–	–	–	–	–	–
Learning to use computer	7	6.5	11.75	7.2	1	1.1	.50	.4
Other	5	4.7	8.50	5.2	1	1.1	1.50	1.1
Total	107	100.0	164.00	100.0	87	99.7	142.25	100.2

CASE STUDY 1, WINKES				CASE STUDY 2, MITCHELL				CASE STUDY 2, SCHULZ			
Tasks	**% Tasks**	**Hours**	**% Hours**	**Tasks**	**% Tasks**	**Hours**	**% Hours**	**Tasks**	**% Tasks**	**Hours**	**% Hours**
3	4.9	2.50	5.6	–	–	–	–	–	–	–	–
9	14.8	3.75	8.4	–	–	–	–	5	10.4	4.00	6.3
5	8.2	1.25	2.8	–	–	–	–	3	6.3	3.25	5.1
1	1.6	.25	.6	–	–	–	–	–	–	–	–
18	29.5	14.00	31.5	–	–	–	–	–	–	–	–
1	1.6	.50	1.1	–	–	–	–	–	–	–	–
3	4.9	2.75	6.2	3	8.8	8.00	6.9	35	72.9	51.25	80.7
4	6.6	8.00	18.0	2	5.9	6.00	5.2	1	2.1	.50	.8
3	4.9	1.00	2.2		–	–	–	–	–	–	–
–	–	–	–	–	–	–	–	–	–	–	–
9	14.8	8.50	19.1	29	85.3	102.50	88.0	4	8.3	4.50	7.1
1	1.6	.25	.6	–	–	–	–	–	–	–	–
1	1.6	.50	1.1	–	–	–	–	–	–	–	–
3	4.9	1.25	2.8	–	–	–	–	–	–	–	–
61	99.9	44.50	100.0	34	100.0	116.50	100.1	48	100.0	63.50	100.0

APPENDIX 8

OTHERS INVOLVED IN ACTIVITIES

Others	CASE STUDY 1, DUNCAN Tasks	% Tasks	Hours	% Hours	CASE STUDY 2, KAMBORIAN Tasks	% Tasks	Hours	% Hours
None	66	61.7	95.50	58.2	47	54.0	62.50	43.9
Reference librarians	5	4.7	1.75	1.1	2	2.3	3.00	2.1
Research assistants	13	12.1	33.75	20.6	9	10.3	35.25	24.8
Professors	21	19.6	31.50	19.2	16	18.4	14.50	10.2
Professional colleagues	–	–	–	–	6	6.9	12.00	8.4
Secretaries	–	–	–	–	4	4.6	11.50	8.1
Friends	2	1.9	1.50	.9	1	1.1	2.50	1.8
Others	–	–	–	–	2	2.3	1.00	.7
Total	107	100.0	164.00	100.0	87	99.9	142.25	100.0

APPENDIX 9

LOCATIONS OF ACTIVITIES

Location	CASE STUDY 1, DUNCAN Tasks	% Tasks	Hours	% Hours	CASE STUDY 1, KAMBORIAN Tasks	% Tasks	Hours	% Hours
Brown University Library	34	31.8	41.50	25.3	22	25.3	28.00	19.7
COWAA	45	42.1	76.25	46.5	56	64.3	95.25	67.0
Juergen Schulz's office	–	–	–	–	–	–	–	–
IRIS	–	–	–	–	4	4.6	7.50	5.3
Harvard University Library	–	–	–	–	–	–	–	–
Fogg Art Museum, Harvard	1	.9	1.00	.6	–	–	–	–
Tufts University Library	11	10.3	16.50	10.1	1	1.1	8.00	5.6
Boston	2	1.9	6.50	4.0	–	–	–	–
New York Public Library	–	–	–	–	–	–	–	–
Home	14	13.1	22.25	13.6	–	–	–	–
Other	–	–	–	–	4	4.6	3.50	2.5
Total	107	100.1	164.00	100.1	87	99.9	142.25	100.1

CASE STUDY 1, WINKES				CASE STUDY 2, MITCHELL				CASE STUDY 2, SCHULZ			
Tasks	**% Tasks**	**Hours**	**% Hours**	**Tasks**	**% Tasks**	**Hours**	**% Hours**	**Tasks**	**% Tasks**	**Hours**	**% Hours**
42	68.9	37.50	84.3	–	–	–	–	41	85.4	56.75	89.4
–	–	–	–	–	–	–	–	–	–	–	–
16	26.2	4.75	10.7	–	–	–	–	6	12.5	5.75	9.1
–	–	–	–	–	–	–	–	–	–	–	–
2	3.3	2.00	4.5	–	–	–	–	1	2.1	1.00	1.6
1	1.6	.25	.6	–	–	–	–	–	–	–	–
–	–	–	–	–	–	–	–	–	–	–	–
–	–	–	–	–	–	–	–	–	–	–	–
61	100.0	44.50	100.1	–	–	–	–	48	100.0	63.50	100.1

CASE STUDY 1, WINKES				CASE STUDY 2, MITCHELL				CASE STUDY 2, SCHULZ			
Tasks	**% Tasks**	**Hours**	**% Hours**	**Tasks**	**% Tasks**	**Hours**	**% Hours**	**Tasks**	**% Tasks**	**Hours**	**% Hours**
–	–	–	–	11	32.4	33.50	28.8	19	39.6	13.50	21.3
49	80.3	30.00	67.4	–	–	–	–	–	–	–	–
–	–	–	–	–	–	–	–	6	12.5	5.50	8.7
1	1.6	1.75	3.9	–	–	–	–	1	2.1	1.00	1.6
–	–	–	–	–	–	–	–	4	8.3	8.50	13.4
–	–	–	–	–	–	–	–	–	–	–	–
–	–	–	–	–	–	–	–	–	–	–	–
–	–	–	–	4	11.8	11.00	9.4	–	–	–	–
–	–	–	–	–	–	–	–	6	12.5	8.00	12.6
10	16.4	12.50	28.1	18	52.9	69.50	59.7	3	6.3	1.50	2.4
1	1.6	.25	.6	1	2.9	2.50	2.1	9	18.8	25.50	40.2
61	99.9	44.50	100.0	34	100.0	116.50	100.0	48	100.1	63.50	100.2

APPENDIX 10

ANALYSIS OF HOURS BY MONTH

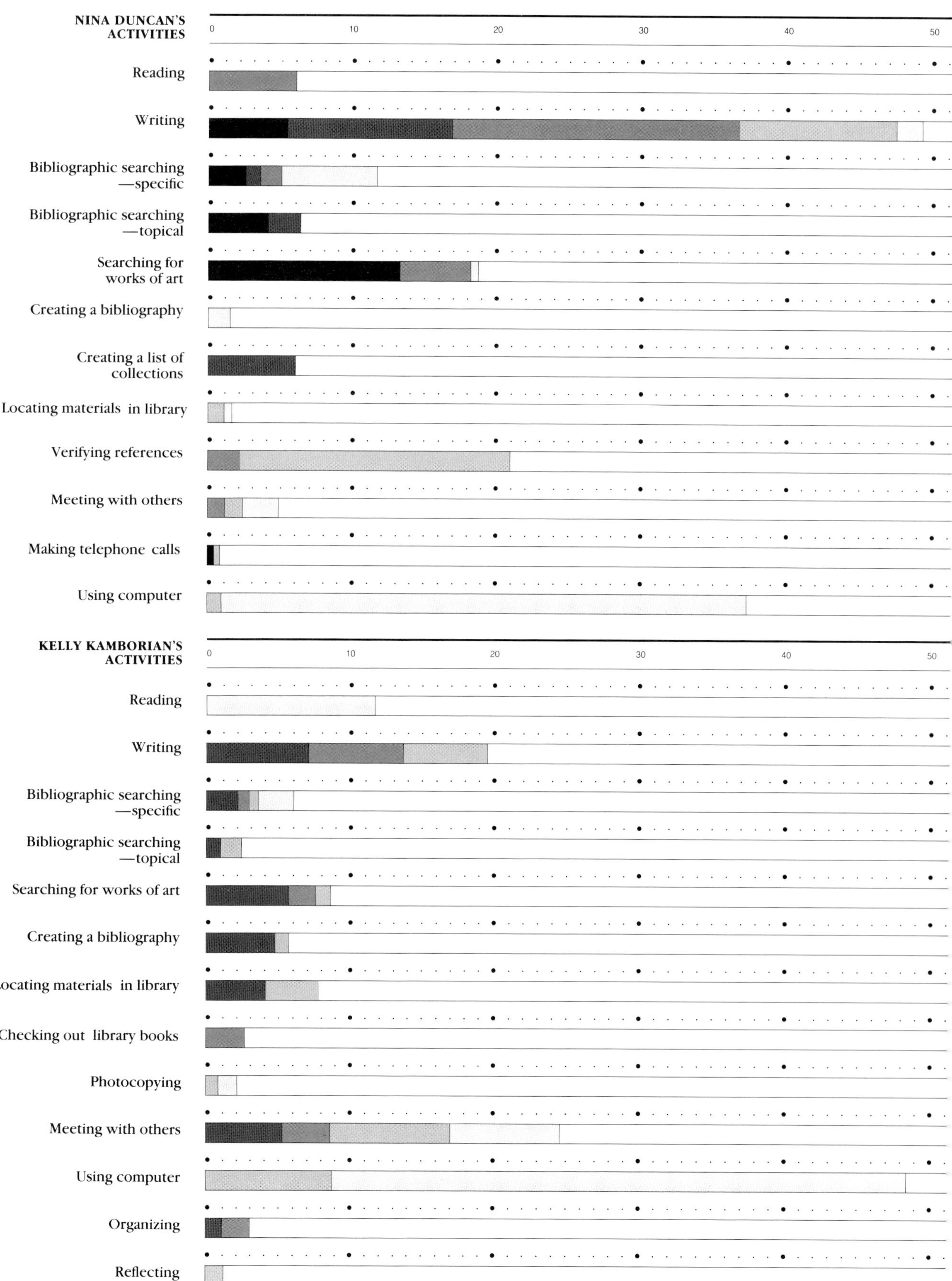

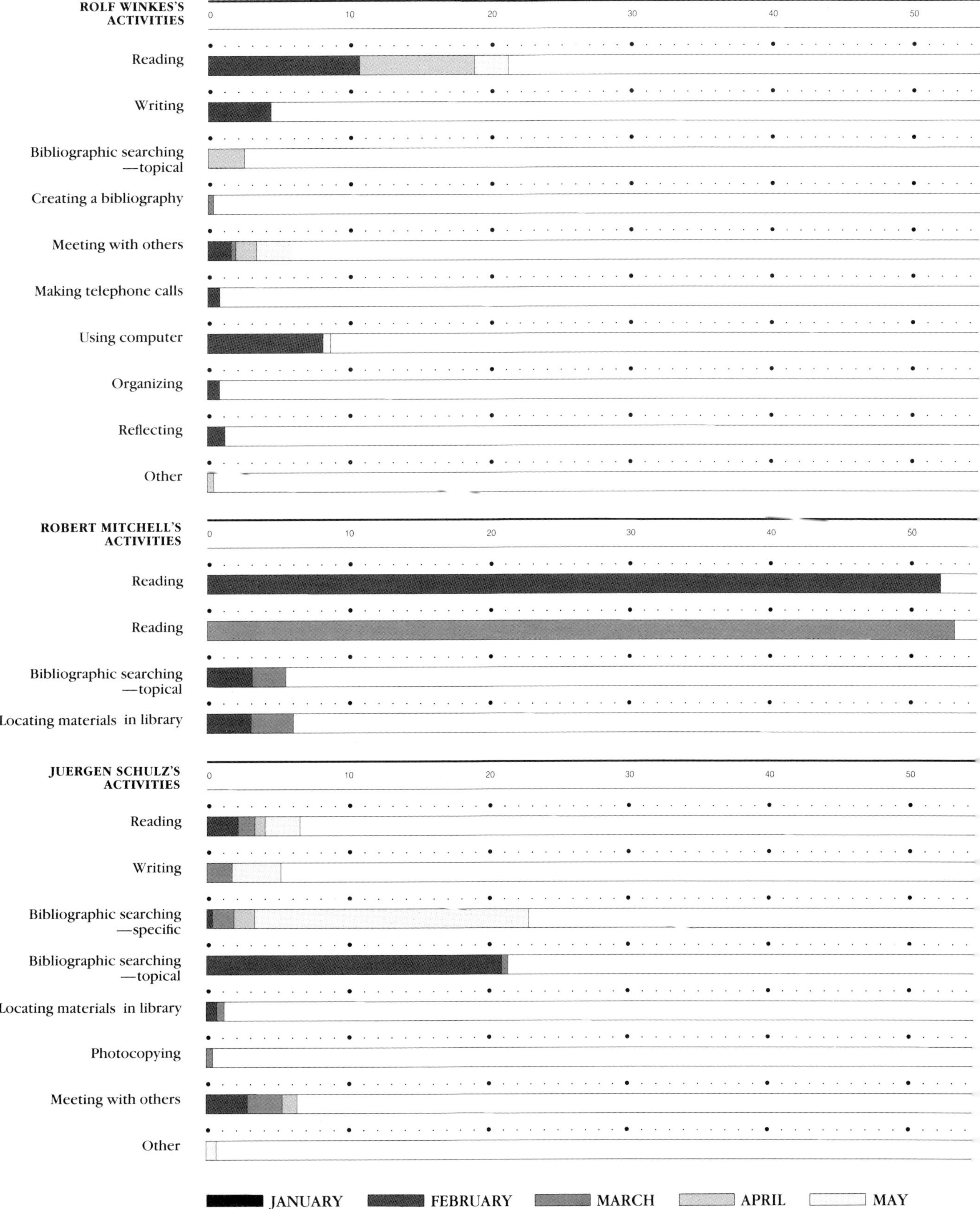
ROLF WINKES'S ACTIVITIES
0
10
20
30
40
50
Reading
Writing
Bibliographic searching —topical
Creating a bibliography
Meeting with others
Making telephone calls
Using computer
Organizing
Reflecting
Other
ROBERT MITCHELL'S ACTIVITIES
Reading
Reading
Bibliographic searching —topical
Locating materials in library
JUERGEN SCHULZ'S ACTIVITIES
Reading
Writing
Bibliographic searching —specific
Bibliographic searching —topical
Locating materials in library
Photocopying
Meeting with others
Other
JANUARY
FEBRUARY
MARCH
APRIL
MAY